MAKING PSYCHOTHERAPY WORK

MAKING PSYCHOTHERAPY WORK

*Collaborating Effectively
with Your Patient*

Steven A. Frankel, M.D.

PSYCHOSOCIAL PRESS
Madison, Connecticut

Library of Congress Cataloging-in-Publication Data

Frankel, Steven A.
    Making psychotherapy work: collaborating effectively with your patients / Steven A. Frankel.
        p. cm.
    Includes bibliographical references and index.
    ISBN 1-887841-57-1
    1. Psychotherapist and patient. I. Title.

RC480.8.F695 2007
616.89'14–dc22

                                                    2003070651

Manufactured in the United States of America

For Diane, my beloved wife and incomparable soul mate

Table of Contents

Acknowledgments

My debts are many. This book is the product of all of the 34 years I have spent in the field, trying to understand how people work. It all began in 1969 at Mount Zion Hospital in San Francisco under the guiding hand of Cal Settlage, together with Shirley Cooper, Phil Spielman, and Joe Afterman. Robert Wallerstein, chief of the psychiatry service at Mount Zion, created an atmosphere that made it possible for us to teach and inspire each other, regardless of the discipline in which we were trained. A challenging inpatient rotation with Lars Lofgren gave me a good start. The following 3 years, while on the faculty at the University of Michigan, working at Children's Psychiatric Hospital, certainly helped. Then and afterward there were countless others, far too many to name, so many of whom remain dear to me.

Here, in addition to my three good analytic friends Phil Erdberg, Paul Gilbert, and Spencer Bloch, and the added visionary support for my ideas from Ken Appel, I want to mention just four people who have been unfailing sources of support and influence. My wife Diane, who is also my partner at the Center for Collaborative Psychology, has never failed in the love and wisdom she has provided for this project, and, of course, for my very existence. My only wish is that I will never fail to do the same for her. Cal Settlage, whose legacy I believe I carry, has for all these years set a model of scholarship and integrity that I believe few people ever encounter in their professional lifetime. Gweneth Kerr Erwin my personal editor, friend, and confidant, exposed me to a new standard of love from a friend. In ways,

x   *Acknowledgments*

Gwyn was my collaborator on this book. And Margaret Emery, editor-in-chief at International Universities Press and the Psychosocial Press, deserves credit beyond any words I can offer for supporting and nuturing this project. She has been stalwart in support of this book, helped shape it when I wandered, and repeatedly breathed the life I needed into it as my spirit languished along the way.

And, finally, there is my love and admiration for my grown-up children, Peter and Cara, and my excitement about the future with Diane's children, Hilary and Tracy, and my son-in-law, Iishwara.

Preface

A psychotherapist has a fascinating life. What could be more interesting than the question of what makes people tick? There are an infinite variety of people, each with layer upon layer of psychology, and there is the haze of subjectivity that covers both therapist and patient. For anybody who likes to solve puzzles, this is the work of more than one lifetime, and it is always challenging.

I began my training as a psychiatrist in 1970. I was trained in a program that was an offspring of the San Francisco Psychoanalytic Institute, so traditional psychoanalysis was my first frame of reference. The analyst to whom I went for treatment, to embellish my experience during my residency, spent much of our time sounding definitive and attacking my "narcissism," which she believed was the reason I was so self-critical. Then, there were my supervisors. But, each one, when you cut it to the quick, seemed to have a different set of explanations for how the mind worked, and, it seemed to me, probably conducted themselves accordingly when with patients. Some were cold, withholding, and explicitly judgmental, others thoughtful. Then there were the few who seemed less shy about being directly interactive and even friendly when with patients.

You can imagine how surprised I was when, as a candidate at the San Francisco Psychoanalytic Institute, I stepped into my training analyst's office several years later and discovered how much he respected both my style and my knowledge. To him, I seemed to feel guilty about having any ambition whatsoever, and simply needed to be bolder and more comfortable with myself and my aspirations. In stark contrast with my first analyst, he was always ahead of me in approving every step of my progression within the Institute, from early candidacy to graduation.

It was striking to me that almost all my teachers, and the two analysts with whom I had therapeutic contact, *claimed* to hold the same point of view, with only minor variations. Then I observed other candidates, each of whom was in a training analysis, who did not necessarily benefit from their analyses. In fact, it seemed to me that after years of treatment they often emerged more constricted and less flexible and creative than they had been at first.

As I developed the courage, I began to allow myself to see the obvious: not all therapies—even if they were called by the same name—worked, and, by inference, it was clear that not all therapists or even psychoanalysts did the same thing in their offices. Those observations, of course, highlighted my central dilemma: I was treating patients, using valuable minutes, hours, and even years of their lives, charging them money, and, yet, it seemed quite clear to me that neither I nor most of the people who taught me had the answer to the question of what makes therapy work; or, for that matter, what makes it possible for one human being to help another to change.

I have always assumed that all therapists ask this question all the time; that is, all therapists who can think for themselves and don't simply go by the books, laying out the principles of the particular system in which they are trained. Yet, I am not sure my assumption is accurate. It is not always possible for therapists to practice their craft comfortably and continually question themselves. In some ways, it is just too damned hard to incessantly question yourself and have the firm ground erode from under you.

I came together at least 20 years ago with one of my closest current friends, a former teacher and head of the department in which I was trained, and we admitted to each other that the techniques we used in our offices frequently differed from the standard techniques in which we were trained. Of course, things were different then, distinctly more oppressive. Psychoanalysis was in its ascendancy, unchallenged both within the psychiatric field and by the public. We viewed ourselves as being on the cutting edge of traditional psychoanalytic thinking. We both believed that analysts needed to be a great deal more flexible and open than standard technique allowed. We thought we knew what was missing in psychoanalytic technique. And yet, as we met over those years, we discovered, to our dismay, that neither of us could be absolutely sure we were getting it right. We each felt repetitively tormented by a sense that we were somehow guilty of a kind of blasphemy, of a nonbelief in the system in which we were trained, for which we could be ultimately crucified. More importantly, we had no way to prove to others or ourselves, except by assertion, that we were correct. That was our experiment. We did our best to get beyond the constraints of ideology, and yet, ironically, in the end we were in some respects as lost as we had been at first.

Like most therapists, we struggled valiantly to find the answer to the question of what makes psychotherapy work, and like many, we originally thought we might be close. What we were left with, however, was something we had known for a long time: there are many therapies, an infinite number of types of therapists, each with their theoretical convictions and personal styles; some succeeded and others did not.

I have written this book with these problems in mind. It is the third in a series, and like the first two books, it lays out my own theoretical ideas and point of view about psychotherapy practice. In it, I directly address the question of what makes therapy work. I do think I have arrived at some sound ideas about how some therapists—often with dramatically divergent points of view—are successful, and why others are markedly less effective in creating change.

The answer to what makes therapy work has everything to do with trust and respect. Those factors always have to be shared between therapist and patient, deployed bilaterally. Incidentally, I believe that this point of view is in accord with the results of most of the recent research on psychotherapy, the consistent conclusion being that the key to understanding how therapy works is the character and quality of the therapeutic relationship (Roth and Fonagy, 1996). That notion puts the emphasis on therapeutic process, that is, the character of the emotional ebb and flow between therapist and patient, and far less on the content of their discussions. When the vector, the flow of thought and emotion, between the two therapy partners is even slightly unilateral, the therapist is stuck. When the flow tends to be in one direction, usually from therapist to patient, the therapist is deprived of meaningful feedback. He is not able to be free ranging in his therapeutic experiments, searching for the therapeutic action that will make a difference at any point, and he has no one to truly confirm or disconfirm the validity of his thinking. One-directionality, where the therapist is the expert on the therapy, in my view, invariably leads to a kind of personal stasis for the therapist. His beliefs and biases become at least somewhat frozen, impervious to influence. I believe that is what was plaguing my friend and myself. We had not gone far enough in recognizing the extent to which psychotherapy needs to be a collaborative endeavor. We were neither fully collaborating with our patients, nor with our colleagues. We had not taken the final, most personally frightening step of being absolutely authentic in our interventions with our patients, and publicly about our views. My objective in this book is to overcome that final barrier. Central to my ideas are such concepts as *collaboration, not knowing, authenticity,* and *self-revelation.*

It is not that I have discovered how psychotherapy works—that discovery needs to be made with each psychotherapy, in an absolutely open and dedicated collaboration between therapist and patient. It is the quality of that collaboration that actually counts, and brings the therapist and patient along therapeutically, to points where the therapist has a fairly good idea about what is going on in the therapy, enabling him or her to make organized, clear interventions in the form of words or actions. The path to these points of clarity, however, requires the therapist to endure the always agonizing experience of not knowing, often for long periods of time. This experience is so painful in part because all therapists feel accountable to their patients, and yet, if they think the way I do they need to be able to relinquish virtually all sense of conviction that they understand the forces at work in the therapy, at least for periods of time.

Ultimately, one lesson I learned as I carried out the project leading to this book, and the message was powerful, was that the complexity of therapy consists of an overwhelming number of verbal and nonverbal messages passed back and forth between patient and therapist, each providing instantaneous feedback to the other, both partners striving to understand the patient's latent goals for the treatment and searching for ways to make the therapy work. The answer to the question of what makes psychotherapy work, I now believe, lies in reciprocity, and that give-and-take cannot be understood outside of the complexity of the therapy interaction.

Introduction

Success in psychotherapy is primarily a function of the power and authenticity of the collaborative therapeutic interaction, not its formal structure. Frequency, for example, generally helps, but how often have we as therapists known of people in multiple times a week therapy who make little progress throughout the course of a prolonged treatment. This book describes a unique, dynamically informed psychotherapy, no less effective than formalized psychoanalysis, and capable of being carried out on a flexible, face-to-face basis.

I am advocating a psychotherapy able to penetrate the most subtle barriers to patient and therapist joining. In it, ground rules are revised as the therapy moves on, therapist and patient always monitoring whether progress is occurring. The forces aligning therapist and patient are also optimized, allowing the two to influence each other most powerfully in the direction of the patient's therapeutic goals. The challenge is always how to support the therapy interaction so that therapist and patient impact each other most compellingly.

My method of psychotherapy focuses on the ways in which therapist and patient find out enough about each other so that they can genuinely appeal to one another. (1) What makes the interaction productive? (2) Who takes the initiative and when? (3) What are the special therapy conditions required for a profound level of transformation to take place? (4) What happens in the interaction to allow therapist and patient to impact each other so powerfully? These questions are the subject of this book.

1

The alternative to asking these questions is disquieting. Therapists like myself are likely to be at least subliminally aware of how often therapy fails to produce substantial, lasting change for the patient. It would be hard to overestimate the amount of well-intentioned but unacknowledged guesswork that occurs in psychotherapy or psychoanalysis, and the risk that the resulting impressions and interventions will be off base (Schachter, 2002).

Mismatches between people occur all the time; some are overt, most are subtle and never understood by the participants. The subject of how people fail to understand one another may sound straightforward, but it isn't. The barriers to understanding, collaboration, and change can be as elusive as the effect of a tone in one partner's voice warning the other not to expect or risk too much, or slight hesitations in delivery that signal the partner is withholding. Both participants have secrets that obscure emotions and thoughts. People know by experience to expect this kind of privacy from others, making them hesitant to open up fully, especially when they detect some risk.

The disconnections I am talking about are explained only minimally by the psychodynamic concept of resistance, attitudes the therapist attributes to the patient based on the patient's earlier troubled relationships. In addition to the patient's transferences and the therapist's problematic countertransference distortions, there are also cultural, biological, and temperamental differences between the two, and the demands of each person's actual life. All of these factors influence and color the interaction. To this list may be added a lifetime of experience that shapes the way each person approaches the world, as well as different levels of perceptiveness, intelligence, psychological mindedness, and emotional endowment. All of these factors influence and limit the faithfulness of any interaction and the extent to which two people can understand and rely on each other.

I have briefly described factors that result in any two people maintaining a zone of isolation around themselves (Winnicott, 1963). This distancing happens even in psychotherapy and is amplified by the contribution subjectivity makes to confounding the interaction. Alternatively, distinctly less is written in the psychodynamic literature about the way participants in a therapy are drawn to each other, facilitating the progress of a therapy. The pull to affiliate is a most basic human phenomenon. Its role in psychotherapy certainly has been discussed (reviewed by Frankel, 1995, pp. 116–120), especially in developmentally oriented writing. Empathy as a therapeutic subject is particularly found in self psychology. Relational theorists such as Aron (1996) talk about the importance of authenticity in forging the mutuality they believe is needed to make therapy work. Then there are the writings on the variations of the therapeutic alliance, each acknowledging the imperative value of establishing a framework of safety and trust within therapy (Greenacre, 1971; Loewald, 1960; Meissner, 1996; Schore, 2003; Settlage, 1992; Stone, 1961). Research findings suggest that the quality of the therapy relationship is a uniquely influential factor in psychotherapy (Bergin and Garfield, 1994; Roth and Fonagy, 1996; Wallerstein, 1986).

In my work I place great emphasis on interpersonal affiliation. Here, I include the value of empathy, mutuality, and the alliance with the patient, but I also extend its reach to a depth of responsiveness not usually embraced for psychotherapy. Integral to my therapy model is collaboration, overt and subtle, between therapist and patient. The therapist's authority to lead derives in large part from the careful, moment by moment, attention paid to the patient's feedback within collaboration as the therapy moves on.

Neuropsychological research (Cozolino, 2002; Schore, 2003; Siegel, 1999; Westen and Gabbard, 2002; Siegel, 1999) and elegantly conducted infant studies (Beebe and Lachmann, 2002) argue that much of what transpires between people is unconscious and nonverbal, often based on early affective memories, never articulated. Given these findings, it would be hard to argue for the validity of a therapeutic procedure based on theory that minimizes this level of experience, as, for example, in the position taken by the psychoanalytic traditionalists in the conflict versus deficit debate during the 1990s.

Such concepts as the therapeutic alliance mainly describe the atmosphere created for a treatment, and tend not to be specific about the intrapsychic events accompanying the interpersonal ones associated with the alliance. In contrast, in my model collaboration and the notion of therapist and patient joining in ways that create fundamental change are absolutely specific as part of this process. Interpersonal influence, moving a therapy forward, calls for unique relational configurations leading toward the patient's personal evolution in internal controls, personal and social competence, and the capacity to trust and lastingly reach out to another individual. As part of my model of psychotherapy, I offer a schema, identifying and mapping these configurations (Bromberg, 1995; Frankel, 1995; Westen and Gabbard, 2002), for use in plotting a therapy's direction and course.

Included in this network of interrelated relational configurations are the traditional notions of transference and countertransference as they operate in psychodynamic psychotherapy. Therapist and patient using my model follow the unconscious as best they can through its identifiable manifestations in their work. But, more essentially, they *live out* the unconscious themes, collaboratively choosing those aspects to embrace and those to mitigate. Distancing between therapy partners, then, is reduced through at least two means: the first via dynamically informed understanding, and the second, and often the more powerful, through thoughtfully conceived interpersonal influence.

As the therapy partners track themselves and each other, they begin to change. Much of this change is not tightly linked to the formal therapy dialogue, because it is the product of both the verbal and nonverbal words. While this observation makes perfect sense when considering the commanding role of the nonverbalized dialogue in therapeutic experience and influence, the thrust of the literature is on explaining how psychotherapy works. But what if, as is frequently the case, there is no available or convincing explanation and the process works anyway? In that instance one would have to speculate that the two therapy partners are doing a good job of intuiting what each requires and of the patient's latent therapy goals. Much of this book is devoted to the therapeutic challenge of tolerating and making use of the nonexplicit aspects of the therapy experience, leading to ever more profound bilateral change.

Sticking to the mission of finding an ever truer alignment, of course, is precisely the way I see the psychotherapy couple working. Tracking occurs both verbally and nonverbally; the nonverbal may be followed through derivatives found in thought and behavior, or intuitively. Therapist and patient struggle to verify their impressions collaboratively. They progressively develop a consensus about what action is next required to move the therapy along. Each successful experience brings the partners closer, in an enhanced commitment to the other and their therapy goals. At the culmination of this effort barriers are down, and sweeping changes are occurring.

My therapeutic method recognizes ingredients of a conventional connection between two people, such as empathy and support. Omitted, however, from that description are the sophistication, complexity, and power of this bond as it occurs in psychotherapy, and the laborious preparation required for two human beings to have such a moving emotional impact on one another. I call this powerful coming together of therapist and patient *conjunction*; the therapeutic activity involved is the *conjunctive process*.

I want to make the point that developments of the sort I am describing are not restricted to psychotherapy. People can make personal changes in other interpersonal situations; for example, marriages, friendships, or even through inspiration. The minimum requirement for such transformation, I believe, is a thoroughgoing belief in the integrity and wisdom of one's partner, and his or her commitment to one's welfare, the ingredients also basic to a viable therapy. Still, it stands to reason that a therapy meeting these conditions is most likely to produce sweeping change because it is dedicated to that end. In therapy both partners are committed to the arduous process of discovering, rediscovering, and achieving the patient's most essential goals.

The patient's willingness to open his floodgates and drop the powerful, mostly invisible, protective force fields he brings to relationships, is unlikely to develop unilaterally. Therapy will be limited in depth when the therapist remains doggedly anonymous. The required trust, the desire to open up, the credibility of the therapist's ideas about how the patient might evolve, can be seriously circumscribed by the therapist's anonymity. One antidote for this deficiency is judicious self-revelation by the therapist that is more informative and more persistent than most authors recommend. I also believe that "real life" contacts and timing should be encouraged in treatment if they do not impinge on the patient's prerogatives or violate his or her boundaries. I am referring, for example, to the patient leaving telephone messages between sessions, varying the length and frequency of the sessions as benefits the treatment, the therapist seeing a spouse for a few sessions, or even a home visit or two.

As a treatment tool, I make no distinction between the kind of treatment I am recommending and psychoanalysis. I would agree that formal psychoanalysis generally offers a more standardized research environment and more anecdotal clinical material than the therapy method I am describing. The sheer amount of information obtained from multiple meetings each week and the standardization that traditional psychoanalytic conditions afford make it more possible to compare treatments conducted in that way, as contrasted to treatments carried out less intensively and with more variation in technique. As a treatment, however, there is no reason to assume that a psychoanalysis is *not* being conducted when the meetings are less standardized. The conjunctive method I describe, treatment based on a deliberately and carefully cultivated bond of authenticity, carries enormous personal weight, its results not infrequently more powerful than those of more intensive treatments based on formal, less emotionally moving analytical procedures. Therapists using my method need to be proficient at psychodynamic formulation and capable of taking the lead at any moment; but they must have a healthy respect for the inexplicable and be willing to yield their ideas and control to the collaborative process with their patient.

The now widely accepted view of therapy as an interactive process, ensconced by subjectivity, makes the therapist's unilateral judgments about therapy progress suspect. In its place I am recommending an intense and intricate process of collaboration between therapist and patient, the two continually assisting the other to find their way. When, however, the partners become stalemated or lost, I add a technique of consultation by an outside therapist as a way of introducing an independent perspective into the work.

Many of the clinical phenomena I describe for my model require names that distinguish them from clinical events that bear familiar labels in other models. The term *disjunction* (Frankel, 2000), for example, encompasses resistances, the typical disconections between therapist and patient deriving from intrapsychic or interpersonal conflict. But the causes of disjunctions, as I conceive of them, are a great deal broader. Commonly, disjunctions in therapy have the subtle, impenetrable character of the barriers that disconnect people, which I described several paragraphs earlier. The therapy partners seem to be working well together, believe they are in sync, but, uniformed by the other, may be so far out of attunement that only limited therapeutic progress is possible.

The therapist's accountability also distinguishes my technique. Discerning the patient's goals and making sure they are realized is the final objective of this kind of therapy work. In my method, the therapist is accountable for attaining these ends. The therapist needs to keep the therapy moving, always searching for some way of documenting whether the desired change is occurring. If it is not, and the difficulty cannot be remedied collaboratively, the therapist should call in a consultant and, in this way, find additional help for himself and the patient.

In this book I deal extensively with the topic of the therapist's accountability and its consequence, therapeutic asymmetry, in the context of my recommending as well a high degree
of symmetry, shared power, and respect between therapist and
patient. Therapeutic action and intervention are traditionally limited to techniques designed to overcome psychological block-
ades, through either interpretative or corrective action. The
deliberate use of personal influence, confrontation, and compassionate warnings to the patient that he is jeopardizing himself,
for example, may be avoided within a therapist's given repertoire. My view, in contrast, is that so long as the therapist has
been willing to become involved with the patient's most essential
needs, and receive payment in the form of the patient's time and
money, the therapist has an overarching responsibility to make
sure the sought after progress occurs.

This book, then, is about influence, the kind of influence
that moves both therapy partners to make fundamental changes
through their shared experience. It is not primarily about differences between people and how these are understood and resolved, except when they further therapeutic understanding and
repair. Placing one's welfare in someone else's hands requires
enormous trust, achievable reliably only in small, precarious in-
crements. Attaining those steps involves solving disconnections,
but also importantly, developing a rapport unique enough to
overcome deep-seated misgivings. The sequence of these attainments is both highly technical and intuitive. The process is an
exceedingly busy one with therapist and patient engaged in fact
finding and collaborating on the most microscopic levels. The
conjunctive result is unique to both partners, and indelible for
each.

A word now about how I conducted my project and amassed
the data that I needed to develop my ideas. I meticulously reviewed 54 sets of detailed therapy notes, that I took while conducting 14 intensive, analytically structured psychotherapies and
psychoanalyses, and 22 therapies conducted on a once a week
or less frequent basis. These cases were not selected according

to any specific criterion. They included all the cases that I began and on which I did process recordings during a five year period. The style of the therapies within the second group was much more varied than with the first, and at times included conjoint sessions with the patient and his or her spouse, or meetings with people other than the patient but closely associated with his or her life.

My goal in this study was to isolate factors associated with therapeutic change. For over 25 years I have taken detailed process notes during and after psychotherapy and psychoanalytic sessions, writing down everything I notice, including my own mood and response. I wanted to minimize the distortions in recall that occur when notes are recorded after clinical events occur. I refrained from note taking in the session when it interfered with the patient's therapy experience, or my ability to pay close attention to the patient's communications and my own responses.

Later, I randomly selected clinical sequences from each therapy and scrutinized them, identifying those influences that appeared to lead to change. I chose sequences by opening my notes to any page and reviewing them for a predetermined time interval, in this case three to six months. One other experienced psychotherapist also carefully studied these notes, recording his or her impressions along with my findings.

Obviously, this review effort does not qualify as a formal research project. My colleague and I studied only my own work. My therapy work, note taking, and review were influenced by my personal biases and reactions. However, this method of note-taking and review has been remarkably useful for reassessing my clinical work. During all of the therapies, I reviewed the notes periodically throughout the course of treatment, checking and revising my earlier clinical impressions. The discipline of note taking and review by myself, and at least one other psychotherapist, has continually moved me to see the therapy at issue from a new perspective. It is as if I am repeatedly offered second opinions, even if those opinions come from myself at a time when I am more removed from the therapy and in a different subjective state of mind. In addition to data recorded during the therapy, in over two-thirds of these cases I have been able to meet with the patient periodically after the therapy is over. These follow-up meetings provide me with information about whether progress has occurred in the therapy, which interventions have been most effective, and whether the therapeutic change is enduring.

Additionally, in fourteen of these cases, I have had the benefit of input from a psychologist consultant whose job was to provide information, using psychological testing and clinical interviews, about the patient's psychology, the value of the therapy, and whether progress had taken place. I have carried out this procedure, whenever possible, for the past 10 years, with two different psychologists, Philip Erdberg, Ph.D. and Diane Engelman, Ph.D. In addition to testing reports, we assiduously kept notes, recording our clinical experiences throughout the consultation.

While none of the procedures that I have named is part of a formal research design, they do represent a disciplined approach to monitoring a psychotherapy and addressing the question of what is and is not working. All the patients I mention in this book were included as part of this project. I used the data provided by the psychologist consultant to search for different types of information: for example, in chapter 4 for information about the therapist's responsibility to actively move the therapy forward; in chapter 5 for the patient's equivalent role; in chapter 7 for the topic of authenticity and its role in the efficacy of a psychotherapy.

1

The Conjunctive Model of Psychotherapy

The psychotherapy process requires the deliberate joining of two human beings, mainly orchestrated by one, and requiring heartfelt collaboration by both. Breaches in the relationship are plumbed for the information they provide, the two continually surprised and inspired as they move to new, uncharted views about what the patient needs and how to get there. Indeed there are rules, procedures, and boundaries, but knowing when these guidelines contaminate the therapy's authenticity and sap its power is one of the therapist's most subtle challenges.

Therapists constantly work to identify how their craft differs from the commonsensical stuff of everyday relationships. They are not supposed to hug their patients, attend their weddings, or even have the smallest need for their patients' approval. The therapy process is not to be corrupted by patient and therapist embracing too much of their *real* relationship, as if the technical, less personal aspects of therapy are the most authentically therapeutic.

As therapists, we do not talk much about wanting the patient to respond to the personal influence we may bring to bear in creating desirable change. Struggling, even suffering, in the service of establishing and maintaining an ever more profound connection to the human being otherwise known as "the patient," may be labeled overinvolvement.

11

Yet, the pull toward connection, uncomplicated human connection, pervades the therapy experience. Much is known about the ways in which this therapeutic connection can be distorted internally via transference, countertransference, projective identification, and developmental distortions and lags. These complicating developments in therapy represent one source of the impasses I call *therapeutic disjunctions* (Frankel, 2000), in this case intrapsychically generated. Gender differences, cultural background, and real life influences on mood are a few examples of the other category of disjunctions based upon mismatches between people, deriving from their personalities and their actual life circumstances. When any of these disjunctive factors is at work, the disconnect between therapist and patient can be profound, without necessarily being obvious from the surface appearances both parties maintain. Their words may be right, as if they agree on key issues, but they may be infected by silent skepticism or tarnished by the tone in which they are uttered. Many of our theories of technique are directed at understanding and healing these interpersonal rifts.

Underrepresented in our theory making, however, are the ways in which therapist and patient actively breathe life into each other, collaboratively facilitating the other's healing when required and encouraging ongoing personal and therapeutic development. These creative forces are as present as the divisive ones, making therapy a remarkably complex set of activities that encompasses multiple pulls at every moment. In order to distinguish it from other kinds of therapeutic joinings, I call this coming together between therapeutic partners the *conjunctive process*. In this book much space will be devoted to delineating and illustrating the driving force in therapy I call *conjunctive*, as well as addressing why therapists tend to be uncomfortable about actively encouraging this kind of connection with their patients. I use the term *conjunctive sequence* to refer to a series of linked interpersonal steps involved in therapeutic unification. Finally, at the heart of the matter, *conjunctions* are points of joining where the two therapy partners clearly influence each other toward depth of understanding, and are aware that the conditions for change are being engaged.

But the actual uniting, that which convinces the patient to comprehend in a deep way what he and the therapist have been struggling for, is actually closer to magic than anything I will be able to describe. This magic consists of a special conglomeration of words, intuitions, feelings, emphases, and pauses. The order in which pain and disappointment, and elation take place is all-important to the final result. The moment at which comprehension occurs, however, is often surprising, and is not so easily linked to the quest to find psychological meaning.

Even contemporary, relationally informed psychodynamic therapies tend to accord the therapist prerogatives in orchestrating and leading the therapy that give him or her an edge on knowing. In this chapter I begin to develop a point of view that, while recognizing the therapist's responsibility to make sure the therapy progresses, argues forcefully for therapist and patient sharing authority and taking full advantage of each other's wisdom. These conditions are required for the two to move effectively toward bilateral change in the direction of the patient's therapeutic goals, the interpersonal and therapeutic development I call conjunction.

How Equal in Influence are Therapist and Patient?

The notion of therapeutic symmetry pervades this book. The underlying principle is that the therapist and patient are both human beings. They make judgments, cooperate when they feel doing so is reasonable, and yield to each other's influence when they are convinced that the other makes sense, deep interpersonal sense. This picture of interpersonal symmetry does not contradict the notion that, indeed, there is an inherent asymmetry in the therapy situation, with the therapist being responsible for guarding its outcome. Other asymmetries are based on the wisdom that each partner brings to the table at any point. Yet, understanding the conjunctive driving force behind the therapy requires a focus on the sharing and collaboration that constantly occurs between the two therapy partners.

Shifts in psychodynamic thinking acknowledge the individual and shared subjectivity of the therapy situation, as well as the mutative influence therapist and patient may have on each other and provide a contemporary theoretical backdrop for establishing conjunction as a major activity of therapy. In these views, the balance between therapist's and patient's authority to know and lead in the therapy is shifted toward parity, each having moments of greater knowing. My understanding is that this reciprocity, or sharing of influence, occurs whether it is acknowledged formally or not. The undercurrents coloring the therapy experience are always there, with therapist and patient sending a complex array of signals to each other, embellishing the formal work of therapy. In this picture, the therapist is a human being, as fallible and as open to constructive influence as the patient. This statement captures the essence of my own position, emphasizing the equivalence of the two partners, each with his or her role in making the therapy work, each willing to be the authority when needed, each changing through the other's influence. Therapy is a human experience, the two people involved willing to be interested in knowing the other as fully as is necessary for the patient to discover and achieve his or her most personal goals.

In spite of this movement toward acknowledging and sanctioning shared authority, and in contrast with my own view of therapy as embracing mutuality and collaboration, many theorists still *emphasize* the asymmetry of the therapy situation, with the therapist's authority deriving from his formal training, personal therapy or training analysis, and his professional responsibilities for orchestrating and maintaining the therapy. However, the problems with overvaluing asymmetry are well documented:

its potential for pathologizing and devaluing the patient's wisdom and agency. Compare, for example, Bachant, Lynch, and Richard's (1995) position where bilateral influence is viewed as a contaminant in psychoanalysis, with Mitchell (1997), who speaks about the "voice" (p. 6) in which an interpretation is given as central to therapeutic action and the "suppression generated by the noninteractive framework in which the analytic process has been understood" (p. 12). Mitchell states, "One of the best-kept secrets in the psychoanalytic profession is the extent to which analysts often grow (in corrective emotional experiences) through a surrender to the influence of patients whose life experience, talents, and resources may be different from their own" (p. 26).

Finding the balance between mutuality and the therapist's edge in knowing and leading is elusive. As I read them, most modern relationalists, such as Lewis Aron, Irwin Hoffman, and Stephen Mitchell, argue for more unbroken authority for the therapist than I do, even if they agree that the authority is subjectively grounded, offering only another viewpoint or version of reality (Mitchell, 1997, pp. 52, 225–227). Closer to my view, authors like Darlene Ehrenberg (1992), Karen Maroda (1999, 2002), and Owen Renik (1998), and perhaps Donnel Stern (1997) are especially up for surprises, following the patient as much as possible to the unformulated edge of experience or to the depth of "mutual emotional honesty" (Maroda, 1999, p. 45). Influence in therapy is bilateral, with the patient frequently cueing, advising, and inspiring the therapist. These cross-currents can become incorporated into the therapy interaction when they are acknowledged and valued. Otherwise, they are there anyway, coloring the outcome of the effort. Added to these givens is the interpersonal concern and honesty I believe are required for therapy to work at its best. No therapeutic procedure lacking these qualities will be convincing and engaging enough to command the depth of change sought after in a dedicated therapy.

The themes of subjectivity and symmetry, therefore, pave the way for recognizing that the essential action in psychotherapy is based on two human beings struggling to understand and assist each other. Both make errors in judgment, have driving ambitions, stylistic preferences, which are partly cultural and partly temperamental in origin, and more or less of the usual affiliative needs to be cared for and understood accurately, as well as to share deeply felt personal experiences. A comprehensive picture of the psychotherapy process needs to consider each of these factors.

Like all human experiences, therapy is characterized by the shifting subjective status of both partners. Each moves from one focus or mood to another in a moment: optimistic on awakening, suddenly grumpy when remembering a failing account at work, and then delighted when his 4-year-old offers him a flower. In contrast are those attempts to describe the psychology of one or the other partner in fixed terms, reducing the other to a few nouns and adjectives, as irrefutably knowable. A model of how psychotherapy works needs to spell out how people come together to influence each other successfully: identifying the intersubjective entity created in the moment from that process, how therapist and patient act differently to achieve their goals, and the nature and durability of the relationship that follows.

Psychotherapy, as I conceptualize it, is collaboratively based. It takes place in a two-person, intersubjective field, and the actual relationship is instrumental to the therapist's and patient's ability to influence each other and change. Therapist and patient join forces persistently, at points effecting an equivalence of authority and wisdom, at other times locating these functions mainly in one member of the pair. The therapist works actively to move the therapy toward its ever redefined goals, discovered by the therapist and patient in their interactions and shared work. Depth of involvement is critical to success in therapy, the therapist always struggling to go beyond the edge of the familiar. Authenticity is a core value to which therapist and patient continually aspire, the therapist disclosing relevant emotional information about himself to this end.

As I conceive of it, psychotherapy builds toward the end product of a dedicated, yet convoluted, conjunctive process, built on the ever shifting foundation of subjectivity. Within this atmosphere of disconnections and joinings is the tightest bond between therapy partners that can be forged. A committed therapy process is demanding, with therapist and patient alternatively losing themselves in "not knowing" and braving sometimes shocking disappointments in order to get to know each other more accurately. Often this process occurs nonverbally, but in a way that is as complex as any verbal exchange. Stripped to its barest essentials, the therapy process I describe is among the most intense, trying, and exalting interpersonal experiences conceivable. Engaged in this manner, the two partners reach a new, unanticipated level of clarity about clinical issues, and, in the best of therapies, influence each other to change in fundamental and unexpected ways, that is, creatively. *Neither* member of the couple escapes change, both feel or act in fresh ways, sometimes strikingly.

In spite of my emphasis on therapeutic symmetry, none of what I have said is meant to undercut the therapist's responsibility for directing the therapy toward the patient's goals and guarding its integrity. Neither patient nor therapist deliberately sets out to change or fix the therapist. Rather, inevitably, as the therapist's biases and limitations are exposed, as he discovers new and exciting potentialities in the patient and himself in the process, the therapist is changed along with the patient. Involving himself in this bidirectional experience, while keeping clear his responsibility for making sure the two move toward the patient's ever-evolving goals, is one of the greatest technical challenges for the therapist.

Conjunction

So here we arrive at the kingdom of conjunction. The path leading from disruption to repair of the therapy bond, the conjunctive process, can be as tortuous, treacherous, and terrifying as it is transformative and thrilling. With the therapist dedicated to understanding the patient inside out, and the patient committed to discovering the therapist similarly, conjunction, when it is arrived at, is a majestic place. Geographically, it stands apart from anywhere either partner may have been before. Each time therapist and patient are lucky enough to come to such a pivotal point, the place is different. There are no two episodes alike; distinguishing them is the fact that they are so different from any other sort of experience.

My experience with Jessica, an analyst friend from whom I sought advice several years ago, following my divorce, illustrates the surprise and illumination so typical of a conjunctive episode. She told me she was shocked, even hurt, when I questioned the depth of her interest. "Steve, it seems that sometimes you're not sure people are really there, caring about and feeling for you." "But," I sputtered, "how is that possible?" Intimacy, committed relationships were my calling cards. Over the next few weeks, however, as her alleged misreading of me converted in my mind to brilliant clarity, my view of myself began to change. I started to see that the discovery was actually a gift. If at times my sense of others' constancy was subtly compromised, I could, in the future, be able to expect a kind of loving from people beyond anything I had known. How, I wondered, could Jessica have seen so much when no one else before her had, and why did she care so deeply? No matter, she affirmed, she did.

My description of therapeutic conjunction may sound exaggerated, and I can see why. The truth is that it is difficult to describe the landscape. Most people who arrive at this place have only a limited idea of how they got there. Certainly, that was true in my experience with Jessica. A microscope would reveal hundreds of poignant moments between us, some discouraging and others inspiring. Like us, therapy partners experiencing conjunctive joining will remember the frequent disorientation and consensus seeking that kept getting them back on course. But so much of the process is intuitive: guessing how to handle the other's needs, assuming agreement between yourself and your partner, just reacting. Skeptics argue that this pathfinding, tracking the disruptive and reparative forces in search of therapeutic repair and change, sounds too random, lacking in scientific rigor (e.g., Strenger, 1991). Experienced therapists, knowing how accurate the nonverbal therapeutic dialogue can be, have their own ways of following it, most important of which is joining with the patient as collaborator.

Strange, isn't it, that conjunction is such an exciting and complex place, worth almost any struggle to find? There are some regular landmarks along the way, but the process of therapist and patient combining is anything but smooth, each step integrated with the last. False conjunctions (often covering gaping disjunctions) consist of puffed up enthusiasm for an idea and appear regularly. Ordinarily, false conjunctions represent temporary solutions to disjunctions, states of mind that may precede conjunctions. Returning to Jessica, her confrontation caught me by surprise. Moments of resonance with patients and in personal relationships had always reassured me about my capacity for recognizing and fostering intimacy. What was hidden was the difference between my giving to others, a situation I favored, and being given to, one far less comfortable for me. Also, of course, points of discouragement or misunderstanding between therapy partners appear regularly and deepen or confound the conjunctive process. Resolving these disconnections successfully provides part of the point-by-point joining that results in a conjunctive union. Finally, there are the moment-to-moment experiences of connecting and reconnecting, understanding, and being emotionally in tune with the other person that are the hallmarks of the conjunctive process.

When looked at closely, therapeutic joining is more characterized by discontinuities than seamless connections, new developments occurring by surprise rather than design. Therapeutic change is similar, often taking place outside of the therapy plan and in unforeseen ways. The discontinuous nature of the therapy, and, in particular, the process leading toward therapeutic conjunction, mandates a microscopic appraisal of the forces at work in a therapy, if one is to understand its action.

From the patient's side, the therapist's ability to empathize and willingness to struggle is not the only precondition for him to want to enter more fully into a therapeutic union. The therapist may need to be uniquely smart, able to wrestle with ideas, or provide guidance, for example. Therapists, also, look for more from patients than rapport, intelligence, and even the subtle ability to minister to some of the therapist's own needs. Some patients capture the therapist's imagination; others are intriguing because of unusual traits or experiences they have had, or maybe because they are honest and willing to work hard. The therapy process is incredibly complicated, with verbal and powerful nonverbal components, multiple joinings and unjoinings, disorientation and struggle by both partners, and finally, luck and good timing for it all to work together.

The Conjunctive Model at Work

While there are an infinite number of paths to a therapeutic conjunction, each different, it is useful to separate out two types: one characterized by turmoil and dissension, which leads to the discovery of information critical to understanding the patient and therapy interaction, the other smooth and uncontentious. We have all experienced the reward of successfully struggling to work out differences with another person, both emerging wiser from the experience. In therapy, the counterpart occurs when a disjunction separates the two partners, impeding their ability to work toward the patient's therapy goals. When the therapist is partially responsible for a therapeutic disjunction, he will have to change as part of its resolution. When the disjunction is of the patient's making, the therapist will still benefit from the struggle by becoming more intimately acquainted with the patient's psychology. In contrast, some conjunctions have an inspiration-like quality, where two people intuitively understand one another and move ever closer.

The truth, however, is that all conjunctive experiences are mixtures of both processes, especially when broken into their component parts. The following case examples illustrate these principles. In the first, with Brittany, the pathway to conjunction was tumultuous, in the second, with Karen, it was smooth. But, Karen's initial result was limited and our initial conjunction was followed by a much stormier period, resulting in an even more profound and enduring connection between us.

Brittany

On this particular day Brittany, age 36, was not going to cut me any slack. Usually when she was like this she assumed I would be like her always preoccupied mother, or her unrelentingly critical father. I would listen on a level that considered only her material well-being, and the rest would hardly matter.

As soon as I entered the waiting room, I sensed trouble. Brittany's face was haggard and gray, and she refused to look in my direction. I forced an animated "Hello," hoping to make the point that I wanted to be there for her. But her powerful nonverbal warnings grew, her tone and posture distant and rejecting, causing me to fight even harder for the rapport that had been there at the end of the last session.

A few minutes passed, and Brittany's silence took a turn for the worse. Now words would not even come out. We sat staring at each other, me struggling to make sense out of the developing stand-off, not having a clue what it was about. My mind was racing: had I offended her with something I had said? Was I crowding her with my enthusiasm for restoring our rapport? Or maybe her silence had nothing to do with me? The problem was that Brittany wasn't willing or able to help, and it seemed as though everything I did made her recede further.

Of course, we had a history. We had worked together for many years, on and off. The problem was that Brittany was an emotional Geiger counter, more sensitive to nuances within an interaction than perhaps anyone I'd ever known, and brilliant at being able to accurately understand another person's experience. This combination of sensitivity and brilliance was intimidating; she was often better at reading me than I her.

So, there we were in the grips of a therapeutic disjunction; Brittany unable to help me even begin to understand what it was about and I knowing that if she could, the therapy might jolt forward.

My interest here is in demonstrating the sequence of disruption and insight, disjunction and conjunction, as they occur in psychotherapy. Unsolved, our standoff would defeat the therapy work and simply fester and get worse. My active, deliberate, and intuitive attempts to move the therapy forward served only to make our separation worse.

To my dismay it took several more weeks of twice weekly visits before I began to achieve even a modicum of clarity, and several additional months to fully understand and move beyond our disconnection, Brittany always arranging for me to feel helpless and stupid, lost in my apparent deficiencies. Naming my feelings during this time was one thing, experiencing them was quite another. The situation was a bit like being buried alive in a silent tomb, all other human beings out of earshot. As I learned later, Brittany's insistence on not giving me a reprieve was an integral part of that exercise. This time I needed to know what it was like to be her, how desperate she became when she let down her guard and wasn't acknowledged. In the end I did get it, both of us often at our wits' end as I too slowly absorbed what I was learning about her.

Oddly, my speculation at the beginning of the described hour had been right, we had connected well in that previous session. What I learned later was that she had been excited when in that session she confided her interest in alternative healing to me, talked passionately about it for 30 minutes, and experienced my response as interested, even enthusiastic. However, over the next few days she began to distrust me, and privately made the decision, once and for all, to test my sincerity. After all, there had been several instances where, after confiding in me, she experienced my responses as too superficial, and it was time to deal with these judgements directly. The question was always whether I could be excited by her ideas, or would I use them to degrade her as others had done, evoking hope but then leaving her even more emotionally stranded.

By the end of this sequence I understood Brittany better, her desires for a comprehending relationship, and her repeated experiences of desolation when disappointed by people she had started to trust. Also, we felt more at one with each other, our therapy bond tighter. That development, the strengthening of our conjunctive process, was the product of the disruption in our rapport, and our painstaking efforts to understand and repair it.

Karen

In contrast to Brittany, Karen at age 48 trusted me from the start. Ordinarily, she lived in a nightmarish world of betrayal and deceit. I became the best thing going, and she held onto me for dear life. She brought dreams, shared confidences, and proferred small gifts she handcrafted. She voraciously devoured our discussions about her abusive father and promiscuous mother. She digested insights and each time she recovered from a period of despondency, usually associated with a temporary disappointment in me, she had an even better capacity to tolerate the vicissitudes of other relationships.

When I asked her why she thought things went so well with us, she said I usually was right in tune with her, and when I wasn't I would struggle to find out why not. That I took her so seriously made me different from any person in her life; the others were indifferent or wanted to use her for their personal gain. Conjunctions between us generated all kinds of nonverbal energy for her: social, sexual, and the courage for her to find a career. They also served her as a defense, at times, protecting her from doubting my motives, the possibility that I would prove as needy and competitive as the rest of them.

Then, as our work progressed, Karen found it more possible to notice and challenge my failings. Through a painful series of disjunctions, led by Karen's censure of me, I was confronted with my discomfort about Karen's intolerance of others' needs. During this period, the therapy almost came to an end, because of my reluctance to comprehend her allegations that I was irked by her. I was shocked when I could see the degree of my disapproval, undermining our original rapport and how little I noticed I was feeling this.

As I came to understand my contribution to our difficulty, I was forthright with Karen. She was correct I had become less responsive, implicitly judgmental. In turn, she was grateful that I could be self-critical, in contrast to her always blaming mother and verbally abusive father. However, as with Brittany, reconciliation came only slowly. First, Karen needed me to work hard at comprehending my part in our disruption and to be certain that I would not repeat her parent's rejecting behavior. She required that we understand what had happened between us, and insisted on proof that I was appropriately contrite. In the end, in a triumph for the conjunctive process, we knew each other far better and were far more solidly connected with each other. We had endured Karen's terrors and vindictive rages following betrayals, as well as my withdrawals as I struggled with her to make sense out of our experience. Repeatedly, we savored the relief of finally finding our way; our result: an immutable bond between us as human beings, superseding the patient–therapist relationship, in some part a repeat of affirmative but lost relationships from childhood.

With both kinds of conjunctions, those growing from disjunctions and those developing outside of disjunction, therapy partners finally experience the thrill of establishing a heartfelt connection to another human being. Being understood so well, with continuity and earnestness, is a relatively unique development in ordinary human experience. The excitement, when it is at the level of conjunction, is bilateral. Both partners feel it. When each changes in response to the other, the result is a special situation I label *creative change*. Creative change and its legacy, *creative development*, are the desired end product of psychotherapy conducted according to the conjunctive model.

In the end, that was what happened with both Brittany and Karen. They and I, working collaboratively, were transformed, transcending the possibilities we had imagined for ourselves. Brittany was astounded when I cared, time and time again, to follow her to the depths of her despair and stayed with the emotional detail she required me to comprehend in order to join with her. Karen ultimately discovered that a committed relationship could survive her stinging criticism, exposing me in turn to ways that my initial pleasure in her adulation limited the authenticity of our exchange.

Therapeutic Change and Conjunction

The smooth, unidirectional character of a true *nondisjunctive conjunction,* Karen's early unconditional admiration of me being an example, precludes the confusion and turmoil associated with the discovery and resolution of most disjunctions (Frankel, 2000). The creative, bilateral experience of therapist and patient together discovering an entirely new interpersonal world as they comprehend their differences, may not take place. Change in this kind of straightforward joining tends to be along customary, developmentally prescribed lines, with therapist and patient roughly in an involvement like that of a parent and child. I call this kind of therapeutic change *renewed development,* connoting a continuation of an expectable developmental process.

Self psychologists (Stolorow, 1995; Wolf, 1993) and child developmentalists (Beebe, 2004; Beebe and Lachmann, 2002, 2003) have studied analogous processes, concentrating on disruption and repair as these events occur between mother and child, as well as in psychotherapy. Here is one of the few places in the literature where the terms *disjunction* and *conjunction* also appear, the distancing and joining being varieties of attachment and detachment associated with human bonding and the development of a sense of self and other. Refocusing on the conjunctive side of this continuum, Karen sought relationships she could trust, but she didn't know how to 'find and develop these. She needed a teacher who could directly model that kind of relationship with her. Through my personal care and the insight gained in therapy, Karen grew; she made and kept relationships, including ours, and was successful in her work.

Contrast this picture with my wrenching experience of Brittany's antagonism toward me, an example of a *disjunctive conjunction*. We both came out of that episode with a fresh understanding about what people need from each other and the lengths to which they might have to go emotionally to find it. Originally, our rift—Brittany experiencing me as obtuse, unable to comprehend the acuteness of her dissatisfaction—exacerbated her despair and threatened to bring the therapy to a halt. But the result of our laboring day after day with the grim, unnerving cancer of her hopelessness made it possible for us both to grasp her conviction that she would never be understood, that her wish to be appreciated for her pressing interest in spirituality, in this case the topic of alternative healing, would be buried forever. Our struggle established the depth of connection required for us to build toward our ultimate personal and therapeutic alliance.

The result, creative change, is the product of the conjunctive process, comprised of multiple disconnections and joinings, disjunctions and conjunctions, where each partner discovers ways of being that are radically different from anything he or she has experienced or perhaps even imagined. The conjunctive process, leading to creative change and creative development, always involves episodes of disruptions and disorientation, and usually painful readjustments by both patient and therapist.

The line I am drawing between nondisjunctive conjunctions, leading to the resumption of the patient's expectable course of development, and disjunctive conjunctions, resulting in creative change and creative development for each partner, is, of course, too absolute. No one would ever deny that magical, ineffable episodes of connection occur regularly between two people, transforming both. These moments of reciprocated inspiration represent another category of nondisjunctive conjunction, with the emphasis on shared, not one-sided, change. A complex and sophisticated verbal and nonverbal dialogue occurs between the two people involved, both coming to understand each other deeply, often without words. To the extent it is nonverbal, this process, in spite of its complexity and power, may take place unobserved, its effects appearing suddenly as alterations in therapeutic mood. The timing of these shifts often has little that is obvious to do with the deliberate work of the therapy, surprising patient and therapist alike. It is not unusual for them to retrospectively attach an explanation for these developments that fits some formal conception of how therapeutic change occurs; however, a careful look exposes the explanation as forced.

The Nonverbal Underpinning of Conjunctions

In this section, I want to extend our understanding about the nature of the therapy process by pointing to the powerful, intricate nature of the nonverbal exchanges between therapist and patient. Whatever they do or say, much of what flows between therapy partners is nonverbal, and this communication is in large part purposeful and sophisticated. Its goal is to accomplish either partner's ends, while both are equally active in engaging the other in this way. How this nonverbal activity and the words used by the therapy pair relate, and the effect on each component on therapeutic change, is anything but straightforward.

Watchwords useful in understanding the therapy process, therefore, include symmetry and nonverbal communication. In my view, psychotherapy is collaborative, with the therapist's acknowledgment of his "not knowing" especially valued, and understanding arrived at through reciprocal, verbal and nonverbal exchanges between therapist and patient, often involving *transfers of authority to know and lead* between therapist and patient. Desires, interpersonal agendas, and unspoken motives defining what each partner wants from the relationship are communicated, always with the patient's therapeutic welfare in mind. These desires and agendas, it is important to emphasize, have their source in both therapist and patient, and may represent strictures on the relationship that are often unappreciated by either. Taken together, it becomes clear how intricate and personal are the deeper, less articulated layers of the therapy interaction.

Given a mandate to steer our therapy, Karen, for example, made it plain to me at first that she mainly wanted a trustworthy relationship. She and I could sense the potential for emotional meltdown if I even slightly disappointed her. In her own language, devoid of words, she made the emphatic point that, at least to begin with, we both needed to be safe from interpersonal assault. Considering the intensity of her later storms, her messages to me were intended to firm up the initial therapy bond, almost deliberately preparing us for the later, less pleasant work. Here, I initiated the shift of the authority to Karen so that she temporarily determined the ground rules for the therapy.

My conjunctive model of therapy argues for a greater degree of therapeutic reciprocity and more regular self-disclosure than most other versions of psychotherapy, the two individuals steadily extending its authenticity and eradicating contaminants. Collaboration is constant in my model, both partners working assiduously to pick up the other's subtle communications, ultimately searching for clues to the patient's latent goals and needs. Therapists, no matter how seemingly omniscient, cannot probe the subjectivity and complexity of the therapeutic interaction by themselves. The best they can hope for is a productive exchange with the patient; the partner whose perspective is most accurate at any one point put in control. After repeatedly sampling each other's thinking, one of them, more often but not exclusively the therapist, in a move I call the *leap of inference,* offers an opinion about what the therapy requires. The statement may be made nonverbally, in words, or with actions, exchanges reminiscent of the fine-tuned mutual regulation process between mother and child (Beebe & Lachmann, 1988, 2002; Grossman, 1999; Schore, 1994, 1997). Its counterpart with adults is more egalitarian, but here too, as I will discuss later, the therapist usually has the ultimate responsibility for steering the therapy in the direction of conjunction.

Words, of course, are central in the therapy encounter and have a significant place in the conjunctive process. But much of the experience is communicated in a language of tone, gestures, and timing. This activity may be both affective and cognitive, even if the cognitive part is formulated in pictures or patterns, not words (Emde, 1990; Schore, 1994, 2003; Donnel Stern, 1997). When people do understand each other, it may be largely in this second language. Therapist and patient communicate non-verbally in powerful ways about their psychological agendas, needs, and moods. That influence is always in the background determining more of the therapy experience than either partner imagines; interesting, given the importance we as therapists tend to place on the deliberate, verbally formulated aspect of therapy. The agendas are familiar to dynamically oriented therapists as transference-countertransference, enactments, and projective identifications.

However, needs are also important. Needs are common fare for therapy, but usually only when they are the patient's needs. However, less discussed is the topic of the therapist's moods and needs, especially those that are not pathological; yet they are there, are expressed interpersonally, and influence the character of the therapy. Further, the therapist's needs may even be welcomed by the patient who, by responding, can feel valued, making his own critical contributions to the vitality of their therapy bond.

Implications of the Conjunctive Model of
Psychotherapy for Technique

Therapists, no matter how dispassionate their technique, always have an interest in helping the patient. They may attempt to do this by enlisting the patient's introspection, providing a selfobject function, giving the patient an opportunity to reprocess damaged internal self and object representations, or by believing in and offering the reparative value of a new, developmentally relevant relationship. Because of the formal and informal theories of therapeutic action held and personal style, however, every therapist will achieve a different result. Consistent, also, is that formal psychodynamic theories are generally about disjunctions, within or between individuals: instinctual conflict, false self, maladaptive relational patterns.

Yet the way a therapist works includes his or her own deliberate or inadvertent style of facilitating the therapy process, including contacting, understanding, helping, and taking from patients. Personal theory may make special provision for empathy, authenticity, mutuality, real relationship in the therapy, or conjunctive activity may be intuitive, mainly carried out nonverbally. There is also the wizardry, the ways in which disjunctions are harnessed in the service of patient and therapist coming close, such as the one Brittany and I tolerated when she worried I wouldn't understand the importance of her interest in alternative healing. Here, the distinction between two different facets of conjunctive activity fades: the distinction between arriving at conjunction through resolving disjunctions and directly through interpersonal influence.

One could categorize therapists according to whether they do or do not deliberately seek conjunction with their parents, or if they do, what kind of conjunction they attempt to produce. Are they inclined to target disjunctive or nondisjunctive conjunctions, and beyond that, which type of nondisjunctive conjunction are they emphasizing, with the therapist, for example, representing an improved version of a key figure from the past or unique in guiding the patient through a difficult life juncture? It occurs to me that the best and most versatile therapists can work in many types of disjunctive and conjunctive formats, and are skilled at moving from one to the other as needed.

The Elusive Nature of the Conjunctive Process: Karen

All this talk of conjunction and techniques for achieving it may underrepresent the place of the therapist's skill in successfully negotiating therapy. Doing good therapy is more like conducting a symphony than carrying out technical maneuvers. At one moment, the patient is listening for a mournful, resonant note from thc thcrapist, signaling the therapist's comprehension of a lonely recollection. Even then, though, there is likely to be rising tension in the background, like the ominous trill of a lone flute, while a muffled drum beat builds a slow cadence. The symphony is not its parts. Instead, its parts play with and against one another, each moment intricately sequenced with the next. The symphony is the final dynamic configuration, parts precisely arranged to achieve an effect.

The following detailed clinical segment from a single session with Karen, illustrating our own efforts to achieve musical harmony, is intended to demonstrate the complex, significantly nonverbal nature of the conjunctive therapy process. As will be my preference throughout the book, I chose the clinical segment randomly because I wanted to use typical clinical material for illustration.

Karen's husband, Carl, has developed a fatal illness; he will die sometime soon. His conviction that he will be betrayed has peaked, as Karen withdraws from his irritability, making him even more argumentative than usual with Karen. Everything she says and does evokes a surly response from him. She is forced to reexperience through Carl her father's torrents of abuse. With her father, these episodes were about her ''uselessness'' and alleged promiscuity. More relevant, she says, she will be left to fend for herself, another abandonment in the making. Worst of all, she is prevented in the moment from feeling either sad or sympathetic, since Carl's attacks are so relentless.

There is nowhere to turn apart from me. She is ambivalent about my suddenly becoming indispensable in her life. I somehow should have prevented this crisis, warning her that Carl could become this way. Yet I am all she has. She would like to roast me on a fire, but she needs me.

According to Karen, Carl's demands and irascibility keep getting worse. Last session she talked about his escalating requests for time together, heightened by a proposal that they visit his family in a month and then take a cruise a month after that. These plans are to be added to three other trips planned over the next five months. Since Carl has become so difficult to be with his new requests push Karen past her limit. Karen earnestly wants to do what is right for Carl, yet she can hardly stand being with him.

Karen enters my office. From the moment we begin, her tense stare sets me on edge. My immediate sense is that there is something I was supposed to comprehend but failed at. Clearly, Karen means business: the thinly disguised knife edge of her opening words scrape harshly on my brain. "My nephew Alan loved the gift I sent him . . . such a remarkable boy." By implication, she is commenting on my imperfections. In response, I greet her cautiously, listening for projections of her rage incorporated in dark statements about people in her life. Cowering inside, I find myself wanting to assuage her.

She continues, "Carl's getting worse. He throws things at the neighbor's irritating dog, cursing at the top of his lungs. He's started to smoke again, so his condition will progress even faster. Still, there are people around me with integrity. It was so calming to be with my Austrian friend Frieda for a few minutes. She's like a rock." The atmosphere in my office is heavy with my dread as Karen runs through her litany of Carl's abuses and the virtuous people, excluding me, who are free from his pestilence.

But it is not entirely uncontained dread that I am feeling. I am also used to Karen being this way when she feels under siege. Tapping into our past experience, I try to position myself so our interaction can be constructive. From the moment we greet each other, I attempt to understand and manage her assault so we can eventually get on track and again work clinically.

I have to admit, I never like being with Karen when she gets this way. Her influence casts a shadow that makes the world seem like a terrible place. Also, I can easily find myself on the verge of becoming angry at her because she eventually becomes so cold during these episodes, assuming that my loathing matches hers, and forgetting how frightened Carl has become.

My personal reactions aside, by now I know that if I'm patient, and a bit compliant, Karen's angry detachment will pass, and she will be in a better position to make sense out of her rage. Automatically, I find myself knitting a temporary cocoon around myself, intending to hibernate a bit until the storm subsides.

Be aware, my described reactions and behavior are not the part of my posture associated with proper dynamic therapy technique. Simultaneously, I adhere to both standards. I am considerate, work hard to understand the manifest and latent psychology of my patient, as well as the current clinical situation. Also, I am judiciously opaque when I think it is clinically indicated.

Still, I have come to the point in my clinical development where I am willing to discuss and show my emotions, such as my tenseness or dread, with a patient like Karen, when I think doing so will serve our therapeutic ends. In this instance, I believe that Karen wants to know I am affected by her, and so I indicate through my tone of voice and body language that I am. I take fewer pains to disguise these cues than I might consider doing with a patient with different needs and tolerances.

An observer in my office would see only indications of the moods I have described. He or she would find me in my tie, smiling mildly as I greet Karen, politely gesturing to her to sit.

My voice would sound modulated, reasonable, while I wait patiently for Karen to speak. My statements are as considered as I can make them as I sift them through my comprehending therapeutic net. The ambiance is set to allow as much self-reflection as possible for Karen and myself.

But the observer would also perhaps notice that the substance I have come to sacrifice less and less in my work is authenticity. I encourage it in the patient, and continually, deliberately, reorient myself, making sure to talk about and collaboratively examine my reactions, give evidence of my enthusiasm, express concern, whenever this kind of honesty will not confuse or burden the patient with the idea that I need her support for us to move on.

All that aside, we are also two human beings together in a moment of urgency and part of my reaction is to that reality. The person I am with needs my help. I know how to give it using the principles of dynamic therapy. However, if I am too reserved, I am likely to deprive or disappoint the patient in reality. How, I continually ask myself, do I strike the proper balance? With Karen, I made the decision that I would best achieve this goal by being thoughtfully willing to be intimidated and remain so until I sensed her return as my collaborator.

Back to the clinical material, I get the point. Karen is suffused with rage. Carl will leave her when he dies, and he doesn't care to make his exit even slightly easy for himself or her. There is no one there to care for her, and all the available supplies are rationed so they flow to Carl. In that circumstance, she is convinced that I will be like her self-centered mother, not bothering to try to comprehend her suffering. As Karen's rage grows in the moment, these anticipated crimes expand in her mind. She begins to have thoughts like: he'll screw me not just emotionally but also financially. And you, Steve, should have warned me, done what you could to prevent this outcome. This progression, from a mild sense of dissatisfaction to utter catastrophe, happens in the first 15 minutes of our session.

I am both participant and observer in this process. From the moment our eyes met, Karen and I were figuring each other out, with me automatically comparing the ambivalence of our encounter to all of our other experiences together. This one was familiar. I understood not to speak too quickly; Karen would need time to decompress or she would be further inundated with her experience as a victim, even less able to take distance from and evaluate it. Also, rather than repel the intimidation I felt, I knew from experience that we would benefit most if I became interested in it, regulating it so it could suffuse through rather than decimate me. In this way, I was most likely to understand why Karen needed me to feel that way and come up with a formulation she and I could begin to work with.

Even while she tested my tenacity and motives, part of Karen always understood how therapy works. She knew and respected the principle that the therapist is not entirely a real life participant in the process, more a catalyst for the patient to inventory, process, and reintegrate inner experience. Nonetheless, the tenseness in our interaction began to feel remarkably real to me. I had the sense that Karen's metered assault was about to degrade into a raging torrent. My temperance was wearing thin, and I could hardly contain my irritation at her lack of sympathy for Carl and her ingratitude toward me. My cocoon became more than just a regulatory device to moderate my response, so I could work with it. I was beginning to need some place to hide so I would keep my irritation in check and keep myself focused on the fact that I was probably becoming the victim in an enactment, Karen's experience of victimization being displaced to me.

The orchestra deteriorated into dissonance; Karen and I were out of synchrony. I was thrown back on my dynamically informed repertoire, tempted to make a transference interpretation, groping for something to do to heal the huge rift that was widening between us. And, then, the unexpected. Karen inexplicably relaxed. "I'm worried, Steve, I've been doing everything to make Carl comfortable, even agreeing to travel with him when I don't want to. I'm keeping my rage to myself. You'd think that inside I would be fed up. But, strangely, I'm spending much of my time crying. It's not just that Carl will die; it's also that I'll feel such a vacuum.''

I experienced a slight hope. Something seemed to have worked. I began to relax, only to be jolted back to Karen's cynicism, once again. Carl, Karen opined, led such a self-indulgent life. I picked up the familiar signal. Here we go again, the litany of Carl's sins against humanity. One false move and Carl's filth would become mine.

This back and forth shifting occurred in only a few clinical moments. I was off-balance again, doing everything I could in the midst of my confusion to indicate to Karen that I was following her, taking her seriously. I wanted to inquire about her new attack, and ordinarily would have done so, but it took me by surprise with no time to recover. I felt myself coerced into delivering the nonverbal message that she and I were of one mind about Carl. I felt straightjacketed. I could have articulated my experience, wondering what the shift meant about the scenario being enacted; I might even have concocted an on-the-spot dynamic formulation, but I did neither. Instead, in response to her intimidation, I held fast, deciding not to challenge Karen's allegations, honoring instead her insistence on being heard.

For a minute I thought my rapport with Karen had returned, but it was quickly lost and for no reason I could identify. She actually had launched me into a brief sentimental reverie, allowing me to privately picture Carl seriously ill, musing sadly about his death, and then she pulled the rug out from under me. The segment I have described lasted for 15 minutes. During it, I was buffeted between irritation at Karen and sadness for Carl, constantly being warned, nonverbally, that this was no moment for therapeutic exploration. In the end, I found myself unable to do anything but defer, waiting until a more auspicious moment to intervene.

And, then, out of nowhere a sweet, wistful melody entered, Karen saying:

> The women in my cycling group are a hardy lot, you know. Two have lost husbands, and one has lupus. They're in their 50s, but

they imbibe life, drinking in the good and bad equally, and prevailing. And I like that they don't ask too many questions, are easy about accepting me. I didn't tell you that I made a stylish necklace for one of the women, the first piece of jewelry I've made in years. She seemed so grateful, both she and I were thrilled by the workmanship.

I still hadn't made my transference statement about Carl's abuse and anticipated abandonment, reminding her of her childhood experience of her father's defection, with Karen's mother unable and unwilling to rescue her. It was now 45 minutes into the hour, the interpretation superfluous. Not only was our rapport returning, but Karen was showing signs of healthy acceptance of herself and others, in addition to Carl. Somehow my lungs were starting to fill with clean air; the wistful melody was gaining body, even resounding. Suddenly, the whole orchestra became involved, parts integrating rather than playing against each other. Carl was comfortably being incorporated by Karen as someone to be understood, but more importantly, the two of us were playing well together.

I defy anyone to describe this clinical sequence scientifically. It certainly has form that, with work, can be comprehended, and the principles governing its development are not all that hard to explicate. But the way the parts aligned themselves is so elusive. How did I know to pull back in the beginning? What could have informed me that such a bleak start could be a prelude to an epiphany for both of us, especially after my encouragement was dashed a second time as Karen again began to recite Carl's vices? What in my manner and tone convinced Karen that I was taking her grating complaints seriously enough for her to finally put them aside and dredge up a deeper optimism?

What did we really accomplish? Did we achieve a genuine conjunctive shift, with Karen and I moving our perspectives from loss and death to life? What was the enduring therapeutic value of my strategically managing Karen's irritation and readiness to blame? Did she know anything more about herself by the end of this hour, the background and motives for her fear of Carl's assaults and his medical condition, her need to enlist me through intimidation? In my opinion, the answer is "yes," on two accounts. My belief is that Karen's internal representation of Carl, me, and, I would guess, people in general was made safer, more benign, through this experience. Maintaining that change will, of course, require that the experience be repeated, grooved in. Second, to the extent that the achieved state can be repeated and retrieved, Karen is in a better frame of mind to examine the psychology of her reactions and to explore their reworking. She is ready to be a better therapy collaborator. She and I will be in an improved position to examine the components of our therapy experience, acknowledging the realistic stresses, such as Carl's tendency to be offensive and the fear engendered by his progressing illness, as well as by my personal contributions to our experience.

Notice the power and pervasiveness of the nonverbal negotiation in this passage. Karen's recovery occurred as if by magic, apparently in response to my developing the affective intensity she required to relax. Given my limited ability to objectively read the fine details of the process, this development seemed nearly inexplicable, almost transcendent. What I can clearly see, however, is that her revival was the product of an intense negotiation between the two of us. Always present, and critical to the ultimate conjunction, was the fact that we were striving for rapprochement. We were both doing everything we could to reconnect in a meaningful and constructive way. In contrast to traditional views of how therapy should be conducted, I became strategically reticent, willing to be nondefensively intimidated and ostensibly contrite, timing my affective recovery with her readiness to accept it. My contention is that these kinds of maneuvers are heavily distributed throughout any clinical sequence and are primary ingredients in moving the sequence along toward success.

The apparent lack of therapeutic content, the absence of exploration and interpretation in this therapy session is, I contend, just that: apparent. Within this sequence, I learned nonverbally about the extent of Karen's distress and the character of its violent underpinnings. She discovered that I was not the depriving mother she anticipated me to be, and that in fact I respected her pressing need to be helped and heard. She must also have noticed my censure of her harsh views of the dying Carl. In our rapprochement, she shifted to a view of Carl that was closer to the more humane picture that I implicitly advocated. Together, we created a new affective connection that allowed her to begin to mourn Carl's anticipated death. We achieved an emotionally creative solution, both of us shifting to a view of the other that represented a marked departure from the ghosts of our pasts.

Concluding Statement

Therapeutic conjunctions are in the moment. They happen when all the voices and sections in the orchestra are synchronizing. They cannot be fully mapped or anticipated. They consist of the kinds of episodic, inexplicable developments contained in my clinical hour with Karen. The therapy partners are involved in a deeply personal process, spontaneous and creative by nature, usually guided by one or more theories that lay out therapeutic and psychological principles.

The conjunctive therapy process is facilitated if and when the therapist does not shy away from actively pushing it along. He is well advised to move toward optimizing the attunement and consensus between himself and the patient. Strengthening his personal commitment with the patient by using these measures makes excellent clinical sense. None of these actions will interfere with the possibility of the two more formally exploring and elucidating the patient's psychology.

There are so many types of therapeutic joining, some arising out of utter despair, others bursting forth like crystalline fountains, always discovered by therapy partners together. To continue our more formal journey toward exploring conjunctive therapy, we will, in chapter 2, undertake a detailed examination of the conjunctive process. In chapter 3, we will look, in detail, at the interpersonal field in which therapy takes place. Then, in chapters 4 and 5, we will check in with the people most intimately involved, the patient and therapist, detailing their job descriptions, delineating what each is responsible for contributing to the therapy enterprise. From that point, culminating in an overview in chapter 9, we will explore in detail the requirements of the conjunctive process.

2

The Structure of the Conjunctive Therapy Process

Intuition and nonverbal negotiation permeate therapy as it moves toward conjunction, requiring the therapy couple to negotiate the steps and fulfill conditions I call the *conjunctive sequence.* But within that sequence the conjunctive process is marked by discontinuities, which under the therapeutic microscope may emerge as radical fractures in the therapy process. First though, we will explore the concept of conjunction in its component parts: (1) those forces that align therapist and patient; (2) complicating factors including intrapsychic themes and interpersonal agendas imposed by both therapist and patient; and (3) the therapist's responsibility for actively moving the therapy along while always making room for the patient's contributions. Framing therapy in this way leads to new technical recommendations for conducting therapy that are designed to enhance the intensity and accuracy of the work.

According to the conjunctive model, psychotherapy is a virtuoso performance, two people playing together magnificently. But parts of the production may be complex and discordant, like a modern composition, sections of which sound like a jangle of dissonance and are designed to make a psychological point. In that case, magnificent means creative, often with a radical edge. If you admit that there is something electrifying about the idea

41

of "radical," would not you want to know more about the com-
poser's personal elation and torment, making his or her creation
possible? It's the same with therapeutic conjunctions. On the
surface, the idea of conjunction may sound sweet, rhapsodic, not
that complicated. But peel away the surface, and you will find
intricacy and surprise, the surprise being emotionally jolting if
it is going to fit its purpose. Karen, at the end of chapter 1,
illustrates the incongruent picture of turmoil and delight that
emerges. The uncertainty, the clash of emotions, can be devastat-
ing, the experience overwhelming and confusing, mandating that
the path to conjunction be traversed only with a safe and skill-
ful partner.

We are seeking the technical know-how in this chapter.
Moving from a reassuring view of therapy built on beautifully
executed music, we are after the sometimes exalted, sometimes
tedious, often wrenching, but always creative experience that
inspires the composition. We know that attaining to such an
epiphany, especially in a two-person therapy world, is infinitely
complicated, fraught with anxiety and confusion, and usually
only becomes rewarding as the therapy partners catch sight of
their destination. Skills need to be precise, requiring data to make
strategic decisions. When applied to the music of human experience, they need to be particularly rigorous.

Our task in this chapter, then, is to put the musical pair
under a microscope, recognizing that the individual components
of the performance, when most magnified and detached, may
bear only an obscure relationship to the whole. When a small
section of the composition is played alone, it may sound thin or
ragged, thoroughly lacking in appeal, a far reach from a creative
victory. My experience with Karen for the first two-thirds of our
session, reported at the end of chapter 1, was more like the
arduous experience of learning the first screeching scales on a
violin than anything we associate with well-played music. Of
course, the end point in my session with Karen was ecstatic,
both of us thrilled we had survived, shocked that we could again
become enthralled by the music we were making.

Fine Tuning: The Component Parts of the
Conjunctive Process

So many factors, personal characteristics and emotional pulls included, work to connect people in therapy. In the following section I have placed these in four categories. The first are implicated in the *alignment* between therapist and patient and include trust and safety, attunement, nonverbal communication augmenting growth in both partners, as well as each partner coming to accommodate the other's temperamental style and developmentally based limitations. A second category, which I call *Grappling with Distorting Influences,* includes the therapist experiencing and understanding the patient's cognitive and emotional invitations to enact transference scenarios, as well as the therapist becoming clear about the ways he similarly contaminates the therapy field. Third is the therapist's responsibility to *take the initiative to move the therapy along,* including clearing his mind of preconceptions as a prelude to discerning what the patient and therapy require, tolerating and using disorientation constructively, as well as nondisjunctively helping the patient meet his needs and goals. Finally, in any therapy, there are always *disjunctions developing, interacting with and eroding conjunctions.* Naming, ranking, and charting all these influences establishes direction for the therapy work.

Alignment

Fit makes all the difference in psychotherapy. Patient and therapist struggle for a purpose, the patient repeatedly needing to test the therapist's most basic motivations and skills. They sense comprehension in each other, building the trust necessary to keep the therapy afloat during difficult times. Each partner also welcomes the extra effort the other makes to be comprehensible, intuitively compensating for that partner's temperamental and emotional style. But more specifically, to make a therapy experience persuasive enough for the patient to give himself over to the change process, it has to be set upon the following foundation:

1. *Interpersonal trust and safety:* Comfortable, productive interpersonal relating requires trust and respect for each partner's vulnerabilities. Unflinching basic trust may be more important to the therapy situation than almost anywhere else in life because of the requirement to reveal oneself to another. But building such trust is an arduous process, necessitating that breaches are reliably and rigorously examined and healed. To achieve conjunction, attaining reliable trust and interpersonal safety must become a given.

After Karen decided I might not be realistic enough about Carl's abusiveness, relocating trust was the overriding goal for both of us as we built toward her realignment with me. At the beginning of that hour, Karen needed room to breathe emotionally and required me to step back and create that space. Karen's ability to come through at the end is evidence to me that she was privately mining for this trust all along. In this therapy sequence, the powerful joining forces at the core of the conjunctive process, although buried, had been solidly set down previously by our tireless conjunctive efforts.

2. *Attunement:* Analogous to the music created between mother and infant, an attuned experience is sought moment by moment by the therapy couple, each feeling the other's pitch and rhythm, reading his or her needs and availability to shift to a comprehending stance. Attunement to the effect of the other, particularly the therapist's attunement to the patient's affective shifts, lends a silent but thoroughly vital coloring to any interaction that is indispensable to its success.

3. *Nonverbal communications augmenting growth in both partners:* People understand a great deal of what each other intends, often the message is delivered without words. In fact, I believe much of this communicating is as specific as any verbal statement, informing the recipient about the communicator's meanings and motives. This nonverbal conversation is supported

by attunement, as the two listen to each other's tone, pitch, and rhythm.

Karen makes the statement, without words, that she needs me to recognize how desperately unhappy she is living with Carl as he prepares to die. She wants me to know her misery and help her to do something about it. As a child, her parents had been too self-involved to care when she was in trouble. I doubt that she could have drawn as powerful a response from me with words alone. Instead, her angry withdrawal, her words disappearing before they came out, prodded me to feel just what kind of response she needed. From my side, I allowed myself to be sucked under by her whirlpool of emotions until I got her message.

The interaction between Karen and me is reminiscent of mutual regulation between mother and child. When it works well, they reciprocally stimulate each other signaling need, danger, and responsiveness (Beebe and Lachmann, 1988, 2002; Grossman, 1996; La Barre, 2001, 2003; Schore, 1994, 1997). While both mother and child participate in this process, the mother from the start has the primary function of identifying and reversing these disruptions (Beebe and Lachmann, 2003; Greenspan, 1997; Schore, 1996, 2003). In fact, the "good enough" mother described by Schore (1997) "[inadvertently] induces a stress response in her infant through a misattunement [and reinvokes] in a timely fashion her psychobiologically attuned regulation of the infant's negative affect state that she has triggered" (p. 16).

In another modality, children and adults are capable of implanting their feelings in others not just by eliciting a mood, such as sympathy, when they feel a loss, but by relocating their own unwelcome inner experiences in the other through projective identification (Ogden, 1982). Karen's despair and anger about Carl's immanent loss became mine in our interaction. Experiencing it so powerfully helped me to understand just what kind of response she needed from me.

Added to their discoveries about each other, therapist and patient also locate within themselves levels of experience that are unformulated or barely formulated (Fourcher, 1992; Donnel Stern, 1997). That concept explains my experience of surprise as Karen led me to acknowledge her penetrating ability to understand Carl. I had intuitively appreciated her uncanny reading of people all along, but barely registered it consciously. At times, unformulated experience may first be discovered only after it is transferred, nonverbally, to another person through projective identification (Bollas, 1991), and then, "decontaminated" (Bion, 1967, p. xiii), as it is taken back to be owned again by the subject.

Neurophysiological research is demonstrating how nonverbal and affective communication occur as a result of interactive cerebral activity; for example, the right cerebral hemisphere of one person relating to the right hemisphere of another. There is now substantial neurobiological research evidence that an individual's internal representation of him- or herself in interaction with others and the associated affective states can be accessed and modified throughout life. This notion is based on research demonstrating capacities for plasticity in the adult brain (Cozolino, 2003; Grigsby and Stevens, 2000; Gross, 1985; Johnson and Hugdahl, 1993; Schore, 1997). Affective states are mediated by the right cerebral hemisphere, in particular through the right orbitofrontal cortex, which has a unique role in social and emotional behaviors, in the regulation of body and motivational states, and in the adjustment and correction of emotional responses (Schore, 1994, pp. 34–42). A therapist and patient together can reactivate these structures, reviving the affectively powerful experiences of a mother–child or father–child interaction. The two mutually regulate each other and thereby may effect "structural transmutations" (Schore, 1997, pp. 231, 448–453). The therapist and patient together create an interdependent dyadic growth-promoting environment (Greenspan, 1981, 1997).

4. *Accommodating the other's temperamental style and developmentally based limitations:* Everyone has needs and preferences colored by temperament and engendered by deprivation, trauma, or indulgence during childhood. These preferences and needs are sensed and accommodated by partners in successful human interactions.

For a therapist to connect effectively with a patient he must sense areas where the person's development was skewed or incomplete and adjust his or her behavior accordingly. Although less sanctioned as appropriate therapeutic technique, patients, in fact, do the same for therapists. Neither patient nor therapist will respond with emotional depth, or even be able to understand the other, unless he or she makes the appropriate adjustments to the other's developmentally based idiosyncrasies. Returning to the example in chapter 1, Karen could quickly lose any assurance that my commitment to her could be reliable, regressing to the insecurity of a rapprochement age child with an unresponsive parent (Mahler, 1971). In that instance, Karen experienced me as not just critical but as unreliable as well, with Karen losing the sense of basic trust that had started to develop in our relationship.

But it worked the other way, too. My father could be as cold as ice, distinctly short on emotional availability. When Karen withdrew, I felt her loss, perhaps more acutely than would a therapist with a different developmental history. When I tried to fill in the emotional void in the way I had learned as a child, by struggling to understand her, she responded. I was doing my job as therapist by making her feel recognized, but I was also, inadvertently, quelling my sense of loss after she withdrew. To claim that my more private motives were entirely altruistic would be disingenuous. I liked, even needed in a limited way, to reconnect with Karen affectively.

Failure of alignment, whether reflecting breaches in trust, attunement, verbal or nonverbal communication, or mismatches between partners based on developmental idiosyncrasies, are all implicated in some of the most subtle, at times, lethal disjunctions arising in therapy. In *Hidden Faults* (2000), I call these disjunctions, reflecting mismatches between partners, *external disjunctions.* Since they are frequently nonverbal, there is often no way for either of the therapy partners to verifiably recognize them. Mainly the therapy duo feels the limitation in their rapport and either registers or accommodates to it. Karen's idealization of me early in our work is one variety of an external disjunction operative at that time, since it prevented her more ambivalent feelings from emerging.

Grappling with Distorting Influences

Therapist and patient live in a hot, complicated interpersonal world. Without the heat, the tensions and excitements, the participants would be stick figures, with the challenges of their union only practical. Tolerating, understanding, and taming internal and interpersonal storms are a major facet of psychotherapy technique, with patient and therapist grateful to the other for doing his or her part.

1. *The willingness of each to tolerate the other's cognitive and emotional invitations and then attempt to understand them:* These pulls, of course, come in the form of transference–countertransference distortions and related enactments, where one or both members of the couple feel misunderstood or idealized, and projective identifications, where a partner feels infiltrated by emotions not belonging to him- or herself. As with Karen, when she alarmed me to get me to understand her anguish, an invitation to enact a distressing role or experience a projective identification can be offered with the goal of furthering the work of therapy (Frankel, 1997). The hoped for product of this kind of collaboration is a closer alignment between therapy partners.

2. *The therapist's effort to know his limitations, and free himself of distorting unconscious agendas:* For patient and therapist to achieve the highest level of attunement, based on their striving for progressive authenticity, the distortions and unconscious personal and interpersonally enacted agendas they bring to the therapy need to become known to them. This often strenuous,

personal and shared introspective process, described in detail throughout the book as *controlled disorientation,* is instrumental in achieving conjunction. Controlled disorientation, orchestrated by the therapist and linked with moment-by-moment collaboration between therapist and patient, supersedes, but incorporates, one-sided introspection as the most effective way to carry out this activity.

The main parts of the conjunctive process tapped in this section have to do with collaboration. That collaboration occurs verbally, but also, as in my experience with Brittany and Karen, in hundreds of microscopic nonverbal incidents, all aspects of the process I call *reciprocal knowing.* The objective of this collaboration is to understand and resolve disjunctions, in this case those arising from expressed-in-action aspects of the psychology of both therapy partners. I refer to this class of disjunctions as *internal disjunctions* (Frankel, 2000). A more deliberate category of collaboration involves *transfers of authority to know and lead* in the therapy, with the shifts usually instigated by the therapist. My claim is that the successful outcome of the clinical sequence at the end of chapter 1 with Karen was largely the result of my switching the responsibility for timing the resolution to her. In that case the initiative and shift were carried out nonverbally and Karen then paced our exploration of the rift she experienced in our rapport.

The Therapist's Initiative:
Its Many Forms

The view that the therapist–patient relationship is, in many ways, symmetrical, meaning that each partner usefully has authority to direct the therapy, does not contradict the necessity for the therapist to take ultimate responsibility for the success of the therapy. I believe that even therapists who advocate a relatively passive role for the therapist take more initiative in giving therapy direction and encouraging the patient's progress than they acknowledge. There are several requirements for carrying out this function.

1. *Nondisjunctive aspects of the therapist's behavior and the therapist's commitment to making therapy work:* Over and above everything, patients want to know that a therapist is committed to making therapy work, not by standing on ceremony but by being active in furthering the therapy goals. This aspect of the therapy work is nondisjunctive; it is experienced as caring, the therapist's willingness to go out of his way to carry through on the promise of help that is latent in every therapy contact.

2. *The therapist's ability to tolerate and use controlled disorientation to understand the patient and the work of the therapy:* The key to this activity is timing. When the therapist experiences psychological or emotional forces from within or outside himself that he doesn't understand, he needs to embrace and tolerate these until he comes to know and make use of his understanding, sharpening his connection with the patient. Controlled disorientation applied in this regulated way, is a profoundly useful epistemological device in therapy; its use also functions as a signal to the patient that the therapist will endure anxiety and confusion in his struggle to understand the patient.

3. *The therapist's responsibility to refresh repeatedly his perceptions about the patient and therapy by clearing his mind of preconceptions:* This activity goes hand in hand with the therapist continually searching for a fresh, unique sense of the work, always maintaining a creative edge. Since therapy is so subjective, mind clearing combined with collaboration is a precondition for finding direction through controlled disorientation. Moment by moment, therapist and patient supply feedback to each other, as they strive to overcome their biases and misperceptions. Maximum creativity is facilitated by the therapist, and, when possible, the patient, by going beyond the edge of what is known and understood by the two, as well as by tolerating the massive disorientation this activity produces. The therapist being described

is proactive, always searching for new, generative perspectives to further the therapy work.

4. *The therapist's, and at times the patient's, responsibility for discerning what the patient and therapy require at a given moment, and then acting on this knowledge:* As we have seen, when you closely monitor a productive therapy hour, you will find that the therapist develops a conviction about what is happening in the therapy and what the patient needs at any given point. The therapist then acts more definitively, sometimes making a verbal statement about his belief, sometimes communicating it nonverbally through behavior.

This event, the *leap of inference*, comes at a critical time in a therapy hour. Therapist and perhaps patient have been gathering information collaboratively, attempting to discern what the therapy requires to move forward. When either therapist or patient, but usually the therapist, is reasonably convinced his impression and timing is correct, he acts, making his position known. While the leap of inference may include interpretative aspects making the psychology of the patient clear, it is fundamentally about action. The therapist acts using words, timing, emphasis, and initiative. The leap is carefully timed and orchestrated with the goal of achieving a result. The leap is often bold, moving beyond the familiar territory covered by the therapist and patient. It has a key place in the therapy sequence, bringing the partners distinctly closer to the patient's therapeutic objectives.

In my view, an additional requirement for this step to succeed has to do with the therapist's humility and willingness to check repeatedly with the patient to confirm or disconfirm his thinking. In fact, the collaborative process I envision for therapy requires that authority to know and lead in the therapy be regularly moved between therapist and patient, with the therapist generally being responsible for orchestrating these shifts.

My leap of inference with Karen involved recognizing that I needed to pull back and let her deliver her message. I made it clear that my discomfort with her critical behavior made it hard for me to evaluate my part in having caused it and that I was willing to be patient enough to understand her reaction. I indicated my comprehension of what she needed by drawing back into my "cocoon," and staying there until she could contain and process her annoyance *with me*. The entire sequence, as I pulled back, reflects my most critical decision in that session, a leap of inference through which I delivered a clear message to her that she was in control and that I could tolerate and work with her to understand her rage.

Most defining about the activities of the conjunctive process subsumed in "the therapist's initiative, its many forms," is their basically disjunctive nature. The key concept here is that disjunctions, plumbed for the information they contain and resolved collaboratively, are one of the main vehicles for arriving at conjunction. This aspect of the conjunctive process is the most tumultuous. It requires the best "sight reading" and collaboration skills by both partners. Learning to play this symphony tends to occur according to steps of the conjunctive sequence. This series of attitudes and procedures encompasses the technical challenges two therapy partners encounter as they strive to connect conjunctively. The steps in the conjunctive sequence include: incipient conjunction, disjunction, controlled disorientation, reciprocal knowing, and transfers of authority to know, the leap of inference, the principle and techniques involved in going beyond the edge of what is known, the yet to be described challenge of finding a fully alive part of the patient with which to connect, the powerful influence of the nonverbal therapy dialogue in the therapeutic exchange, the requirement that the therapist be proactive, and conjunction. These steps are all taken with the objective of achieving creative change in both partners; that is, patient and therapist composing truly great music together. Conjunction rests on the bedrock of finding ever more pure forms of authenticity, requiring ongoing interpersonal rubble clearing to eliminate distorting blockages. Altogether, there is a direct correlation between the extent of the disorientation, turmoil, and sheer determination of therapist and patient, and the creative result of this shared experience.

How It All Fits Together, Establishing a
Direction in Pursuit of Conjunction:
An Integrated Example

At each point, the conjunctive process actually consists of multiple simultaneously developing conjunctions and disjunctions, each with its own theme, and each having more or less influence for the individual and couple. Without an assessment that accounts for each of these activities, their relative importance in the therapist's or patient's personality or interaction at that moment, and how they are or are not dynamically related to one another, it is impossible to get a clear picture of the type, character, and source of a hoped for conjunction, and the most reasonable means for achieving it.

This case illustration of Brittany covers our conjunctive experience, its expansion and decline, over a period of 20 years, highlighting one year when she was 33. The issue of attunement and the requirement that the therapist be proactive are emphasized, as are the disruption and repair of the therapy rapport, with contributions to its recovery by both Brittany and myself. A critical step in the success of this segment is my willingness to be straightforward with Brittany about my opinion of her desire to change jobs. Further, a critical discontinuity leading to a distinct deepening of our rapport occurs when Brittany empathizes with me, as she becomes aware that I am distracted by a life crisis of my own.

Brittany speaks with a whisper, when she can find her words. She is hunched into a shape that reminds me of a bent broom. She lives in a dingy studio apartment, never escaping the din of the delivery trucks running beneath her window. Although she had a fine education, first at a small southern college and then at an excellent graduate school of journalism, upon finishing graduate school she withdrew to bed for 6 months, wracked with depression, muscle pain, and headaches. Talented, she finally found a job in a company she came to hate. In therapy, she felt no hope of inducing me to care about her agony, as if I would simply be contemptuous of her disability.

I know a lot about Brittany. I treated her in psychotherapy for 3 years beginning at age 15. Even then she was feeling tenuous, moving from one of her divorced parents' homes to another, watching as her four siblings, including her twin sister, slid into drug use and academic failure. The hope by the end of that period of therapy and her graduation from high school was that Brittany could capitalize on her talents, throwing off the weight of her parents' and siblings' troubles.

I think I fueled that hope, often implicitly, when she won a scholarship to study in England during her junior year in high school and I rejoiced, privately harboring the wish that my own daughter would be as visionary as Brittany when she reached 17. I believe Brittany could sense my hopes and appreciation for her, even when I did not express them aloud. This is the kind of nonverbal cuing that provides a framework on which the tapestry of collaborative therapy is woven.

Brittany and I saw each other occasionally, for a few sessions each time, after she finished high school. When I did hear from her, I clammered for evidence that she had moved beyond the prison walls of her childhood. Also, even though our contacts were few, we never forgot the odd ways she could induce me to comprehend her mood, an experience we called "reflecting" (as in reflections from a mirror), presumably based on her powerful early connection to her twin sister.

Neither Brittany nor I expected her catastrophic decline, beginning soon after we lost all contact, 4 years after she left college and in the second year of graduate school. Petrified about what she would do after graduation, she began to turn every comment made by any teacher into a condemnation. She barely made it through those three postgraduate years, every relationship becoming tarnished by her growing paranoia.

Back in treatment, barely short of suicide at age 30, Brittany was almost unreachable emotionally. The expectable moment of cordiality at the beginning of every session vanished rapidly,

Brittany's ability to think and speak evaporating. The evil force attending this phenomenon eluded me each time; it was just suddenly there again and again infecting everything that followed. Strangely, I could hardly escape the feeling that I was the chemist creating this putrid mix, Brittany the victim of my despicable plot. The poisoning always seemed to begin with the golden moment of our initial contact.

Brittany's despair was overwhelming for both of us, hardly the setting for a future conjunction between us. It frightened and exhausted me because no matter how hard I tried to help she seemed to get worse. Hospitalization would have simplified matters, at a minimum removing Brittany from my care for a while, giving us both a rest. But something made me resist that solution; I could not shake the belief that for Brittany to recover I needed to hold onto her for dear life and not yield to the temptation to take an easier way. My tenacity was sustained by the connection to the promising, emotionally brilliant kid I had met years earlier.

Still, I kept picturing Brittany's suicide, worrying in tandem, to my chagrin, about what, in the event of her suicide, an imagined malpractice suit would do to my career. Was it worth the risk for me to remain true to my intuition that Brittany needed proof that I cared enough to struggle to understand her experience and help her?

Several episodes, traceable to at least age 15, became the main ingredients of our ultimate conjunction. (1) The early psychological romance was pivotal, where I regarded Brittany like an ideal daughter, she experiencing me as the connected, devoted parent she never had. The "reflecting" phenomenon thickened our potion by enabling us to intuit each other's needs. From early on, then, there was a unique bond, a powerful one, between us. (2) Brittany's desolation after leaving home, putting her childhood behind her, created a vacuum between us. Her sense of security imploded, forcing her back to feeling entirely alone as when her parents went their own ways during her childhood, neglecting all their children. Brittany's aloneness was bone chilling for me, filling me with dread, but paradoxically it drew me in, mandating that I help her. (3) Then, years later, back on the scene, I felt Brittany's despair more poignantly than ever, but this time I was caught up in it as a perceived perpetrator. After all, it was not so easy for me to make her life better any more. Here then was the disjunction, one of mammoth proportions, giving me firsthand experience of what Brittany's subjective experience of abandonment, victimization, and rage felt like.

Everything I have mentioned was explored between me and Brittany, often with the anticipation of enlightenment. But the results were unimpressive, Brittany's ability to speak-up faded, leaving me dangling each time as she progressively lost her bearings in life. Her pain persisted, hardly responsive to treatment. Yet, we did make progress of a sort as I came to understand her better, the mechanism being less related to our words than our actions. Slowly, through wrenching episodes like the one described with Brittany in chapter 1, where by creating experiences in me paralleling her own, I understood that Brittany required me to listen to her in a new way. For one thing, I needed to reduce my pace, wait for responses. The waiting often had the sense of pleading, imploring Brittany to show me what I misunderstood, in what ways my tone or rhythm was off. More importantly, she had to help me understand why my misattunements were so toxic for her, reminding her of the emotional desolation of her childhood when the only place she could turn was inside.

In short, in struggling with our disjunction, I was able to understand the grim reality of Brittany's original sense of abandonment by her overburdened parents, as well as her ongoing experience of isolation. By my not abandoning her, we were able to salvage and refurbish our time-tested, affirmative connection. In this instance, our conjunctive process involved both threads, the disjunctive alienation Brittany often felt with me and the affirmative as we repaired our rifts. The result for us was to engage more deeply to understand Brittany's conviction that her inner life would never be of consequence to anyone, and the counterpart in our interaction as she found my responses unsatisfactory.

In another episode many months later when her despair was in a phase of escalation, it became clear that Brittany needed to leave her job, convincing me how destructive the job was for her. When, with the help of therapy, she arranged to quit her job and even collect a stipend as she began to retrain, she became riddled with misgivings about her decision. She was petrified she would fail and could not maintain the conviction I would continue to have faith in her as she changed career direction. After all, she alleged repeatedly, perhaps I had never experienced the kind of hostility she encountered from her parents as a young adult when she wanted something for herself; if so, how could I ever understand why making this change was so agonizing for her? The therapy process was rocky during this time, movement toward restitution melting into despair as she experienced me as hostile to her decision to leave her job.

At about this point my own divorce process began. Privately, I was in agony, and knew that Brittany, because of her profound sensitivity, could sense I was subtly pulling back. In response to my withdrawal, Brittany became even more distressed with me, making it mandatory to tell her I was somewhat immobilized, freeing her from blaming the temporary change in our rapport on herself. I was shocked when upon telling Brittany about the divorce, she immediately became enlivened. She even said she wanted to help, to understand the nature of my pain, and expressed profound relief as I explained to her that in the divorce process I may have experienced distress reminiscent of her own. While she was sorry for my struggle, she observed that, paradoxically, because of it, we were in a better position to feel for, understand, and, I say this with some embarrassment, nonexploitively help one another. The disjunction caused by my personal retreat became the basis of a more exact understanding of each other, fueling our developing conjunction.

The shift in Brittany's mood from this point was striking, emerging as the current bleakness in each of our personal lives intersected. It was helpful, of course, to have our time-tested commitment to one another to steady us, at least at first. But witnessing and weathering Brittany's despair, while giving her the opportunity to retrieve her dignity through empathizing with my own anguish, proved in the end to be the best combination for joining us.

Therapies always begin with therapist and patient assuming they will succeed, each trusting the other to do his or her best. This initial connection may soon disintegrate as anxiety and distrust enter the picture, but if the therapy is to survive, that connection cannot disappear entirely. In *Intricate Engagements* (1995), I called this part of the therapy relationship *the facilitating relationship* and made the point that even as psychotherapy progresses and the facilitating relationship seems to fade, the fundamental commitment it reflects has to remain alive in the background for the therapy to remain viable, creating the backbone of the conjunctive process and sequence.

Over time, regardless of how despondent she became, Brittany retained hope. Her heated dissatisfaction with me in the hour described in chapter 1, following her monologue about alternative healing, was simply the inverse of the importance to her of our original therapy pact. At the end of that sequence Brittany believed I cared to listen, even that I was excited by her ideas about spirituality. Coming this far with another human being was exalting for Brittany, but also for me. We had achieved our goal, joining in a conjunctive process marked by bilateral, creative change. Mapping my experience with Brittany in subsequent hours extended the path of that sequence, consolidating Brittany's faith in the ultimate reliability of our bond. As important as my willingness to tolerate the affective heat generated throughout those hours of Brittany's insistence on being heard and taken seriously, was Brittany's welcoming a chance to see me in human terms and express concern for my personal distress.

The following are major themes in this part of my work with Brittany: (1) Brittany easily felt criticized by all men who reminded her of her father, including me. She saw us as insensitive beings who enjoyed humiliating women like herself. I responded sympathetically but, privately, felt falsely accused. (2)

Brittany desired to be respected by the men she admired, including me. She wished to impress me with her innovative mind and aesthetic sensibility. I felt approving. (1) and (2) are about equal in potency, leaving Brittany confused, withdrawn, and erratically seeking and rejecting relationships with men. (3) Brittany was extraordinarily perceptive about emotional issues, making her ideas relevant to any conversation, though she had difficulty speaking of them. (4) Brittany felt responsible for quelling her mother's, father's, and siblings' pain as the family crumbled when she was a child. She continued to lose her sense of herself when anyone suffered, and she felt criticized when she believed she failed in her responsibility she felt toward them. In therapy, she could become disoriented when she believed she hurt me by being critical or too self-focused.

This mapping of vectors predicts that a conjunctive stance with Brittany required me simultaneously to respect her fear of being unnoticed and even humiliated by me and her yearning to be admired by me. To accomplish this contradictory feat I needed to work hard to understand each of her complaints that I was not following closely enough, while at every opportunity recognizing the remarkable quality of her writing and insightful observations. In working with Brittany, I needed to remember to attend to every nuance of Brittany's experience at each moment, recalling that her shifts between disjunction and joining came quickly.

In contrast to Brittany, an assessment of the conjunctive and disjunctive forces in the early work with Karen seems so much simpler. It includes her limited expectations for herself professionally, the belief she would be abused and disappointed and that people would be unreliable and envious, all in contrast to the anticipation that I would be different. In effect, there was an overriding nondisjunctive conjunction protecting our relationship and work. What I gave her through this part of our conjunctive process was very helpful to her. Later, we discovered it was semistable and rested on the implicit disjunction created by Karen's belief in the near perfection of our relationship, thus keeping the good of our relationship apart from the abusive, bad of her internalized parental representations.

Radical Discontinuity: The Nonlinear
Character of the Conjunctive Process

Following any therapy hour or sequence of hours very closely, microscopically, can be unnerving. Clinical sequences that look logical and continuous on the surface come apart and seem fragmented, hardly related to one another. Suddenly the mood of the session shifts, the patient was being impossible and is now cooperating. A paralyzed therapy springs free without explanation, or, the opposite, is going well and inexplicably grinds to a halt.

Brittany's foul mood, lasting for weeks following our upbeat alternative healing session reported in chapter 1, is an example of the latter situation. In that case, her ruminations about how I might fail by not taking her ideas seriously created a disjunction between us, one I couldn't make sense of at first.

The disappearance of Karen's ill temper toward the end of the session presented at the end of chapter 1 was even less explicable. The outcome of that session was successful, although the beginning and middle were profoundly discordant, and few words outside of Karen's diatribe were spoken. We have established that a conjunctive process was present from the start of the session, our disjunction, brought about by Karen's frustration and despair, obscuring that part of our interaction. My conscious experience during that session, however, was largely of the disjunction, Karen's rage felt entirely personal to me, making me cower inside. Both the conjunctive and disjunctive forces were there in full force, creating the uneven, unpredictable character of that session.

The *discontinuities* to which I refer, leading eventually to joining, are found throughout all psychotherapies, a view supported by reference to the psychological literature on nonlinear dynamics (Grigsby and Stevens, 2000, pp. 104–130; Schachter, 2002, chapter 6) and the clinical use of surprise (Bromberg, 2000). I am using the term *discontinuity* in this instance to describe the incongruent relationship of clinical events to one another, not to denote what each of these events is made of thematically or psychologically. Discontinuities in therapy are sometimes, but not always, based in therapeutic disjunctions, separating the therapist's and patient's interpersonal experiences. At other times they reflect gaps between levels of relating; for example, with therapist and patient joined on one level consciously and unaware of other levels separating or connecting them. The dramatic change in Karen's mood in the example just cited, her laying aside her insistence that I was too easy on Carl, is an example of this kind of startling discontinuity.

It seems worth reiterating that only some discontinuities are associated with therapeutic disjunctions. There was little disruption in flow and rapport in my early work with Karen, a process that was almost always smooth. Yet, so much was left out. A close look reveals striking discontinuities between her upbeat mood in therapy and her ability to focus on disturbing psychological elements in her life. During this period of treatment, she had hideous dreams even as she was celebrating her improving life; also she had periodic panic attacks, all of which occurred outside of her capacity to process them therapeutically. Most of all, toward the end of this segment, she insisted on marrying Carl, despite a profusion of evidence that the marriage could repeat a pattern of abuse from men. Missing during this period of therapy were overt disjunctions that could have provided the cutting edge for understanding the contradictions between Karen's expressions of pleasure in psychotherapy and her symptomatic productions. However, the discontinuities between these realms of experience did point toward the critical therapy work that remained to be done, and became the focal point for us over time.

Radical discontinuity refers to a juxtaposition of disparate clinical events or perspectives, which is particularly sharp; for instance, marked by striking, often unexplained, shifts in the tone or rhythm of the therapy. As an example, my conscious experience of discord with Brittany over the several weeks following the "alternative healing" session, contrasted starkly with the hidden, more powerful conjunctive forces joining us. Radical discontinuities represent particular opportunities for creative discovery and change. Handled thoughtfully they provide launching points to new perspectives for the therapy pair. Radical discontinuities provide therapy partners with opportunities for unexpected, fundamental shifts in experience, challenging their beliefs, expectations, or modes of interpersonal relating.

Several steps in the conjunctive sequence create or harness discontinuity deliberately, each having the potential for moving the therapy forward. The procedures involved include disjunctions recognized and embraced clinically, controlled disorientation, and the leap of inference. The number of potentially generative discontinuities in the therapy is endless. Two examples are the discovery, as a therapist, of how far your partner's subjective experience is from your own or the extent to which your assumptions about how people think has colored and distorted your perception of the patient.

As time goes on in a therapy, each participant discovers in the other partner a person quite unlike the one he or she originally thought was there. This inevitable, potentially disruptive development may be resolved methodically through a series of interpersonal or technical maneuvers designed to address transferences, countertransferences, or projective identifications, or the discovery may be more inadvertent and the resolution less easy to predict and understand. In the latter situation, even with painstaking exploratory work, it may never be fully clear how the therapist and patient move closer to and even transform each other, though the results may be substantial.

The management of radical discontinuities is a key concept in understanding the timing and magnitude of disjunctions and conjunctions. Therapists need to be prepared to encounter, and when looking for ways to move the therapy along, search for radical discontinuities in therapy. To productively work with discontinuities, therapists need to be friendly to surprises and predisposed to going beyond the edge of the familiar, seeking an alive, inspired part of the patient with which to connect. My trusting the validity of Brittany's claim about my failure to reestablish our rapport as we moved through the "alternative healing" hour; my being confronted with a brilliant sensibility I didn't at first recognize, is a case in point. Taking these steps prepared me to appreciate and use the discontinuity between our perspectives to bring us to a new level of shared experience.

Techniques That Support the Conjunctive Process

Interpretative techniques, from whatever dynamic persuasion, work to align therapist and patient helping them understand the psychology of the patient. The risk in these measured approaches is that such understanding, emphasizing words and cognition, substitutes for deeply felt comprehension. More than psychological exploration is required for two people to make penetrating affective sense to each other. In the service of conjunction, I am adding techniques to the more interactive end of the interpersonal repertoire, where the therapist's personal influence is considered integral to the curative mix (e.g., Muran, 2000; Safron, 2003; Safron and Muran, 2000). The therapy activities I name below are intended to increase the depth, vitality, and mostly the spontaneity, of therapeutic communication. My decision to put forward these techniques is based on experience suggesting that if a high level of interpersonal relatedness between patient and therapist is maintained, the dynamic therapy will grow in power.

The test of the techniques I suggest is whether they succeed, uniquely, for a clinical situation. The ultimate value of each one depends on whether the patient is able to use its flexibility to enhance the therapy work. If, for example, the patient misinterprets encouragement to leave phone messages as an invitation to step into the therapist's personal life, that kind of flexibility will lead to a countertherapeutic blurring of boundaries. Introspection, shared and individual, will be thwarted not furthered. On the other hand, if leaving phone messages potentiates the therapy dialogue, making it more vital in facilitating change, then the technique is desirable.

1. *Flexible use of chair and couch:* The decision of which to use should be mutual and discussed. At times, using the couch impedes analytic therapy by allowing analytic practitioners to shield themselves from uncomfortable interpersonal encounters; at times it serves the same purpose for the patient. In my opinion, the decision of whether to use the couch should be made collaboratively and revised over time as therapist and patient assess its value to their work.

2. *Encouraging the flow of information:* Therapy is often enhanced if the patient can supply information, at will, outside of sessions. For those patients for whom this provision is constructive, not encouraging excessive dependency, the use of voice mail and confidential faxes, or e-mail when confidentiality is less important, increases the freshness and immediacy of the work. Information is exchanged, usually from patient to therapist, close to the time that events occur. The idea that emotionally charged information, for example dreams, should not be processed as close as possible to the time they come up seems illogical to me. In fact, traditional psychoanalysis is scheduled four or five times a week in part to achieve just that end.

The liabilities of such an arrangement include the already mentioned blurring of boundaries. There is a genuine risk of this kind of flexibility of contact inducing confusion in patients who use projection freely when in intimate situations. Also, people who have trouble containing their interpersonal needs or who tend to demand ever more attention when given an opportunity, may have difficulty regulating themselves when the therapy envelope is flexible. From a practical standpoint, the therapist may charge for the extra time required to listen to and send messages, encountering opposition from the patient about doing that, unless the fee arrangement is clearly agreed upon from the start.

3. *Providing advice to patients in response to a request, or accepting advice from a patient:* Advice by either party may be an invitation for an enactment, but withholding advice may also be used to maintain the therapist's authority or his mystique, potentially retraumatizing the patient. One factor that usually encourages therapy progress is whether the patient truly feels

cared about and heard. There is no question that Brittany required advice at points when she was having difficulty leaving her job months after the alternative healing hour. Brittany wanted a clear, practical response from me in those cases, not a clarifying statement about how her expectation of disappointment was based on past traumas. Part of her cure involved knowing she could replace past disappointing figures with helpful, responsive current ones, including me.

Alternatively, of course, the patient may simply need advice within the therapist's area of expertise, in response to a reasonable need. For example, if the therapist is a psychiatrist, this expertise extends, conditionally, to medical matters. After all, the patient has sought professional help and is entitled to receive legitimately sought advice, assuming he will not be confounded by it, misconstruing the advice as reflecting the therapist's advocacy. As another consideration, the judgment about whether to offer advice is especially tricky when dealing with patients who are mired in ambivalence. These individuals tend to reallocate their internal conflict, externalizing one aspect to the therapist. They are prone to switch sides, dropping one argument for another as soon as the therapist makes a recommendation, blaming the therapist if the advice he offers proves problematic or creates uncertainty.

4. *Providing the patient with information about the therapist's life:* The message here is that the therapist has nothing to hide that is pertinent to the therapy work, is interested in an authentic connection with the patient, and is not particularly invested in being idealized. Clearly, such revelations benefit some, but not all, patients. The decisions of when and what to share come as a result of thoughtful, bilateral scrutiny superimposed on the therapist's introspection, determining which course is in the best interests of the patient and what actions will further therapeutic progress. This topic, self-revelation by the therapist, is the subject of chapter 8.

5. *Accepting gifts from patients, and even giving gifts to patients:* Again, the meaning of gift giving needs to be understood. But when the gift giving is mainly a confirmation of recognition and regard, or the gift serves the patient as a transitional

therapeutic device, bridging the deliberate bounded parts of the therapy relationship with its more intimate aspects, gift giving may facilitate rather than burden therapy.

This topic, gift giving and receiving, is complicated, much like the subject of providing or receiving advice. Used judiciously, gift giving can serve to deepen a therapy connection by adding a personal touch, making the experience more real and immediate. Incidentally, the traditional guideline of exhaustively examining the meaning of a gift before it is given runs the risk of depriving the gift of its personal meaning. On the other hand, simply accepting or giving a gift without some deliberation may lead to complications when, for example, the giver—usually the patient—expects reciprocation or sees the other's acceptance of the gift as a sign of corruptibility.

6. *Arranged contacts outside of sessions:* Considerations about contacts outside of the therapy office, in person or by communicating through phone, fax, or e-mail, are similar, although the latter are generally more containable. Accompanying a patient to an important medical appointment or conducting an essential home visit, often adds respect and a touch of authenticity to the therapist's and patient's experience. Though these out-of-office contacts, the two may come to see each other in a different light. The therapist is less cloaked by a professional aura; the patient may appear more competent when in his own territory. The therapy dialogue is often enhanced with the addition of these real-life encounters. Whether extratherapy contacts will dilute or enhance the reflective aspects of a dynamically informed therapy needs to be determined separately in each case.

The Place of Conjunction and the Conjunctive Process in Other Models

Specific references to the conjunctive process and its products, creative change and creative development, are missing from the writings of most modern psychodynamic authors. Reference to a conjunctive-like process is visible in these writings, usually only in a general sense; that is, the therapist and patient are engaged in a dialogue in which authenticity and mutuality are valued. There are writers who are friendly to the idea of relative symmetry between therapist and patient, with the therapist learning a good deal about his personal, stylistic, intersubjective, as well as countertransferential contribution from the patient (Maroda, 1999). These authors tend to encourage bolstering the patient's sense of agency (Pollock & Slavin, 1998; Safron & Muran, 2000), and emphasize reciprocal authenticity (Renik, 1998). So far as I can tell, few if any of these authors advocate the degree and kind of mutuality and symmetry found in my thinking, specifically involving trading the authority to know between patient and therapist, the dedicated quest for authenticity in the therapy relationship, instances of self-revelation by the therapist, and the requirement that the therapist change along with the patient, aided in doing so by the patient.

In the following paragraphs, I will try to locate the position of some of the more powerful current voices from relational psychoanalysis in this debate, for the purpose of highlighting the shades of differences between our thinking. For this exercise I have selected Irwin Hoffman, Darlene Ehrenberg, Stephen Mitchell, and Lewis Aron. There are many important writers, Jay Greenberg (1991, 1999), Jessica Benjamin (1995), Philip Bromberg (1995), Charles Spezzano (1993), Thomas Ogden (1994), Owen Renik (1999), and Evelyne Schwaber (1996), as examples, who I have excluded from this discussion because of lack of space. However, similar contrasts can be drawn between their thinking and mine.

Lewis Aron (1996) presents the therapy relationship as fully mutual but asymmetrical as to "roles and functions" (p. 98). Stephen Mitchell (1997, 1998) is always quite clear about the subjective nature of therapy but holds that someone has to lead in creating new self-state possibilities for the patient, while Irwin Hoffman (1996, 1998) calls authority and asymmetry a fundamental but "ironic" (1998, p. 9) part of the therapy arrangement.

Hoffman's position seems most incisive to me, since he portrays the therapist's authority as being created and arbitrary, existing in part at least to satisfy the need of the therapy pair to have some sense of order and purpose in what they do. The ultimate limitation on the therapist's authority, according to all of these thinkers, is his subjectivity, even though that subjectivity may open the way to new, creative possibilities. The therapist's judgments can never be fully objective. Still, the debate about the balance of influence in therapy, justifying more or less asymmetry between therapy partners, rages in the literature, perpetuating the *impression* that the therapist can be relatively objective, at least some of the time.

Regarding therapeutic connection, Darlene Ehrenberg (1992), speaking on the subjective experience of working from a relational viewpoint with patients, says, "By encounter I mean those moments in which patient and analyst engage in relatively direct and personal ways" (p. 140). "Attending to the most subtle aspects of what goes on interactively in the analytic relationship" (p. 33), her more precise goal is to show "that analytic work is best advanced by facilitating a process in which the patient, not the analyst, is the one to arrive at the major insights on his or her own, and in which the patient has the opportunity to discover resources in himself or herself of which he or she had been unaware" (p. 32). In spite of her dedicated adherence to an interactive perspective and her unwavering commitment to discovering the meaning of the patient's impact on the analyst, the process Ehrenberg describes is in some ways asymmetrical. The analyst is the facilitator of what the patient discovers, a point of view that I suggest may subtly underwrite the analyst's authority and expertise. Not as fully emphasized is the patient's transformative effect on the analytic therapist, the patient's active scrutiny of the therapist, and the disorienting and exacting experience for the therapist when he or she is the subject of the analysis.

Stephen Mitchell (1997), in searching for theories to identify the missing element between interpretation and therapeutic efficacy, cites the "working alliance" (p. 49), holding and empathy within an interpretative model (Kernberg, 1995; Modell, 1991; Pine, 1993), Fromm's (1960) "more personal" approach, and the "authentic way of engaging the patient" (p. 50) advocated by contemporary interpersonalists like Levenson (1972), Wolstein (1983, 1987), and Ehrenberg (1992). Mitchell goes on to describe his position, with commentary that in ways sounds like mine. I will quote him in order to illustrate our differences.

Mitchell states: "but for holding or empathy to be genuinely analytic, the patient must experience it as something quite different from anything found in her customary object relations." His solution (quoting Bromberg, 1991) is that, "Meaningful analytic change . . . comes not from bypassing old object relations, but from expanding them from inside out. This entails new understandings and transformations of the patient's old relational patterns in the transference, as well as new understandings and transformations of the analyst's customary relational patterns in the countertransference, including the analyst's capacity to think about analytic interactions in new and different ways" (p. 52). The missing part in understanding the analytic process, he says, "is to be found in the emotional transformation of the relationship with the analyst . . ." (p. 52).

Mitchell's contribution is both scholarly and creative. I have no argument with it so far as it goes. However, as I read Mitchell, his focus is on "new understandings" and the emotional "transformations" of both partners' relational patterns "in the transference." For Mitchell, it seems to me, the therapy process tends to become more tactical and less spontaneous than the experience I advocate. In spite of his clear support for the bilateral nature of therapy, Mitchell ultimately underwrites asymmetry in the therapy situation, thereby placing limits on the reciprocity and authenticity of the therapy interaction.

Mitchell and I both emphasize bilaterality and interpersonal transformation. Like Mitchell, I believe the therapist needs to be proactive in leading the therapy, making sure he and the patient are meeting the patient's goals. However, in spite of the similarity of the language we use, my recommendations support the therapist being more expressive and self-revealing, as well as more accommodating of the analysand's needs in the service of personal and therapeutic engagement, than I think Mitchell's do. Like Mitchell, I selectively exercise my prerogatives as therapist, but almost always do this as the end product of *collaboration* with the patient. I also believe that one of the therapist's main functions is to orchestrate the transfer of authority to lead and know in therapy between the patient and himself.

There is plenty of talk about authenticity in the current relational literature with some describing therapy as a mutuality. My impression, however, is that this mutuality is almost always conditional. For example, for Aron (1996), mutuality consists of bilateral regulation and influence, and shared data gathering (p. 99). Few dynamically oriented authors, apart from myself, call therapy a "relationship," and they certainly do not do so without qualifying it as asymmetrical and limited in the extent of the therapist's personal involvement and the openness of his self-revelation. Aron (1996) seems to substitute "intimacy" for "relationship." His use of the word *intimacy*, however, may remove it a bit from the strictly personal when he says it involves, "similarity and difference, mutuality and autonomy" (p. 150). My point is that the perpetual limitations that most authors, including Aron, seem to place on the intimacy of the therapy relationship and the use of self-revelation by the therapist, threaten to limit its authenticity, restricting the depth of the conjunction achieved. Dynamic therapy, as they describe it, risks becoming a bit of a staged performance, limited in spontaneity, totality of engagement, and in the transformation achieved.

In contrast to the authors I have cited, my conjunctive model of therapy requires that both partners take reciprocally active roles in striving to eliminate distortions, deriving from developmentally based deficits and unconscious agendas, as well as inauthenticity within their relationship. One of the main vehicles for reaching the depth of authenticity I describe is self-revelation. The variety of self-revelation I recommend for the therapist requires his full emotional presence, serving to bring the therapist and patient closer. In my model, this level of disclosure frequently goes beyond that described by others in the literature. Safron and Muran (2000), Renik (1998), and Frank (1997) come closest to my view. I am advocating genuine and profound emotional exposure by both partners, or the conjunctive process will be restrained. According to my conjunctive model, authority and leadership repeatedly change hands between partners, in small ways from moment to moment, and from day to day on a larger scale.

Conjunctions by definition are creative: Patient and therapist influence each other in ways that are often radically surprising to them; discontinuities in experience are fostered that separate present and past. Therapeutic conjunctions of the disjunctive type are almost always preceded by disorientation and pain. A true therapeutic conjunction leads to creative change, which, when sustained over time, affects both therapist and patient deeply and becomes creative development for both.

Excluded from this description are the arduous technical steps required to achieve conjunction. By using the term *technical* I want to convey that these steps require precision to implement; I do not mean to imply that they are always negotiated deliberately. As I hope I demonstrated with Brittany and Karen, the process is infinitely complicated and much of it occurs nonverbally. The critical point here is that the depth of connection sought, based on the struggle of each therapy partner to get to know the other, is often beyond the expressive capability of words. No one knows the full flesh and blood, ecstasy and horror, of another's private world. Finding out usually requires daring leaps of imagination and credulity. The process of moving from the surface to these depths cannot happen unilaterally; and, with this statement, I temporarily rest my case, hoping I have begun to place my system squarely at the interpersonally responsive end of the spectrum of two-person dynamic viewpoints about psychotherapy. I have the rest of the book to elaborate.

I want to underscore that my system does not do away with asymmetry. I hope I have made this point clearly when describing how important the therapist's leadership is in orchestrating shifts of authority, and in his role in the leap of inference. Yet, there is a fundamental, humbling paradox about psychotherapy that does not similarly plague any other kinds of work. Psychotherapy, carried out in a two-person field model is one of the only professions where the professional is also an integral part of the subject being studied. In most other lines of work, the subject and the person conducting the work are separate, allowing the subject to be evaluated for the most part dispassionately, as for example, when a mechanic fixes a car engine. Traditional analysts have tried to solve this provocative challenge by objectifying the patient and his pathology, invoking their blank screen technique as its solution. Their one-person field perspective allowed them to argue that psychodynamic therapy should be considered a science (Wallerstein, 1992), believing the therapist's personal countertransferential contribution to the therapy field could be minimized. Acknowledging the conflict inherent in having the therapist both lead the therapy and be its subject, forces the view that therapy has to be a thoroughly collaborative activity. There is little that is certain about the observations and decisions made in therapy outside of the powerful, largely nonverbal righting mechanism that two people deeply engaged in therapy work can develop, when the therapy works well.

There are also some practical explanations for why the literature may not support the kind of symmetry and involvement I advocate in therapy. (1) Some therapists will experience my system as removing too much of their authority and prestige, as too greatly deprofessionalizing the therapist. Therapists work hard to achieve their professional role and some may not want to relinquish it. Others may believe their training gives them an edge on understanding that is consistently greater than the patient's. I relocate therapeutic expertise from the therapist's omniscience to the therapist knowing when he should make the patient, or alternatively himself, the expert in the heat of therapeutic activity. (2) Therapists value their professional status as a vehicle for building and sustaining a practice. Making the therapist less of an expert, may, in the minds of some therapists, interfere with the marketability of their skills. (3) Therapists legitimately may not want to endure the degree of exposure, and inevitable disorientation and painful readjustment, my system requires. They did not enter the field of dynamic therapy to be exposed and therapized by their patients. (4) My system supports extratherapeutic availability by the therapist when it furthers the ends of the work. For example, I see no reason why, when used thoughtfully, in the service of the therapy, patients should not be able confidentially to leave voice mail or e-mail messages or send faxes. In my experience, this additional contact can enrich the therapy dialogue, as can judiciously arranged meetings outside of regularly scheduled sessions. However, these contacts are an additional requirement for the therapist and, at times, may become burdensome for him or her. (5) The system I am proposing requires enormous depth of feeling and empathy from the therapist. Some therapists may be incapable of working on this level; others may prefer not to.

I hope the reader is now feeling oriented about where my model belongs in the contemporary dynamic spectrum. Characterizing it is:

(1) the interpersonally complex, ever layered, and shifting nature of the conjunctive process, both partners working to engage the other and deepen their connection;
(2) that the therapy takes place in a field bounded by the two subjectivities of the therapy partners and their intersubjectivity;
(3) while mine is a relational theory, heavily weighted toward the interpersonal, the therapist's hope for the therapy and his willingness to advocate for it is instrumental in achieving therapeutic change;
(4) further, the power of the unconscious remains, but so do developmental considerations, explaining a good deal about the patient's unique preferences, interpersonal strengths, and

limitations; while ongoing personal development stays in the foreground, influencing technique, and underscoring what I believe is the potential remedial value of the current therapy relationship.

In my model, the effect of experience, verbal and nonverbal, sets the therapeutic stage for deliberate and spontaneous revision of the patient's inner life, while not excluding the value of dynamic understanding in achieving therapeutic change.

A model of therapy such as mine, based on disruption and repair cycles, where the two therapy partners continually experience and remedy disconnections and benefit greatly from conjunctive developments, places personal influence at the center of the therapy stage. Therapist and patient are pictured as regularly blocked in their progress by personal and interpersonal factors beyond their grasp. Whether the understanding they work toward is convoluted, based on needs and defenses that are obscure to each, the point is that the therapy pair is committed to finding its way. That commitment is heartfelt, shared between the two, each progressively trusting the other to be a full collaborator, dedicated to knowing about himself and his partner, and to a level of authenticity distinctly greater than is usually found in ordinary life.

Lastly, many analytic views, traditional Freudian or Kleinian, for example, or for that matter some interpersonalists (Levenson, 1996, 1998), tend to discourage the therapist from taking an active, cure-seeking role, one that advocates the judicious disclosure of personal information. Rightfully, these writers cite fears of overstepping boundaries and subversion of the patient's sense of agency (Slavin, 1994; Slavin and Kriegman, 1998). But in doing so, they risk making therapy artificial, interpersonally limited, potentially placing a cap on the depth of exploration and personal change that can occur.

From here, we will take a microscopic look at the therapy field. Then in chapters 4 and 5 we will explore the therapist's, and after that the patient's, initiative as each contributes to moving the therapy forward.

3

The Influences in the Therapy Field

Missing still from our picture of the therapy situation are the influences in the therapy field outside the conjunctive process, including specific ways in which therapist and patient interact, each an identifiable relationship configuration. To organize these observations, I have developed a model of the mind describing each configuration from an affective, self, other, and self-with-other perspective (1995, pp. 55–78). I call this aspect of my model of therapy the *self and other relational matrix*.[1] Additionally contributing to the therapy field, are:

(1) the unique parameters distinguishing psychotherapy from ordinary interpersonal relating;
(2) internal agendas (e.g., transferences and countertransferences) brought to the therapy table by both parties;

---

[1] In *Intricate Engagements* (1995) and *Hidden Faults* (2000) I called this view of the mind relating to others the *self-and-object-unit model (SO model)*. I prefer now to call this aspect of my model *the self and other relational matrix*. I have also changed the name of the relational entities I picture as being involved in an interaction from *self-and-object units* (Frankel, 1995, 2000) to *self and other relational configurations* or *relational configurations*. The new designation sounds less mechanistic, a move in keeping with a nonlinear, nonstatic model of the mind, emphasizing a mind built significantly of distinct but interrelating self and other states (Bromberg, 1995).

(3) the therapist's and patient's personal limitations based on
    unfinished or skewed early development;
(4) cultural background;
(5) current events in each person's life;
(6) biological influences on the therapist's and patient's life and
    mood; and
(7) the personal and formal theories the therapist and patient
    hold about how therapy works.

Understanding how a particular therapy produces change
requires that the components of the therapy field be identified,
in addition to those that are intended to be specifically therapeutic. Each factor needs to be weighed in terms of the way it
effects and gives direction to therapeutic action. The conjunctive
process exists within this milieu, not apart from it. However,
even with all the factors that become known, a significant part
of what drives a therapy and creates change always remains
unarticulated and mysterious.

Let us turn our attention to a new metaphor: cliff scaling.
El Capitan is a magnificent rock face gazing down on visitors
to Yosemite Valley in California. Its regal blues, greens, and
grays mingle, shifting playfully as the sun moves across its ho-
rizon.

An illusion? No and yes. From the valley, all is majesty.
But, when a climber was stuck on an overhanging ledge, had
lost part of his climbing gear including his two-way radio, and
the first in a series of winter storms suddenly invaded the valley,

---

Also, note that in *Hidden Faults* (2000), my model of the mind and
psychotherapy was focused on disjunctions that impede the therapy process,
and I called it *the disjunction model* (2000, pp. 4–5) in keeping with the
theme of that book and also with the disjunctive focus of most psychodynamic
theories. In this book I am broadening my viewpoint to include and often to
emphasize the conjunctive process. Since I see the conjunctive process as the
overriding influence in therapeutic progress, and since conjunctions are
largely built on the resolution of disjunctions, I will incorporate both viewpoints, *disjunctive* and *conjunctive,* under the title *conjunctive model.*

both the climber and his would-be rescuers were stranded. There was nowhere to turn; a helicopter couldn't get close to the climber because the wind and snow were already so turbulent. The climber, a bit too inexperienced, had started somewhat under prepared, without warm enough clothing for a storm and with food and water for only a few days.

For that climber, a straightforward climbing challenge, beginning from the top of El Capitan, suddenly became a nightmare of considerations: equipment, clothing, food, nightfall, temperature, wind, cramps in one leg, and outjutting of rock just barely long enough to stand on, all in all a technical challenge for which he was not prepared. The majesty of El Capitan became a web of horrors.

For the therapist, at the outset of a therapy, the field of operations also looks uncomplicated. Partway into the trek, however, the terrain invariably begins to change. Not that all the excitement turns to horror, but the therapist's original clarity becomes murky, handholds familiar from past therapies disappear, and for the moment at least, the terrain seems impassible. At the point, ironically, when he is least able to do so, the therapist, like our climber, needs to reorient, calculate into his mapping the multiplying factors influencing the therapy. He also, with the patient as collaborator, needs to search for the subtle agendas, introduced by himself and the patient, that move, impede, or color their work

Mapping the Field

How Therapy Differs from Real Life

As a personal commentary, I think it is worth noting that the therapy field I am describing is in many ways a breakdown of real life. This perspective should not be forgotten as one considers the special conditions governing how therapy is structured and conducted and the issues of technique that differentiate the therapy experience from informal encounters outside of therapy. There are significant differences between life and therapy:

(1) The therapist has been sought and employed because of his assumed healing abilities, based in part on his training. The authority supporting this power is context dependent, partially a product of the culture in which both partners live (Greenberg, 1999; Renik, 1998).

(2) The formal arrangements of the therapy, especially the fact that the therapist charges for services, may limit the extent to which both can experience the relationship as authentic (Hoffman, 1998, pp. 3–5).

(3) An important interpersonal difference is that within treatment the ultimate focus is on one member of the pair, the patient, and his or her well-being.

(4) Introspection has a more prominent place in therapy than in most life experience.

(5) To accomplish their ends, therapist and patient, individually and jointly, generally with the therapist taking the lead, develop a self-reflective capability unusual outside of therapy. Their heightened self-awareness enables the pair to appraise progress, seek consensus between themselves and the world of ''reality,'' and make adjustments moving toward the goals of the therapy, whether implicit or explicit.

(6) Finally, in their work together the therapist and patient have to take profound personal risks. Getting to know and engage with another deeply, mutatively, requires jolting encounters with the unfamiliar ways in which the other person experiences life. In ordinary experience, people tend to remain aloof from this kind of dislocating engagement.

Givens

In mapping the field of dynamic therapy, we cannot leave out any of the factors coloring and shaping the experience in therapy, not as theoretical constructions but as interactive, fluctuating influences. Required here is a complex equation with all the influences in the therapy field taken into account, from moment to moment, each with its trajectories and the product of their interactions identified. These factors involve the psychological and cultural, but also the temperamental and biological. The influences of biology on individual behavior, that is, neurological, physiological, and hormonal influences placed on a genetic template (Schore, 1994, 2003; Siegel, 1999), cannot be overstated, but as yet, for the most part, the effect of each cannot be named scientifically with great specificity. Apart from the effect of developmentally based personality distortions and arrests, and traumatic predisposition to dissociation or neurosis, what makes one person inherently better able to intuit another's meaning and warm up, easily encouraging conjunction, while another in a similar circumstance pushes away, predisposing to disjunction?

Cultural background plays a critical role. Brittany's parents were from fourth-generation New England stock, and that fact helped to explain her self-restraint with people and her need to dismiss messy feelings. With Brittany, I was fighting her training in austerity as I did my part to move her to a more expansive and expressive frame of mind; at the same time, we were using all our therapeutic tools to deepen our dialogue and joust with the ghosts who harassed her. Life circumstances, including daily events, also play their part. In the week she felt most alienated from me, Brittany suffered from crippling headaches. It is hard to imagine that I was at my best with my patients while I was depressed about my divorce and working hard to contain its effects on my mood.

In summary, nonverbal, intuitive communication introduced in chapter 2 (Cozolino, 2002; Schore, 1994, 2003), is joined by both participants' biology, past experiences, and current intrapsychic and interpersonal conflicts (Frankel, 1995), and is delivered in a cultural context. None of these factors can be excluded from a rigorous understanding of a given patient and the therapy process. The point of going into this kind of detail is that you can't do therapy and assume any factor is missing. In therapy, you are always impacted to some degree by a variety of influences, as well as their complexity.

The Therapist's Initiative

We must ask, then, how therapy partners achieve their unique goal of reaching each other deeply and authentically, influencing the other to change creatively. Real-life human encounters are complex enough to make mapping daunting, and in therapy are circumscribed and in ways heightened by its special guidelines. Stephen Mitchell (1997) locates therapeutic action in "the struggle of the analyst to find an authentic way of engaging the patient" (p. 50), Philip Bromberg (2000) in "surprise," and Anton Hart (1999) in the analyst's disruptive role. Darlene Ehrenberg (1992) goes further in suggesting that when the patient and therapist take the risk of working at the unarticulated "intimate edge" of the patient's experience, transformative engagement is possible. The emphasis is on new, different, authentic, and then, if you agree with Ehrenberg, risk. As I see it, Enhrenberg is on the right track. The therapist has the charge of maintaining a vital emotional and intellectual "edge" within the therapy. When the interaction falls into familiar patterns, someone needs to release the logjam or the two will be swimming up familiar streams, no matter how interesting their conversation.

In my view, the therapist has the unique function of repeatedly guiding the therapy in fresh directions. He is responsible for monitoring the therapy field and assigning whoever can be most helpful at any one time to direct the action. In collaboration with the patient, he continually and painstakingly searches for the next critical opportunity for progress in the therapy. When reasonably certain, he forcefully, in a leap of inference, acts to move the therapy in that direction, repeatedly checking his impressions with the patient. The therapist's authority here comes from maintaining consensus and attunement with the patient, supported by the therapist's training and experience. In this role the therapist regularly reinvigorates the therapy experience, moving it forward, no matter whether he or the patient is the main author of the clarity he achieves. Often, following the patient's lead, the therapist makes certain that the work of therapy repeatedly goes beyond the edge of what the patient and therapist already know and understand. In my opinion, when conditions of therapy work against emotional risk taking, they deaden and limit the depth to which therapy partners can ultimately reach, thus preventing therapy from achieving its full potential.

The Self and Other Relational Matrix

The therapy field is complex and dynamic, always consisting of multiple, often contradictory, relationship states, each with its own affective, self, other, and self with other aspects. Some of these experiential entities, which I call *self and other relational configurations,* are primarily initiated and experienced by one therapy partner, others are partially or fully shared between the therapy partners. However, all self and other configurations are relational. Each participant's experience is shaped interpersonally, even if it is ultimately owned mainly by one of them.

There are two relational configurations that are central to therapeutic action and found in *all* productive therapies. I call one type of self and other configuration, from which patient, therapist, or both, evaluate their interaction, the *analyzing relational configuration.* An example of an analyzing configuration is found in the nonverbal but shared decision made by Brittany and me when we appraised her guilt-contaminated decision to leave her job and came to the opinion that I'd better take over and help her make it happen. A second type of relational configuration always encountered in a viable therapy, the *facilitating configuration,* involves frames of mind through which therapist and patient actively support each other and the therapy. Several facilitating configurations may exist simultaneously and interact with relational configurations of all other descriptions. At any particular time, (1) Brittany and I separately may want the therapy to succeed (a facilitating configuration). (2) We may work well with each other (requiring two partners with sound analyzing configurations). Yet, simultaneously Brittany may suspect

that (3) I disapprove of her desire to be a writer (the correspond-
ing configuration being a variety of a *general relational configuration,* each one of which is labeled according to the issue being
transacted, in this case Brittany's job change); and that (4) I may
want to resist a dialogue with her about that topic (another facet
of the general relational configurations associated with the proposed job change).

Thus, along with all the other levels, influences, and complexities, understanding the therapy field requires considering
the major relational configurations at work in the therapy at any
one time, their relative strengths and activity, and whether they
work counter to or support the goals of the therapy. Finally, how
constant and fundamental is each relational configuration for a
particular individual; that is, does any also qualify for inclusion
in a variety of relational configurations I call *core relational
configurations?* Note that relational configurations, generally,
draw their characteristics from the subject's past relationship
experiences, but they are always thoroughly anchored in the
present. The balance between loading from the past and the present differs from configuration to configuration. More complete
reviews of the relational matrix concept can be found in Frankel
(1995, pp. 155–178; 2000, pp. 14–30) under the heading ''The
Self and Object Unit Model.''

Joining

The activity I am describing as ''the field'' in which therapy
takes place has direction. As patient and therapist work successfully to engage with one another, they catch on to each other's
preferences, goals, and ways of relating, working more efficiently as a result. The important relational configurations, facilitating and analyzing, develop in this milieu. As mentioned, there
is also a broad spectrum of other, general relational configurations, each organized around a typical theme, including, for example, creative relational configurations involving interpersonal

experiences that are novel for both participants, and work associated relational configurations based on such requirements as sustaining a family and vocation. The path to the joining of minds, the relational configurations of one partner combining with the relational configurations of another, is often a crooked one, however. Relational configurations within the same category (facilitating, for example) are often not developed and available in the same way and at the same time by each partner. The resulting dissonance often results in one partner knowing about a disjunction or potential conjunction before the other, setting a path that the other partner may need to also traverse before he comprehends what the first partner already knows.

Sharing

The relational configurations I have named, for the most part, start out by belonging to each participant, separately. They contain that partner's particular wishes and preferences about how to go about life and relationships. Over time, though, the two develop more of a shared sense of where they are going and how they will get there. Whatever they disagree about, if the therapy goes well, they find they have accumulated more understanding in common, including that which can be communicated without words; that is, their relational configurations become shared at points. The cognitive counterpart of this development is consensus, and the therapeutic triumph is conjunction, where the full array of relational configurations work so well together that therapist and patient are transformed, the ordinary tin of experience converting to gold.

The idea of shared relational configurations has much in common with others' intersubjective views of what happens to players in therapy (Aron, 1996). An example is Ogden's "analytic third" (1994), an intersubjectively created entity that is neither the therapist nor the patient, but like Winnicott's transitional object (1968) has qualities of both. It is the product of a dialectical exchange in which patient and therapist influence and transform one another. I look at the creation of shared relational configurations (Frankel, 1995, pp. 172–174) as a usually desirable development based on patient and therapist getting to know each other intimately. This sharing reflects a consensus about psychological and emotional issues, which has force and evolving presence in the therapy work. Sharing relational configurations refers to a more purposeful development and a state of mind that is more enduring than is the case with Ogden's analytic third. Sharing relational configurations and conjunction are ultimately synonymous. As the conjunctive process builds, key relational configurations of both partners become joined, each partner developing a sense for the other, both enlarging their nonverbal repertoire.

Shared relational configurations and the analytic third actually refer to different stages in the development of psychological structure. The analytic third is an ephemeral intersubjective phenomenon, while the shared relational configuration concept suggests that some reliable change has occurred within the mind of each partner. For relational configurations to exist, it is necessary to posit that persistent organizations of affect and thought regularly develop within people's minds. While each partner's subjective focus may shift between these organizations, that is, between relational configurations, and while relational configurations are constantly modified as they are impacted by experience, the general characteristics of relational configurations can be described and recognized by the subject. Logically, shared relational configurations, which require dedicated cooperation to develop, are likely to occupy a progressively significant place in each partner's mind. In contrast, for the analytic third persistence is irrelevant; what counts is its transitory existence within the clinical situation.

Disjunctive forces are never missing in therapy, always vying with those drawing patient and therapist together. Disagreements arise regularly and come in all shapes and sizes. Often more subtle, however, are places where patient and therapist implicitly lack consensus. As an example, adding to the complexity of the therapy field, is the fact that events in therapy are understood according to personal and formal theories held separately by both patient and therapist about the way people think and how therapy works. These ideas organize what each sees and emphasizes in the therapy.

An Illustration

This case example is presented to demonstrate how a relational configuration analysis is of practical value in understanding and working with the forces in a therapy. I have chosen a relatively simple situation, focusing on one set of relational configurations. In this clinical situation, my assumptions clash with Brittany's and establish a disjunction between us. The initiative to resolve this disjunction was ultimately mine because my failure to understand her desires caused Brittany to retreat, hiding her real feelings.

In this sequence of sessions I attempted unsuccessfully to support Brittany in an encounter with a man who had a romantic interest in her. In relational configuration language, I attempted to author a rather one-sided facilitating relational configuration, emphasizing my advocacy for that relationship. Because of Brittany's reluctance to encourage the relationship, the product of my attempted facilitation was disjunctive, our relational configurations associated with this issue in conflict, mine for the relationship and hers against. My advocacy was based on my conviction, originally prompted by Brittany, that she was lonely and that a relationship with this man would improve the quality of her life.

As it turned out, the "other" with whom my advocacy configuration was interacting was, at best, an outdated version of Brittany, in part predicated on her earlier complaints about being alone and in part on my stereotyped view of the interpersonal requirements of 30-year-olds. It was also based on my wish for a quick fix for Brittany's suffering, since it had been so painful to experience her despair with her. My passion for her relationship with this man prevented me from seeing the current, more basic reason Brittany resisted his invitation. At first, she acted compliantly with me, fearing my disapproval, but did nothing to encourage his interest; only later, when she became convinced that I could give up my advocacy, could she confide that she didn't want to encourage the relationship since this man was a bore, uninteresting to her. It was only when I pulled back—aware, finally, of my misguided assumption that my advocacy would be helpful to her—and convinced Brittany that she did not risk my disapproval, that she allowed her maturing, discriminating judgment to be apparent to me.

Brittany tells me about a man who lives in her apartment house. He is a photographer, and at age 50 leads a somewhat lonely but not dejected existence. She likes him well enough. He came to her apartment several times, obviously seeking a relationship and had just invited her for dinner, "for any day of the week."

Given Brittany's isolation, combined with her previously expressed desire for a relationship with a man, I felt this man's interest might represent an opportunity for her. I assumed Brittany wanted me to help her succeed with him and, as well, required my blessing so she could go ahead without her usual hesitation. I asked her about her fears and finally said, spontaneously, that I thought the relationship could work out as a friendship, even if, as she said to me, it might not be a love affair.

Surprising to me, for the next several days Brittany refused to answer his phone messages, and when they did talk was evasive about her free time. As I came to see it, the problem was me. During our earlier dialogue concerning her desires for a relationship, I found Brittany's depression alarming, and was coercively pushing her to move beyond it, thinking she was now telling me she liked this man enough to spend time with him. At first, I did not understand that it was important for Brittany to resist his invitation, since he really wasn't interesting to her. She equated her recently consolidating self-esteem with restraint; previously, she felt compelled, when lonely, to jump into any relationship available to her.

Brittany felt the loss of my empathy but did not complain about it to me. She just withdrew. As was also true of her successful public relations job, which she did not really value, there was no victory being with a man for whom she had no respect. She did not want to compromise, and was let down by my eagerness to encourage her to do so, first by staying with her job, and then by becoming involved in an unappealing relationship.

To reestablish our rapport, I needed to reverse my stance. To do so I privately carried out the relational configuration analysis described above, exposing the extent to which our relational configurations, our assumptions and motives, clashed. As a result of this assessment, rather than pressing Brittany harder, I inquired whether her message had changed; was I not hearing her clearly? Reoriented, I asked her for guidance. She was clear in telling me I had lost her, that I was too swayed by my misperceptions about her current requirement for a partner. She felt coerced by me, reminding her of her mother's attempt to dominate with her opinions, determining what she should like and do.

Critical to this example is the fact that I hedged with Brittany at first, after she told me I didn't understand her disinterest in her suitor. I was more interested in furthering her social life than in her developing ability to be discriminating about people with whom she socialized. When she stubbornly held her ground, and the oppression of her anger bore down on me, I moved to a relational configuration analysis and began to question my assumptions about what kind of relationship she wanted for herself. As in the case of her career change, I was able to consider a position I really did not yet have.

At first I was caught between my old assumptions and the possibility that my confusion might signal a new message from her. I still insisted she might benefit in this new relationship, assuming she was just too anxious to admit that it mattered to her. My false notion of a conjunction between Brittany and myself, rooted in my desire to help her improve her damaged life, made *me* feel better. I kept being hopeful that Brittany would catch on and see things my way. Of course, I backed up my position with elegant interpretations based on established historical insights concerning the guilt I suggested she might be feeling in enjoying the attention this man was showing her. But at the same time, I was being dissuaded, fortunately beginning to move in a new direction, in part aided by my relational configuration analysis.

I want to make the point that the steps Brittany and I went through for me to join her were all essential to our building conjunction and therefore to the progress of our work together. First, we established ourselves as separate individuals. My agenda, even the one with which I wanted to facilitate what I believed to be her welfare, had to be exposed and modified if I was to understand the Brittany of the moment and contribute to the development of her sense of agency. In that process, I was humbled, forced to examine my limitations in understanding another person's experience, in this case Brittany's. I had to depend on Brittany to help me see what was going wrong between us. Second, I became reflective, invoking controlled disorientation to listen to Brittany more closely. Even then, it required some time for me to believe in Brittany's appraisal of her needs; it took a while for me to come to her side. When I got there, however, I really believed her. Our conjunction was being intricately constructed and becoming durable; we were both changing.

That psychotherapy is a process fueling the patient's sense of agency has been discussed by others (Pollock and Slavin, 1998; Strenger, 1998). Frequently, the patient leads and is the expert on his or her own needs. This view frames therapy as a developmental process, consolidating the patient's sense of having a self, entitled to preside over his or her life.

It may seem contradictory to claim that this disjunction, and then the false conjunction I described when Brittany became compliant and seemed to accept my effort to encourage her social life, added substance to my final conjunction with Brittany. Yet think of what we would have ended up with if we had gone from our initial misunderstanding directly to shared clarity. The product would have been like being taken to the top of our stormy mountain by helicopter, missing all the details, the perils, and the beauty, the actual triumph of the climb along the way.

Exploring the Field

An In-Depth Look at Controlled Disorientation

In the complex field I have described, one or the other therapy partner is more clear sighted at one time or another. I understand the therapy field as ideally supporting the most open and passionate dialogue between patient and therapist, in which the patient is a relatively equal partner, providing perspective and offering solutions when the therapist cannot do so (Ferenczi, 1928/1955a, 1931/1955b; Hoffman, 1983; Langs, 1978a, 1978b; Natterson, 1991; Pollock and Slavin, 1998; Renik, 1998; Searles, 1975). In this scenario, the therapist needs to receive feedback from the patient. This process requires the therapist to make internal room for controlled disorientation, identified in chapter 2 as a set of techniques and responses that the therapist (and eventually the patient) uses when confusion due to the subjectivity of the therapy situation sets in. Controlled disorientation is an orienting device that samples all of the forces in the therapy room, most particularly the nonverbal, and is used to achieve a reasonably accurate sense of the psychology of the patient and the structure of the therapy in that particular moment.

The therapist's task, then, when he does not understand a disjunction and recognizes that the patient may, is to embrace his disorientation and give the leadership for the therapy over to the patient. This is a natural, though for the therapist very disconcerting, part of the ebb and flow of the progress of the therapy. The therapist's use of disorientation in this way is alluded to by Schafer (1997). "One can say that analysts establish their credentials by showing repeatedly and reliably that they are better prepared than their analysands to be unprepared" (p. 188). The two partners may then discuss the therapist's temporary disability, perhaps even its source in the therapist's life and all it brings up for the patient.

For example, Brittany was reassured when I told her I was getting a divorce; she no longer had to speculate about my mood. She also wanted to know that I would engage in a self-reflective process as searching as the one I prescribed for her. The parity we established, Brittany knowing that I might have struggled like her, and could be open about my personal life working to understand myself, assured her that she was not alone in her agony. I could comprehend her through my own experience.

Prior to the session presented at the end of chapter 1, Karen, too, guided me to the realization that I was emotionally removed and not as "analytical" as I thought I was, showing me my discomfort with her critical thoughts about me. In each of these interactions, one of us, the patient, was momentarily seeing more clearly than I, the therapist. This trade-off of authority from therapist to patient is invaluable in that it provides the therapist with information about the therapy from the patient's perspective.

Controlled disorientation is a key technique in my psychotherapy repertoire. I believe that in addition to useful introspection by the therapist and his receiving feedback from the patient (and, at times, other sources), it is the most important epistemological tool the therapist has available. But beware, controlled disorientation requires positioning oneself in a way that usually does not come naturally, and often involves the stressful experience of allowing oneself to tolerate being confused and lost in the service of discovering new and pivotal knowledge.

Disorientation is par for the course in dedicated human interactions. The veil of subjectivity between people mandates that they will only understand each other in approximations and for limited periods of time. Understanding, when it works reasonably well, is a matter of verbal and nonverbal communicating, but given the hefty proportion that is usually nonverbal, establishing certainty about what another person means can be precarious. Some of us are more intuitive than others, but even the best intuition is likely to have its limits of accuracy.

Above plain vanilla subjectivity, people flood the interpersonal field with their unrecognized emotional agendas, in part rooted in their historically based notions about people and relationships. They see others differently from the way that person views him- or herself, and cues that elicit a reaction in one person set off a different response in another. Of course, the agendas I am talking about are transferences, countertransferences, invitations for enactments, and the effects of scuttled aspects of self that are re-created through projective identification.

But there are also temperamental, biochemical–neurological, and cultural factors determining moment-to-moment compatibility. All of these considerations explain why Brittany, who was exquisitely sensitive to being misunderstood, had to work so hard to have me read her precisely. To make matters worse, as with all human beings, she was changeable, and her changes were usually on a personal schedule I found unfamiliar.

Disorientation isn't a complication of misguided psychotherapy; it is a constant diet. A requirement of psychotherapy is that disorientation be unraveled, repeatedly. But, rather than being a liability, disorientation is one of the most useful features of the therapy process. By putting disorientation to use in a controlled way, patient and therapist immersing themselves in it, something close to the truth about the forces at work in the therapy becomes accessible (this use of controlled disorientation has some analogy to the unidirectional effort to tap the unconscious using free association and dreams in psychoanalytic practice). Patient and therapist working collaboratively, providing feedback to one another about their observations and personal experiences, can sensitively pick up the ways each seeks to influence the other. They begin with hunches, such as my surprising sense that Karen could be despondent about alienating me in spite of her brutal attack, (see chapter 1) and develop these to find where their research leads.

Here is where asymmetry comes in. While the collaboration I have described is an ideal, both patient and therapist recognize that the therapist has the ultimate responsibility for the success of their effort. When swept away by the blizzard of disorientation, the therapist needs to keep up the fight for clear vision. Being defeated and giving up is not an option, no matter how inviting either of these solutions might be. In short, the single most useful choice for the therapist at these moments is to embrace, saturate himself with the confusion inundating him. Through this experience, he is likely to be aware of the most probable sources for the disorientation, namely, false identities projected into one another by the patient or therapist, lack of familiarity with the other's assumptions about life, the effect of disrupting outside events, to name a few. Reflexively, he scans his experience for clues to how the other person is affecting him. Is he picking up on the other's mood either directly or through his projections? Is he being pulled into an enactment based on a need of the partner coupling with his own? Is some prejudice of his being evoked, one with which he is familiar. In short, the therapist attempts to be his own observer, making himself, as much as possible, into a reliable sensing device.

Beyond his personal, internal research, the therapist appeals to the patient for feedback. What has he, the patient, noticed about the therapist's behavior? How might these observations provide information about the nonarticulated events in the therapy at the moment? Does the patient need any information about the therapist's experience, and even outside life or background, to assist in this effort? Clearly, in this activity the patient is intermittently accorded the status of the one who is likely to be most clear thinking. For this effort to be authentic, the patient's reports and ideas need to be given their full weight and authority by the therapy pair.

Complications

The technique of controlled disorientation is actually more technical than I have thus far indicated. It requires that the therapist clear his mind of preconceptions about the patient and the therapy process, including the question of what both need to do to make therapy successful. He needs to lose himself in the patient's nonverbal force field: moods, needs, inexplicable behavior. Brittany and Karen made no bones about requiring this level of involvement from me. They were impatient with me until they believed I was earnest about achieving it. The instigated experience when in this state will, of necessity, be foreign to the therapist, frequently entirely unfamiliar. The therapist's disorientation may well get worse before it gets better. It is likely to feel humiliating, challenging the therapist's legitimate need to be competent. Unwelcome responses are generated, like the irritation I felt and could not help but convey to Karen in the example in chapter 1. It is common to believe that the utter lack of orientation and control will continue unabated and may end in the demise of the therapy. Sometimes communication with outside sources of elucidation, a consultant, for example, is required. Always, the therapist needs to be prepared to be stunned by the difference between his preconceptions about the nature of the therapy events and what he and the patient learn, the therapist needing to be ready to change his perceptions and attitudes, at times radically.

Controlled disorientation is one step in the information seeking and action sequence in psychotherapy. Controlled disorientation is a technique, not a blueprint, for the therapy effort. It leads into other methods, elaborated throughout the book, for working toward certainty and deciding how to further the patient's goals. This method of yielding to disorientation, and receiving and giving feedback, expands the therapist's ability to probe his countertransference. The information gained enables the therapist to amend his own introspective findings. It also enlarges his knowledge of factors, other than transference and countertransference, that color the therapy field.

If distortions the therapist introduces into the dialogue are left unidentified and unresolved, they will forever contaminate the work, an unacknowledged influence on the patient's experience. No matter how subtle, such influence is "crazy making" for the patient as it becomes his, once again, unsubstantiated reality.

However, the value for the therapy of the couple focusing on that influence varies, so a cautionary word belongs here. A countertransference focus may be valuable in elucidating enactments, as when Brittany finally helped me to be aware I was becoming moralistic, like her parents, about her wish not to stay with her job. But when the therapist's distortion is a reflection of his own psychology, uninfluenced by the patient, it is appropriate for the therapist to acknowledge this fact and do his own rubble clearing. How much the therapist needs to explain will depend on the patient's sensibilities and whether such an exchange would be a burden to the patient. In Brittany's case, my telling her I was getting a divorce and a bit about my suffering helped her. No one in her past had accorded her that kind of respect, nor had they ever shared their psychic pain without making her responsible for fixing it. Other patients feel deprived or anxious when, beyond acknowledging responsibility for a problem in the therapy, the therapist focuses on himself.

The objective in all of the shared and reciprocal discovery I have described is collaboration within the conjunctive therapy process, leading toward conjunction. An authentic collaboration requires self-searching and self-revelation on the part of both participants. However, openness has its limits. A collaboration requires sensitivity and accommodation to the other's personal requirements as being different from one's own. Although an open, yet accommodative stance is the foundation of the conjunctive process, total openness without considering the other partner's tolerance for emotional intimacy, together with unrestrained probing, is not tenable in a collaboration. Instead, both partners struggle toward an openness and authenticity that considers their own and their partner's needs and limitations. The conjunctive process requires therapy partners to explore these requirements, to identify them as disjunctions that impede conjunction when that is the case, and, when they can, to move toward greater openness and authenticity.

Reconfiguring the Field

Parity

There are many other described ways, compatible with mine, for framing the exchange between therapy partners. Few give the patient opportunities for the same degree of authority-to-know that mine does; nor do they envision the patient taking as much control, in part by examining when the therapist's contribution to the therapy is distorting. As examples, Thomas Ogden (1994) speaks of the dialectical relationship in therapy, emphasizing ways in which patient and therapist communicate nonverbally, especially through projective identification. The therapist is the interpreter of this process, though, and at the same time a participant in it. Richard Moore's (1999) emphasis is on coconstruction, with the therapist most able to appreciate and bring the therapy couple's focus to this process. In both frameworks, the therapist ultimately selects the area of focus he believes is most pertinent for the therapy.

For most contemporary authors, all of whom hold mutuality and authenticity as a core value, therapy is an interplay between two people, one of whom, the therapist, has the prerogative of withholding personal information and setting the rules for the therapy. Irwin Hoffman (1998, pp. 8–10) is more skeptical about the validity of these imbalances than Lewis Aron (1996) and Stephen Mitchell (1997). He discusses the irrationality of the therapist's authority given the elusive, subjective constraints on anyone knowing with certainty about another's experience. Still, even for Hoffman, the therapist is ultimately accorded the balance of power, even if the basis for this power is equivocal. While I agree with Hoffman's skepticism, I believe that even his viewpoint subtly degrades the patient's legitimate role in leading the therapist and therapy at times when his knowledge is the clearest of the two. It perpetuates a picture of the therapy field where the therapist's direction is evident much of the time, even if Hoffman acknowledges that the content and form of the field are coconstructed and context specific.

Kenneth Frank (1997) and Owen Renik (1998) push the balance even more toward patient–therapist parity, emphasizing the patient's role in interpreting the therapist's behavior. Yet, when Frank, in particular, describes an analytic moment, he may make the therapist's insight a bit more definitive than it would be if all experience were irreducibly subjective. I have no doubt that Frank envisions his patients as full therapy participants. I am distinctly drawn to Frank's and Renik's ideas. But, before concluding that our viewpoints are equivalent, I would want more clinical documentation of the degree of parity that Frank, especially, creates as he actually conducts treatment.

The field clearing I propose assumes the therapist is fallible, human, just as is the patient. The goal is an authentic connection, where each participant presents himself for inspection. The therapist, as subject of the therapy, is like the mother being subject to the infant who responds and informs. A good enough mother knows how to listen for her child's subjective rhythms, distinguishing them from her own and to some extent making them her own. Most likely, much of the time each participant has some qualities of both mother and child or the two frequently trade off these roles (Natterson, 1991).

Baring oneself in therapy makes emotional sense only when the other person in the room has become recognizable, with fears, needs, and blemishes not so vastly different from one's own. With that kind of emotional safety, neither will feel judged, misunderstood, or victimized. Watching the therapist receive and use patient feedback respectfully assures the patient that he will feel valued, be an equal team member, not just be tolerated or patronized.

Reciprocal rubble clearing makes the field more comprehensible and negotiable for both participants, therapy becoming a coordinated process where the partners progressively share goals and methods. The pair develop ways of approaching ambiguity, for example, about each other's integrity, and then can mine the emotional ore they are prospecting from each other. In the illustration in chapter 1, Karen progressively wondered what to make of me as, over months, I receded emotionally in response to witnessing her suppressed fury with the ailing Carl. As she realized our rapport was slipping, Karen alone developed a system for alerting me about our decline. Painfully, I learned how to use her feedback to correct the disjunction I had helped to engineer. In the end of the illustrated session, we came together in a way that was clearly more durable than the one we had known previously.

Using Controlled Disorientation to Find One's Way

Understanding controlled disorientation requires experience with the extreme discomfort of allowing oneself to be stranded in the midst of a therapy situation that has lost rhyme and reason. It can be very distressing, and the disorientation, with its accompanying loss of self-respect and humiliation, can last for a very long time. Communicating the emotional and technical challenge of this experience requires clinical examples. At this point, therefore, I want to return to the pressing crisis for Brittany I described in chapter 2: her despondency as she concluded she could never escape public relations work without being condemned to psychic hell for life by her mother and other such powerful magistrates. Brittany saw the catastrophe coming. She was about to lose herself, slide into a crevasse. My need to believe she was doing well provided me with relief from her suffering, my self-deception like white snow covering her inability to see and breathe but keeping her pristine and beautiful. So she mobilized her emergency training and took over. I was forced to stop, listen, and change direction. She would lead us for now. Her voice would be heard above the wind of her storm and the isolation of my noncomprehension.

Skepticism slowly converted to trust, ignorance moved to knowing; they all converged to move us from a searing disjunction to a preliminary conjunction where I recognized that I needed to join Brittany to make it through the storm, supporting her in her desire to leave her job. Intervening was a period of distraction for me, a false conjunction, a detour on the very beginning of the road to conjunction, when I acted as though I agreed with her but secretly hoped she would stay in her job.

Finally, following the path revealed through tolerating my controlled disorientation, I went along with her as she showed me she meant business; there was no turning back, she needed to leave her job. Soon we meshed and were authentically working together, a thrilling experience for both of us. We reached the peak of our mountain by learning about and surmounting its perils. Our conjunction was a stunning achievement and, for a moment, we were on top of the world.

It wasn't long, however, before we were lost again. New hazards appeared, this time returning with Brittany's conviction that I couldn't really like her and value her choice of a career as a writer. Technically, we were working well enough together, Brittany now taking classes and writing better than ever. Her teacher, the one who only weeks ago, she was convinced hated her, was suddenly praising her at every turn. It was just that at this level of magnification, according to Brittany, I was seeing too much, losing the trees and only seeing the forest. I couldn't see how ''inadequate'' her work was, nor give credence to her conviction that she had become a nuisance for me. I caught onto this shift as her voice fell to a monotone, and she again began to ''lose'' her words. She seemed to be saying, Steve, something's happening, I think you'd better take over or I may crash, but, as was typical of Brittany in her distress, she couldn't say that directly.

I needed, of course, to put my observations into words and begin the process of speculating about the psychological events that were taking place within her, as well as between us. More to the point, I had to let my disorientation take over, enabling me to find a way to understand the ice storm of despair that was moving in and separating us. Intuitively, I thought to hold her hand and did so. In the past, doing that had bridged the chasm while our words were beginning to thaw the places that were iced in. My message to her was that I wanted to stop her slide into despair, even my hands were there to steady her. I knew how rarely anyone had ever done that for her, even in childhood.

The Therapy Field   99

Taking a risk, gambling on a leap of inference, I said I understood depression well enough, since I'd recently had my first real experience with it. That my episode had been something like hers in its sense of icy desolation came through to her. She left a message the next day saying she was writing well again, that she was reassured I had not lost faith in her. Three days later, she brought in two new literary pieces, intricate prose, intersecting, and fitting perfectly. This view frames therapy as a developmental process, consolidating the patient's sense of having a self entitled to preside over her life.

I think it is now easier to understand our storm beleaguered climbing friends from the beginning of this chapter, why each member of the therapy couple has to depend on the other to make sense of their constantly changing terrain. In the midst of these shifts, their resources may seem anemic. As I think about their plight, I feel passionate about their need to depend one upon the other and am reminded of the shreds of help we try to glean in the midst of the profoundly disquieting disjunctions that precede and give birth to conjunctions. The needed help can come from a friend of the therapy, a consultant or supervisor, who brings a new perspective, and at times may use an assessment tool such as psychological testing (Frankel, 1995, 2000). Other sources of provocative, fresh information may be a professional book or article, a comment by a colleague or friend, or even a cloud formation that moves the partners to a slightly new perspective and revitalizes their dialogue.

New Selves Emerge

In some ways, exploring the therapy field, its interlocking relational configuration structure, is like a climbing expedition. When you begin you can hardly predict where your skills will be pushed to their limit, and how you and your partner will manage. The expedition is a shared creation in which each participant has a part and both a stake. The climbers, each with his or her own job, inevitably merge, creating a working unit.

Yet, the structure of a cliff scaling is so much neater than the messy and shifting world Brittany and I inhabited. Like most clinicians, if they're honest, I often don't know what to do next; the psychological place where we live can seem on the verge of collapse. When alone, we humans are often less shaky than when in the heat of relationship. We can retreat into the familiar, again becoming the selves we have always been. While I agree with Mitchell (1991) that the self is made of many, constantly changing, self states, for better or worse there are ways we are accustomed to acting and feeling, and we return to these often.

What happens in a successful therapeutic conjunction is that the two people involved begin to wreak havoc with their familiar ways of being. Together, they create a locus of experience outside themselves, different from their customary selves. This new intersubjective entity is not the usual self of either therapy participant. With the structural reinforcement of the conjunctive therapy process, this new shared relational configuration becomes more influential and competes with the familiar, the core self relational configurations. Now, the personal field has become more complicated. There is the familiar sense of self, a growing new sense of self, and ultimately a set of shared experiences and guidelines for living in a relationship. In time, the new may largely replace the old, and, in effect, the subject will have become a different person, having moved to a vista that gives a strikingly fresh outlook, one that feels different and goes by different rules from the original.

The principles of expansion here are different from those cited by authors who view the field as intersubjective but have an essentially unidirectional view of therapist influence. Robert Stolorow and his coworkers (Orange, Atwood, and Stolorow, 1997; Stolorow, Brandchaft, and Atwood, 1987), for example, understand psychotherapy as occurring in an intersubjective framework within which the goal is to reinstate disrupted development, most particularly of the self system. In my view, the process Stolorow and colleagues describe indeed occurs. It is close or equivalent to the reactivation of arrested development, a type of therapeutic change that I call *renewed development* throughout this book. Therapist and patient, like mother and child, work in attunement, creating optimal conditions for the continuation of halted development. The therapist acts according to the principles of "empathic–introspective inquiry" (Orange et al., 1997, pp. 43–44). Although the therapy process is considered to be mutually constituted, it is still understood to be asymmetrical, with one participant "primarily there as helper, healer, inquirer . . . and the other chiefly [seeking] help from emotional suffering" (p. 9). In contrast, the process I call *creative development* requires that patient and therapist be deeply affected by each other, with self-revelation, confrontation, empathy, care, and as a product, change flowing in both directions. Each partner is influenced to examine and revise his or her core self relational configurations (Frankel, 1995, pp. 165–168).

Of course, it is easy to be fooled into thinking you are being creatively interactive in therapy. The new self or joined selves may solely or largely consist of unappreciated aspects of one's original self. In that case what you get is an expanded version of the original self or a reenactment involving the therapist's and patient's complementary unconscious agendas.

There is nothing wrong with self-expansion, of course. It is sought as a prized goal in psychological and spiritual endeavors by people earnestly looking for enlightenment. However, as I see it, in a successful therapy, self-expansion is short of the goal. What therapist and patient are after is real change, a new state of mind where the patient, and, one hopes the therapist, emerge as changed people, influenced by an experience that is different from what they have known before. Throughout this book I call this change *creative*, and I differentiate between *creative change,* which may or may not be enduring, and *creative development,* which is (Erwin, personal communication, 2002). Creative change and the reversal of arrests in development, which I call *renewed development,* are powerful events for an individual, no matter when they happen; however, if they are not consolidated over time by repetition and deepening, they are likely to be ephemeral.

Our new vista is actually a mixture of all the factors I have named: old core selves, new selves on the way to becoming core self-relational configurations, old shared ways of being including old relationship patterns, and new ways of being with another person. The composition of a climbing team can benefit not just from the reinforcement of old skills but the creative replacement of these as well. Translated into human terms and applied to psychotherapy, the ultimate change involves not only the reversal of developmental arrests, but also filling in holes and distortions in development, leading to creative change and development. Creative development is, by definition, substantial and transformational, the most far-reaching outcome of psychotherapy.

Here is where the notion of shared relational configurations comes in. People instinctively fight against influences that feel foreign to them, that compete with familiar self states (Bromberg, 1995). They struggle to preserve a sense of coherence, to maintain the worldview they have meticulously constructed over time. Said in another way, core relational configurations have enormous staying power, and these states of mind come back into play tenaciously. Familiarity also breeds isolation, boredom, often making problematic attitudes and patterns less approachable for change. When partners in psychotherapy care enough to struggle to understand and to offer help in heartfelt ways, making sacrifices that are beyond the call of duty, and each is willing to reveal his or her fallibility, a unique bond begins to develop between the two. That bond, consisting of individual and then shared facilitating and analyzing relational configurations, progressively separates from either partner's familiar core relational configurations. As it gains precedence, it engages in fierce competition with and eventually replaces the old core relational configurations. The struggle is a mutual birthing process with prolonged labor pains in preparation for a shared emotional product.

The notion of a core self (core relational configurations) is debated in modern psychotherapy. Robert Emde (1990), Daniel Stern (1985), Steven Frankel (1995, pp. 124, 165–168), Karen Maroda (1999, p. 76) all describe the development and functioning of a reliable sense of self, at first in infancy as a variant of a core affective sense of self, and, then, continuing into adulthood. Stephen Mitchell (1997, pp. 21–22) dislikes the idea of a core self because he feels it obscures the observation that the self is discontinuous. Even accepting Mitchell's observations, the idea of the existence of a set of core self experiences, including mores and values, seems critical to me in understanding therapeutic conjunction and its product creative development. The discontinuous, ever changing self is not randomly distributed affectively or cognitively. Within bounds, it is describable, in spite of the observation that self states are always shifting and on scrutiny frequently emerge as discontinuous from one another (Bromberg, 1995). The issue being considered here is how these core relational configurations, making up the core self, are transformed in interaction between therapist and patient (Grigsby and Stevens, 2000).

Recapitulation

As I have come to understand the "field" in which a therapy occurs, it consists of (1) initiatives authored by one partner or the other; (2) authority that is traded between the partners; (3) nonverbal exchanges that convey information about what the other intends and needs; (4) innumerable large and small points of consensus, verbalized or not; (5) disjunctions, points where consensus fails and impasse results; (6) information gathering through controlled disorientation, with moment by moment feedback flowing between therapist and patient; (7) and, finally most influential in achieving creative change, conjunctions: uncanny experiences of intimate connection between therapy partners tied to a sense of boundless possibility for personal expansion. The people who are its major contributors, patient and therapist, are constantly in flux, carrying out numbers of tasks simultaneously, each with a particular job description, moving from one private or shared state of mind (relational configuration) to another.

The therapy field is a fluid, dynamic, and always evolving place. The complex division of labor that keeps it going requires that therapist and patient constantly switch off their authority, with one, usually but not exclusively the therapist, directing traffic. Creating the final conjunction almost always requires that disjunctions—internal wars and rivalries—be identified and healed by the therapist and patient who thereby strengthen and deepen their union. Internal work, controlled disorientation, as well as understanding transferences and countertransferences and how they affect the therapy effort, is always required. And, of course, the work is ongoing; there are always new developments and perspectives to consider.

In the end, there is no getting past the fact that the two people doing therapy, making up the therapy field, are imperfect. Each one's reality is impinged upon by an untold number of factors, his or her subjective preferences and experiences, making up the experience of self, constantly subject to revision. A change in one person invariably affects the other, coloring the atmosphere in which the therapy occurs. Here, along with the blur of subjectivity, is where our determination to describe and predict ends. Humans are in constant flux, are infinitely complicated, and have at least some free will. They are far from predictable and are able, therefore, potentially to make sweeping changes to themselves, and thus in their lives, leading to the hope and opportunity for ongoing creative development.

4

The Therapist's
Responsibility

In the first three chapters I offered my view about the symmetry of the therapy process, highlighting the therapist and patient sharing authority to know and lead. Complicating the notion of authority sharing is the therapist's ultimate responsibility for the therapy's progress. Patients want their needs and ideas to be heard and taken seriously. They need to know the therapist will jump in and take over as required, especially when the therapy is in trouble. They also expect the therapist to monitor himself, search for places where his own biases, desires, and reactions contaminate the therapy. Hence, in addition to being proactive, the therapist has to be self-reflective, acknowledging with humility the ways in which he may impede and should guide the therapy.

The Disruption and Repair Cycle in Psychotherapy

Most modern dynamic therapy systems, whether contemporary or traditional, leave little room for the therapist to take over and *actively* guide the therapy. After all, the therapist's opinions may be contaminated with distortions based on his own subjectivity,

105

and the forcefulness of his actions might rob the patient of initiative. And yet, to pretend that therapists and patients do not take turns leading each other and depending on the other to lead, is to falsify and debilitate the dynamic therapy process. *Falsify*, because leading happens and usually takes up a good deal of therapeutic space. Recommending therapy, encouraging the patient to attend sessions at regular times, and delve into their inner and outer lives, or directing through tone of voice, are all examples of leading. *Debilitate,* because no patient would want to be in a therapy where the therapist does not lead, at least from time to time.

The patient's guidance and support, even when unacknowledged, are also critical for keeping a therapist engaged and directed, as we will see in chapter 5. In this chapter I deal mainly with the therapist's side, his responsibility for repairing therapeutic rifts. This behavior is analogous to the repair half of the disruption and repair cycle familiar from mother–child interactions (Beebe, 2004; Beebe, Jaffe, and Lachmann, 1997; Beebe and Lachmann, 2002, pp. 143–184; Frankel, 1995; Tronick, 1989). While both mother and child participate in this process, the mother (or perhaps more accurately, the parent) from the start has the function of active participation with the child and of regulating the recovery from these disruptions (Greenspan, 1997; Schore, 1996). In fact, the good enough mother is described by Allen Schore (1996) as one who "[judiciously] induces a stress response in her infant through a misattunement [and reestablishes] in a timely fashion her psychobiologically attuned regulation of the infant's negative affect state that she has triggered" (p. 16).

How does repair work anyway? If one partner is competent and wants to help, what makes it possible for the other to hear and realign him- or herself so the two can work together therapeutically? People have their sensors. They each want to know if they can trust the other not to victimize, to be smart enough to comprehend their personal dilemmas and work on them collaboratively, and to be emotionally attuned and responsive—always a two-way street. I am talking about the hard to define ingredients that assure that a therapy, or any productive relationship, will work well.

Authors look in different places for answers to how therapeutic rifts are repaired. For some, the process consists of concern and understanding, communicated nonverbally. For Levin (1991), for example, repair comes from "nuances," nonverbal cues, which are traded between people: "The success of psychoanalysis hinges on the sensitivity of the participants to all nuances of communication, especially what is not verbal" (p. 146). Martin Viderman (1991, pp. 486–487) adds that the relationship developed is of a "special quality," making it possible for a "unique language" to evolve between the two participants.

Others, particularly self psychologists, view the therapist's empathy as reparative. Joseph Lichtenberg (1989) sees "symbolic reorganization" as growing out of "the ebb and flow of closeness between the patient and therapist . . ." (pp. 232–233). Referring to Kohut (1977) he says that through empathy the therapist joins the patient at a point of developmental arrest and brings him to new heights of self-organization.

Theories built around object relations (Summers, 1994) and intersubjectivity (Hoffman, 1991; Mitchell, 1993) give particular emphasis to the bidirectionality of the repair process. Complex mechanisms involving the modification of internal representations of self and other may be invoked to explain changes. Ultimately, a new, additional intersubjective entity is created that is neither therapist nor patient, a creation that stands apart from each (Frankel, 1995; Ogden, 1994).

Here we take a more organized look at some explanations for therapeutic repair and how much initiative the therapist is encouraged to take in each case.

1. *Externalization, transformation, and reintrojection:* The therapist is a vehicle through whom externalizations of aspects of the patient's internal objects and self can be experienced, modified, and reinternalized (Bion, 1952/1955, 1967; M. Klein, 1952/1975a; Scharff, 1992; Slavin and Kriegman, 1998). W. W. Meissner (1981, 1991), for example, sees transference as

encompassing the projection and reclaiming of transformed versions of the patient's introjects. This process presumably leads to a modification of the patient's self system through the patient reincorporating that which was projected. Others describe an exchange between two people where externalization and reinternalization occur alternately (Ogden, 1994).

The repair process, as described here, occurs spontaneously; the therapist's initiative is minimal. Also, the means through which it works, how the modification of that which is projected into the other occurs, is asserted; there is no way to confirm how it happens.

2. *The interfacing of two subjectivities leading to the reintegration of dissociated aspects of the self:* Here change occurs through the interfacing of two subjectivities. It may involve an "encounter [with] another personality as a separate center of subjective reality" (Bromberg, 1995, p. 176). One consequence of this event is that dissociated aspects of the self, experienced as subjectively unfamiliar, may again be linked up in the personality (Hirsh, 1994).

While I ascribe to an intersubjective view of how people influence each other, it is hard to know how a therapist can deliberately use the idea of two subjectivities interfacing for the purpose of repairing, rather than simply understanding the repair of a therapeutic rift.

3. *Cognitive reworking:* Some psychological models associate change with projective and introjective processes emphasizing cognitive reworking. Roy Schafer (1983), for example, describes the therapist as developing "countless mental models" (p. 40), from impressions of the patient he takes in and through a "transformational process" progressively arriving at less "out-of-date" constructions by comparing them with his own experience (p. 56). The described process has much in common with the mechanism named in category 1, externalization, reorganization, and reintrojection, but in this case the activity is mainly limited to cognitive reworking.

4. *The therapist functions as a transitional object:* The therapist and patient constitute a "holding environment" that "symbolizes" earlier developmental phases (Modell, 1990, p. 39). The patient lives out these reiterations of earlier experiences in therapy, and largely through the therapist's interventions moves beyond them to new self organizations (Modell, 1984, 1990; Winnicott, 1954/1958).

5. *The therapist as a developmental object:* The therapist becomes a focus around whom arrested development can be reestablished (Lichtenberg, 1989; Loewald, 1960, 1977; Settlage, 1992; Viderman, 1991; Weiss, 1993). Some authors, like Robert Emde (1988a, 1988b), consider reciprocity through affective attunement the key to this kind of engagement. Others see the developmental relationship as a nonmanipulated, corrective emotional experience where the therapist is available to actively facilitate the patient's progress (Settlage, 1993).

When Calvin Settlage (1993) discusses principles of psychoanalytic technique, he includes: "actively engaging the analytic relationship," "encouraging and acknowledging developmental initiatives," "acknowledging and taking responsibility for disruptions of the relationship caused by failures on the part of the analyst," and "offering and demonstrating availability when such clearly is needed" (pp. 23–25). Therapists aligned with Settlage do not claim to know what the patient needs in advance of collaborative exploration. They are aware of the distorting effect of the therapist's subjectivity. The recommendation of an active therapeutic stance, instead, is based on the conviction that the patient needs to feel the presence of another human being who is striving to understand him and be helpful.

While all of the five mechanisms in this list are found in mutative therapy, I believe the last two views, the therapist serving transitional and developmental functions, come closest to my picture of how therapeutic disruptions are resolved. Both mandate an active, involved role for the therapist. They capture a core process of therapeutic change without which verbalized, dynamically formulated interventions would be ineffective. The therapist and patient work collaboratively, assisting each other to repair a disruption in therapy. Often, though not always, the therapist initiates the repair process. On the other hand, both of these notions of therapeutic repair seem incomplete to me. In my view, the therapist's influence comes not only from filling in for the patient's developmental failures. He or she also connects with and appeals to the part of the patient striving for a new and better existence, different from what the patient had previously known.

The Project

My observations from the project described in the introduction to this book, support the view that therapeutic change is regularly associated with the therapist making an active effort to move the therapy forward to address and repair therapeutic disruptions. The project consisted of a review by two of us of 54 3- to 6-month clinical segments from my own psychotherapies and psychoanalyses. The findings from that project, pertinent to this chapter, follow:

1. When we organized these therapy segments into sequences of disruption and repair, we found that repair was always fueled by my active effort to reengage the patient.
2. An affirmative interaction between myself and the patient was usually a prerequisite for useful insight. Frequently, this helpful activity alone, with a minimum of deliberate therapeutic exploration, was associated with change.
3. It was often necessary for me to openly acknowledge the ways in which I may have been responsible for the disruption, before the patient was willing to be self-reflective.
4. My actively working to repair disjunctions in the therapy, regardless of whether the patient or I was responsible for initiating them, helped keep the therapy on track. Ultimately, I was usually responsible for sustaining the repair, even if the patient

had been the first to recognize and bring our attention to the disjunction.

5. Much of the change in the patient occurred some time during the period of repair and prior to the final consolidation of insight, often in the absence of interpretative dialogue.

Marty—A Therapist's Lesson in Humility

The mandate that the therapist takes ultimate responsibility for therapeutic impasses is much like that of the leader of the rock-scaling expedition. Imagine you are holding the rope positioned to get you and your companion over a treacherous cliff, a situation parallel to the intimidation a therapist often feels when at the edge of a gaping disjunction. You alone have led the way up the rock face because you have done this before, having years of rock-climbing experience and paying careful attention to the techniques. But your companion, trailing many feet below, looks dazed. All he sees is vertical rock with a small tree growing here and there out of its face. He took a short course in rock climbing, but since he is terror struck he has forgotten all he learned.

On the other hand your companion is an excellent map reader and without his involvement you could not have made your way here; yet ironically, cooperation is now almost out of the picture. Just before arriving at this point you insisted on following a stream along a canyon. The walls kept closing in, your distraught partner insisting you were lost, but you wouldn't hear him. Only as rain clouds gathered did you realize how quickly a flash flood could wipe you out, and did you even consider listening. Now, you both have to get over this cliff, and you are the one who knows how.

In this metaphor, the stream running along the canyon was my irritation. Marty, my patient, was pushing me relentlessly with his dissatisfaction about every aspect of his life, as well as his accusation that I was responsible for his suffering. In response, I walled him off. Only when our trek looked as though it would fall apart, be washed away by a flash flood of emotion, did I take my bearings from him. And, then, finally, I was in charge again, straining to be helpful, groping for a new way to understand and resolve our dilemma.

Case Illustration, Marty

My experience with Marty, one of the cases I reviewed for the project, provides a dramatic narrative of a disruption and repair sequence. As was typical with people he asked for help, it was not long before I became the target of Marty's transference assumption that I would cheat and humiliate him. A rift occurred when I defensively retaliated against his questioning a charge for a missed session, and then exacerbated as he challenged my method for increasing my fee. The repair required that I first acknowledge my angry countertransference. Only then could Marty begin to explore his own expectation that I would victimize him.

Marty first came to see me at the age of 40. He had made enough money to partly retire from his retail clothing business. Yet, in spite of his financial success, he felt like a failure. He complained that people did not take him seriously, personally or in business.

From early childhood, Marty's father reviled him for being weak. The father's supposed crusade, masking sadism, was to toughen up Marty. Later, while Marty secretly wished for a relationship with his father, he self-protectively resisted his father's attempts to make him into a "real boy." Although Marty claimed he had contempt for this stereotype, he also felt incapable of achieving it.

Marty described his mother as "a dreamer." She divorced his father when Marty was 11. She then earned money in her own entertainment business. In part because of her work and in part to escape Marty's father, she moved frequently. The moves forced Marty to depend on her for companionship. In spite of this close connection with his mother, Marty remembers both parents as entirely uninterested in his private needs and unable to carry on a "logical" conversation about any important personal issue.

At age 13, Marty's 16-year-old sister committed suicide, eliminating his only shield against his father's battering. From that point, his father's wrath and mother's impulsivity were focused entirely on him.

I should have been forewarned about later troubles by Marty's history of terminating commitments to his future success and by the way Marty found me. A summa cum laude from an excellent college, he left a Ph.D. program in history after passing his qualifying exams, allegedly because his advisor disagreed with Marty's thinking about his thesis topic. Years later he sought therapy, coming to me because my name had appeared in an article in a local newspaper. I found Marty immediately intriguing, attracted by his impressive intellect and apparent motivation to repair his life shortly after a cardiac bypass operation.

For the first year of the therapy, conducted three times a week, Marty was compliant and cooperative. I was optimistic; privately, I think, regarding him almost like a distant family member, someone I could intuitively understand. That was the honeymoon; somehow, I thought it would last forever.

Things seemed to change overnight, in a way that entirely caught me by surprise. After about a year of smooth sailing the familiar Marty rapidly slid away. In his place was an angry, chronically dissatisfied man, arguing that my theory and technique were inadequate. For example, after months of compliantly bringing in long convoluted dreams that he claimed he wanted to understand, he began to use dreams, instead, as proof of the absurdity of my method of therapy. Dreams moved from interesting to "meaningless."

I had found Marty so appealing, his intelligence and his original loyalty to our work, predicated on his wish for an unconditionally committed relationship and relief from his postcardiac surgery distress, that I assumed his antagonism toward me was temporary, reflecting what we then called a *transference neurosis*. But, to my amazement, no manner of patience or therapeutic exploration seemed to shake him lose. It was on this foundation that the incident I will relate occurred, 3 years and 3 months into therapy. By then, I was feeling jangled.

Yet, in retrospect, I privately held onto my optimism for Marty's therapy, and probably minimized his pathology. I especially did not want to think of Marty as terribly disturbed, perhaps predisposed to paranoia. In being so upbeat I was also probably trying to keep my disappointment and frustration in check.

Marty kept pushing me with his obstinacy and pessimism about therapy. Here was the setting for the clinical episode I will relate. It started with my uncharacteristically becoming angry at Marty, in part because of the unrelenting experience of frustration in the face of my desire to think well of him, and in part reflecting the humiliation I was feeling as he labored to defeat my therapeutic efforts. The ostensible provocation for our uncoupling was a contested charge for a missed session that Marty had canceled with little notice. Since he had been thoroughly reliable about coming to his appointments he thought I should reward him by relaxing my policy of charging for missed sessions I could not use for another patient. This issue faded until Marty again went on the attack over my later announcement of a yearly inflation-based fee raise, a procedure to which Marty was accustomed. Lurking in the background was my having granted him a somewhat reduced fee at the start of the therapy.

At the beginning of the current session I reminded Marty that the fee raise would begin the following month. Having felt abused by Marty about the missed session, and originally compromised by his requirement of a reduced fee, I may have delivered this announcement with barely disguised irritation, flaunting my prerogative as therapist. Marty's response on that day was strangely muted. He seemed to accept the fee change without the contention I expected, and for the moment, I was relieved.

In the next session, however, all hell broke loose. Marty's composure was opposite to the previous day's as he angrily told me that the increase I was proposing was incorrect and that this issue "needed to be discussed." I was shocked by his sudden reversal, and disappointed, because once again my hope of the original Marty returning was dashed. Privately, I was anticipating that my good will would be appreciated and reciprocated by Marty. After all, I had maintained my faith in him long after he lost his faith in me, and I had behaved like a gentleman in response to his defections.

As I see it now, my incorrigible belief in Marty was in part valid and in part defensive. It was valid in that, insinuated between line after line of his pessimism and hostility, were moments of breezy, intelligent conversation about topics Marty and I were interested in, mainly philosophical, often about ethics. Also, he was implicitly loyal, conveying respect for me and the therapy process alongside his disdain. My belief in Marty was defensive in my need to see him as relatively undisturbed, a person with a mentality much like mine. The disjunction Marty and I experienced, while predicated on our growing awareness of differences, was still mitigated by a powerful, but unspoken desire we shared to keep working together and find some way to counter Marty's negativity.

My reaction to Marty's angry protest about the fee increase came swiftly and forcefully; it was so powerful, I was shocked. I took Marty's accusation that I had miscalculated the fee raise incorrectly at face value. I felt irritated and abused, certain that the fee I had calculated was correct, nonetheless saying that I would be glad to discuss this subject with him. His attack continued. I asked him why he felt I was being so unreasonable. I said reflexively that I thought he knew how careful I had been to set a reasonable initial fee and establish procedures for fee increases. I added that I had even set a somewhat reduced fee for him as a response to his insistence that he could not afford to work analytically unless I did this.

Clearly, I was feeling hurt as well as angry. After all, I believed in Marty, and consistently made concessions in his favor; for example, by initially lowering his fee and maintaining the discount from my usual fee. I became Marty's advocate for a better, healthier self, and he the naysayer. Our struggle had gotten so bad that nothing I said or did met with Marty's approval. Yet, I persisted in my crusade. And here, originating with the topic of my charge for a missed session, was the meltdown, with me having difficulty containing my feelings of being abused and unappreciated.

As I reviewed this sequence I found nothing unusual about my decision to charge Marty for the missed session. There is no question that his challenge might have been hard to take by any therapist. But it was my reaction to his challenging the accuracy and, by implication, the integrity of my fee raise that was at issue for me. Marty enticed me to believe in him and then punished me for doing so. At first, he made me feel hopeful, and then used and stupid. In retrospect, my mentioning the reduced fee when he challenged the accuracy of my calculated fee increase was retaliatory and irrelevant, reflecting my feeling cheated by him. Marty's original insistence on a lower fee undoubtedly contributed to my response and had not been fully exposed by us. For his part, Marty was convinced I would ultimately humiliate him and steal his last vestiges of self-respect. The more he imagined being attacked by me, the more I advocated for him, the higher the narcissistic stakes became for him. He protected himself from the degradation he expected from me through his constant demeaning criticism of me.

My countertransference to Marty helps explain my sharp reaction to his contemptuous treatment of me. In many ways, Marty's accusations came close to my own father's frequent criticism and distrust of my motives. My father's attacks, which usually seemed to come out of the blue, constantly hurt and enraged me. While this issue was mostly settled for me in my own psychoanalysis, Marty's long diatribe was wearing on me. His attacks reevoked visceral memories of my father's abuse.

During the next few sessions Marty's rage escalated. He repeatedly accused me of being ''unclear in my thinking,'' claiming his challenge had upset and angered me. Since his statements did not make sense to me, I assumed I was dealing with a transference distortion, and I tried to explore his accusations. This response only angered Marty more. ''You believe you're right. You don't want to be accountable for what you did. You think illogically and can't even see it. What do we do about therapizing the therapist?''

Over the next several sessions Marty insisted we put our disagreement down in writing. He wrote a description of the session when I introduced the fee change. He attacked my ''faulty methods of raising fees.'' He ''knew'' I resented his complaints, since all I wanted to do was ''make a buck.'' He believed I did not want to hear him. My attitude ''made it impossible'' to trust me. Also, he insisted, how could I understand him if I could not ''even stay clear for 5 minutes as we discussed this fee issue?''

While I personally believed that I had not done anything to warrant Marty's attack, I found myself peculiarly disoriented. I was aware of feeling justified in my irritation toward Marty; truly he was flouting the good will I had expressed in my dogged commitment to his welfare through therapy, not to mention my maintaining a lower fee and keeping a steady focus on his strongest attributes. His need to humiliate and defeat me in treatment was apparent. I was sure, as well, that his chronic dissatisfaction with his life and with me, forcing my impatience with him, had a transferential basis and should be examined therapeutically. But his insistence that my way of handling the fee and my alleged miscalculation (which meant I could not be trusted to be clear thinking), was so tenacious and seemingly heartfelt that I was forced to question my certainty about the validity of my own response.

I worked hard to understand what was happening, but my effort fell flat. At a few points I even made edgy speculations;

for example, suggesting that Marty's guilt about a financial windfall with a stock might be making him sensitive to financial issues in the therapy. Did he perceive me as envious of his stock bonanza, fussing about the fee to squelch his excitement about his good fortune?

At this point, confused, I decided to describe my experience to him. I said I was puzzled. I recognized he was certain I had made a mistake and was very upset with me. I said I was quite willing to try to understand my part in our difficulty. I had to force this stance, since I was still convinced that his response was emotionally distorted, requiring him to frame me as selfish and irrational. Still, I offered to reconstruct the events at issue collaboratively and said we could do this in writing. This concession, while not yet entirely genuine on my part, put Marty in a more cooperative mood, and he outlined the developments, as he saw them, in words and writing.

Largely because of my desire for reconciliation and restitution of the therapy, I struggled to listen more closely; but I wanted something more than just the resolution of our disjunction. I believe I was still hoping for the return of the Marty I respected and liked. Within me, that view of him had been sustained, not modified, just minimized. My desire to make the therapy and, for that matter our relationship, succeed was still in place. Further, I was aware that if anyone was going to take the initiative to make this segment of our work useful therapeutically, it had to be me. Then, during the next series of sessions I managed to hear him as one more time he described my inconsistency in bringing up the reduced fee when he "had only been talking about the proposed fee change." At that moment I recalled the muted sense of retaliatory pleasure I felt when I brought up the reduced fee; it was relatively easy—once I gained distance—for me to remember it.

I told Marty I was now able to hear him; his perception was accurate. I could understand that my remarks, indeed, were inconsistent. He was right. I had become angry when he challenged my fee raise.

Marty immediately felt some relief. He said my inability to hear him had "made him feel crazy." I replied that I had a similar experience when he kept refusing to listen to my points about charging for the missed session, while attacking me as illogical and stubborn. This reversal was my introduction to understanding his experience of me as dogmatic and illogical.

The events I have just related took place over 3 weeks. Marty's perception of me began to shift as I acknowledged I had made an error by bringing up the reduced fee, and that I was willing to review his complaint about the fee increase. For a while he still distrusted me, but simultaneously, he began to see me as reasonable.

After our work to repair our rift, Marty could then turn to the question of why our experience elicited such a negative reaction from him. Marty's father's attacks on him reflected his father's frustration with his own failures. Marty's defense of himself was of no interest to the father. Further, until Marty gained financial independence, his father used money to tease and frustrate him by offering it and then withdrawing it capriciously. This discussion was an opening for us to explore exactly how Marty originally influenced me to establish a reduced fee, based, we could see now, on his assumption that I would use the money he paid me to enhance my power and control over him. He then balked when I asked him to honor his agreed upon financial obligations to me, in this case by paying for a missed session he failed to give me time to reschedule for someone else. My feeling abused by Marty was similar to his when his father offered Marty a financial gift, and then withdrew financial support when Marty required it for reasonable maintenance. Having broached these topics, Marty noted that he regularly experienced misunderstandings similar to ours with other people. In these relationships he, like his father, would insist on "logical" thinking, requiring in effect that these people read his mind to decipher his personal logic. When they did not comply he retaliated, further angering these people with his obstinacy.

Recapitulation

The backdrop for this sequence is Marty's perception of me as being like his father, arbitrary and bent on humiliating him. To protect himself, he barraged me with criticism. When we started our therapy, in order to avoid being cheated, he made sure I set a somewhat reduced fee. He experienced attempts to explore and interpret topics such as these as attacks, and deflected them. Marty understood my charging for the missed session and then my fee increase through this set of expectations. His impassioned attack on the basis of the fee increase provoked me. I struck back. In effect, I accused him, in part accurately, of wanting to take advantage of me financially.

Marty caught on to my reaction immediately. He could see my statement about my originally setting a reduced fee for what it was: a counterattack. I prevented myself from recognizing it as such, and attempted to go to other subjects. But Marty was not about to let me off the hook. His diatribe was unrelenting. So far as he was concerned, any rapport we may have had was now destroyed. My forcing the issue of my prerogative to set financial policy, brought me too close to seeming like his abusive, humiliating father. For the moment, the paternal background for our debate became glaringly vivid for Marty.

This experience was trying for me. I had to weather Marty's vitriolic assaults. I felt confused and misunderstood. I saw no reality basis for his accusation. Only later did I begin to understand his rage at the perception that I was being arbitrary and illogical in my attitude toward his fees.

In this sequence, I was the first to acknowledge my contribution to our disjunction. Marty forced me to see my angry countertransference. Previously, I tried to explore only Marty's distrustful and hostile transference. These efforts failed, until I made it clear that I could own up to my part in our disruptive interaction.

Marty challenged my charge for the missed session and insisted I was incorrect in calculating the fee increase. He accused me of being vindictive when he questioned it. I finally invited him to show me what he was talking about. I acknowledged that I could have been wrong. Soon, I recognized that while my fee increase was reasonable, my handling of his challenge about calculating his fee was contentious. I could see how, in Marty's mind, I became the father he reviled. To him, I was as arbitrary and hostile as his father had been. He was unaware of his own transference-based provocation, but he could see my anger clearly.

At this point in our dialogue I limited my comments, acknowledging only the irrationality of my response to Marty's challenge about my fee setting. I was willing to explore my reaction to feeling cheated by him. Marty relaxed. Only then did I ask about *his* reaction to my behavior. Then, for the first time, Marty could be self-reflective and begin to notice the historical basis of his expectation that I would abuse him.

In my opinion two factors were responsible for the success of this therapy sequence of disruption and repair. First, Marty observed me struggling to understand my own behavior. He could see I was genuinely distressed and confused. There could be little doubt in his mind about whether I cared to work out our differences. Second, I was willing to ask the same hard questions of myself that I asked of him. Marty's early experience was with people who mainly blamed others. Discovering that I could be modest and self-critical was surprising for him. These events created an atmosphere that made it safe for him to be introspective. He ran little risk of feeling used and humiliated if he was forthcoming. I was only asking him to do what I had done myself.

In the end, after we worked to untangle the fee incident, Marty could better differentiate me from his internal version of his father. But, much more happened between us than is contained in these explanations. Neither Marty nor I were the same people after that experience. I was humbled and reached out to Marty. Like Brittany, Marty was amazed that someone would want to understand his complaint. Change for both of us, not just Marty, occurred as we repaired our ruptured connection, each of us struggling to be heard and understood, each pulling the other out of painful isolation. The most fundamental change, then, was based on the passionate interaction between us, two separate people, both attempting to connect with and constructively influence the other.

Russell: The Place of His Self Revelation
and Authenticity

There are many ways that therapists can take responsibility for repairing rapport in therapy. A disjunction may derive from the therapist's side, as in my experience with Marty. Alternatively, the patient may be responsible for the disjunction, requiring the therapist's initiative for its repair. My psychoanalyst colleague's experience with Russell, a nonanalyst psychotherapist from whom he sought help soon after treatment for cancer, years after his training analysis, is a case in point. The patient, Tom, described his therapy experience.

Russell surprised Tom with his wisdom and his willingness to be emotionally forthright in therapy. However, Tom's pleasure in that relationship also made him worry that Russell might disappoint him, leave him stranded after exciting him about the potential depth of the therapy and what he judged to be their personal connection. Paradoxically, Tom pulled back, requiring Russell to prove that he could be even more fully present. Russell's willingness to do that, to continue to lead therapeutically and emotionally, kept them both on track.

In this session, Tom entered Russell's office feeling sheepish for being 10 minutes late. He usually liked coming, but it had been 2 weeks since he'd been there, and he was feeling empty inside. He justified the extra minutes spent jogging as if a loss of 10 minutes to the therapy didn't matter.

"Hi Russell." "Hi Tom," that big childlike grin of Russell's was quite something for a 69-year-old man. Russell seemed really glad to see Tom; Tom began to squirm. He had the feeling he wanted to get out of there, or at least concentrate on the material he had brought to discuss in the session and stay away from personal feelings, especially those concerning their relationship. Two aberrant thoughts came to Tom's mind. First, was he experiencing some homosexual excitement hidden behind his discomfort, making him uncomfortable? The second was that today Tom would not be able to prevent the session from becoming useless, his usual way of undoing the pleasure he felt working with Russell. He didn't tell Russell about either thought. Of particular note, Tom and Russell had been discussing Tom's conviction that for the therapy to work, Russell would have to feel actual affection toward him: real commitment, consistent with Tom's view of what makes therapy work. Now Russell was offering it, and Tom was pushing it away.

After Russell asked Tom how he was, Tom asked Russell the same. Russell surprised Tom by saying, "Much better, the last six weeks have been difficult because I've been preparing to move." Tom knew something about Russell's mood during the last six weeks: Russell had been a bit removed; helpful, but a little distant. Actually, Tom had blamed Russell's distancing on himself, feeling that by talking about himself, he was dragging Russell down. Here, Russell amazed Tom by confirming not only that the problem had been his, but that he liked Tom's request that he, Russell, be as honest with Tom as Tom was with him.

For the moment, Tom recognized that Russell truly liked him. He knew Russell was typically reticent about sharing his feelings with his patients. Tom even had the thought that Russell might be experimenting with the idea of conditionally depending on a patient for a friendly, even supportive, connection. Tom's excitement quickly disappeared, however, under an avalanche of distraction. Suddenly, Tom could hardly hear Russell anymore. Tom said something to him about being glad he understood Tom's need for authenticity in their work, forcing the words out like putty from a tube rather than a bird being released into the air. Russell simply answered, "Yes, I believe in it fully."

The success of that moment was too much for Tom to bear. Again, he pictured excruciating disappointment—finding out that Russell didn't care much about him, after all. He deflected the focus to his experiences of the past 2 weeks, selecting a related but less emotionally charged topic that had to do with ways he was being self-defeating. Tom said he thought he was overcommitting himself again professionally, and went on to describe incidents where he was able to experience some work related joy and then undermined that pleasure. He continued to get the feeling he was defeating the session, making it meaningless, reversing the excitement he felt.

Finally, Tom said to Russell that he thought he was doing to him what he did with other people with whom he wanted to feel close, pulling them in as if intimacy was imminent and then pushing them away. He was distressed by that pattern also occurring with Russell. Again, Tom was surprised when Russell listened and agreed. However, contrary to his expectation, Russell's assent seemed heartfelt rather than stereotypical. Tom kept getting the feeling that Russell wanted the time between them to be emotionally intimate, and that he cared. Tom also felt more convinced that this was not Russell's usual style, but an acknowledgment of the ideas Tom had introduced: that to succeed therapy requires a real, not stylized connection between therapist and patient. Russell was so convincing that never again in that hour did it occur to Tom that Russell might be critical of his distress, even though he had absolutely expected Russell's criticism, and at first even experienced criticism. By not responding to Tom's anxiety, by believing in the value of his ideas about therapy, Russell managed to prevent the damage to their rapport that Tom was so convinced he would cause.

By that point in the session, Tom found himself believing that Russell approved of him; that Russell liked Tom's ideas and him as well. Most of this impression was conveyed without words. Tom reported that something then shifted within him: he found himself wanting to change, to try out Russell's ideas, to live his life a little more like Russell seemed to live his. Suddenly,

Tom didn't notice the resistance to influence he was used to. By the end of the session, he had the sense that he loved Russell: the actualization, on a bilateral basis, of the sentiment he felt Russell had conveyed to him.

Tom's conversion of Russell's humane interest and affection into anxiety about homosexuality initially threatened to sabotage the integrity of their hard-won bond. Fortunately, Russell understood Tom's requirement for him to affirm his commitment in action. Russell needed to demonstrate his dedication to helping Tom overcome Tom's tendency to spoil his offer of affection and nonexploitive pleasure, giving Tom just what Tom's father had not provided him with in childhood.

How did Russell and Tom succeed so well? The bits and pieces I put together with Tom follow. The conjunction started with Russell seeming so unencumbered and friendly, glad to see Tom. But more important, Russell told Tom that he had personally been somewhat distressed during the preceding weeks. This admission was an astounding revelation for Tom. Was Russell a therapist or a friend? In a moment of confusion, Tom could not tell which.

Tom conceived of most psychotherapists or psychoanalysts as rarely admitting to their moods, or even needs. Tom's experience with his training analyst was traditionally one sided; his psychoanalytic training supported this way of thinking about appropriate therapeutic interaction, even though it was logically absurd to Tom. During his years of analytic training, being an analysand mandated a special set of rules for relating that protected the analyst's anonymity. As a patient Tom could not think of his analyst or therapist as vulnerable or troubled, even though he was both a psychotherapist and a psychoanalyst himself. Underpinning Tom's willingness to sustain this kind of illusion about correct therapeutic behavior was his childhood experience with his mother. Seriously depressed after her brother and sister died, she needed Tom to compensate for her grief and support the pretense that she was better off than she was in reality. Tom believes he did something similar with his therapists, supporting an idealization of them by making the therapy relationship and their authority seem sacrosanct.

Feeling Russell's decency and vulnerability made it possible for Tom to consider his own needs, the requirement that he be easier on himself and respect the severe strains from his medical illness, setting the stage for reincorporating genuine pleasure into his life. Russell's willingness and ability to take over and make sure they didn't lose their bond made a great difference. Russell did this directly by agreeing that authenticity for both Tom and himself was critical to their work. But, perhaps even more important, Russell kept the conversation going even when Tom wanted to discourage it, and the tone and timing of his words and gestures told Tom he meant it.

The building of conjunction between Russell and Tom had started months earlier when Russell stopped to listen to and take seriously Tom's unconventional requirements that Russell disclose relevant personal feelings to Tom, and that, as part of the therapy, they develop a genuine emotional commitment to each other. Originally, the disjunction in their work was Russell's, when he insisted on anonymity. The second was Tom's paradoxical withdrawal once Russell embraced Tom's condition that they be open. The growing conjunction came from their willingness not to let each other off the hook: first, through Tom's initial intolerance of Russell's formality, and then, Russell's insistence that in therapy they live by Tom's request for authenticity.

Repairing Disjunctions, Returning to a Conjunctive Process

Most of the disrupted clinical sessions I studied for *the project* began to succeed when I noticed and corrected my part in a developing disjunction. Initially, when I explored and interpreted only the patient's contribution to the disruption, his or her alienation increased. In contrast, when I, as the therapist with Marty, and Russell in his work with Tom, assumed active leadership over the repair process, engagement and change were reinstituted. Other relevant observations from that study were that repair was always supported by my active effort to engage the patient, that an affirmative interaction between myself and the patient was usually a prerequisite for useful insight, and that a helpful, supportive therapy interaction requiring a minimum amount of verbalized therapeutic exploration was often associated with successful repair.

Using these observations and details from the reviews of clinical material for *the project*, we can construct a typical therapy progression from disruption to repair consisting of the following steps:

1. Ordinarily, therapy is initiated with the patient hopeful that he will be helped.

2. As the patient's involvement with the therapist deepens, complications invariably arise. Ultimately, the patient experiences the therapist as failing him in some way. The therapist may make an error; a hostile transference or countertransference may develop. The patient defensively detaches himself.

3. The loss of rapport with the patient is often disconcerting for the therapist, clashing with his belief that he understands the patient and the therapy interaction. A period of disorientation for the therapist often follows.

4. With whatever limited information he has, the therapist needs to act to stop the widening disjunction. This process ideally requires the therapist to acknowledge his part in creating the rift. The therapist embraces his disorientation searching for what it can teach him about his and the patient's role in causing it. But, because the disjunction is widening, the therapist often has to act before he fully understands the problems in the therapy. An uncomfortable, somewhat premature, leap of inference may be required of him.

With Marty, when I took the risk of acknowledging that I might have been vindictive in my response to his accusation about my criteria for raising my fee, and that I wanted him to help me understand my behavior, the first and most important step was taken for healing our rupture. Going out on a limb to embrace the patient's confusion and then to reengage him is likely to be experienced as proof of the therapist's earnestness. Since this activity can be so strenuous for the therapist, these actions may encourage the patient to enter more deeply into the therapy work, marking the beginning of a therapeutic conjunction.

5. As rapport is reestablished, the therapy becomes more reciprocal and collaborative. However, until fully harmonious, the conjunctive progression is characterized by patient and therapist alternating in assuming the authority to know and lead in their work. At any point in this development one partner may have more perspective than the other, seeing the events in therapy and understanding the other partner most clearly.

In the beginning of a therapeutic disruption–repair sequence, disruption is initiated as the patient draws away, and progresses when the therapist fails to recognize his own part in creating it. The patient reengages and begins to work again as the therapist acknowledges his role in causing the disruption and moves to reinvolve the patient. The patient may be the one who originally points out the rift and even initiates the repair, as Marty did with me. Eventually, however, the therapist takes over, directing the process of resolving the disjunction and fostering a conjunction. Reestablishing Marty's confidence that the therapy could be saved required that I see my countertransference role in our standoff before he did. Through action, interpretation, and self-revelation, the therapist ultimately leads in repairing the rift, often needing to do this before the patient is able to reflect on his own contribution to creating the disjunction.

Therapists who can scrutinize themselves are experienced as personally accessible. They present themselves as humane, fallible, unafraid of the same self-reflection they ask from the patient. Issues of authority and superiority fall away. An atmosphere of safety and personal good will is created that potentially leads to the fervent rapprochement between the two that is conjunction.

In my view, it is hardly surprising that human beings require this kind of reassurance before committing to a process as interpersonally precarious as therapy. The risk of being misunderstood or betrayed in such a relationship is enormous. As illustrated by Tom's experience with Russell, the anticipation of relief from personal isolation and suffering brings with it terror of disappointment and victimization (Mitchell, 1993, pp. 209–214). Paradoxically, I believe that all people enter therapy with the hope and usually the conviction that the therapist can relieve their suffering and that the two will join conjunctively to enhance the quality of the patients' lives (Bass, 1996; Mitchell, 1993, pp. 207–209; Slochower, 1996a, 1996b; Daniel Stein, 2004).

A key difference between my point of view and traditional psychodynamic positions is that within limits I see this hope as reasonable. I believe that to some extent it has to be protected within therapy. Research in child development supports the view that affiliation is one of the pivotal human motivations, with most other motivations subsidiary (Beebe and Lachmann, 2003; Kraemer, 1992; Schore, 2003; Seligman, 2003; Silverman, 1992). Theories of dynamic therapy predicated on this developmental research (Beebe, Jaffe, and Lachmann, 1992; Settlage, 1992; Shane and Shane, 1989; Weiss, 1993) advocate that the therapist take a facilitating role in therapy, actively furthering rapport between themselves and the patient.

Self-reflection is hardly possible when the patient's energies are concentrated on securing himself against harm and disappointment within the therapy. In that case, the therapist is a potential adversary. He needs to be contained along with unacceptable elements of the patient's inner life, including prohibitive ideas and degraded editions of self or other. Until the therapist's goodwill and reliability are unequivocally established, the patient cannot commit wholeheartedly to a shared process involving self-reflection. The risk is too high that the therapy will turn instead into an experience of self-deprecation and victimization for the patient.

I am proposing a model of therapeutic disruption and repair where the patient's expectations have both a realistic and irrational side. However exaggerated his worries about exposure or intimacy may be, the patient's fear of the therapist harming him is in part realistic. Therapists, for example, may promote false beliefs by insisting unreasonably on the correctness of their convictions, or inadvertently retraumatize a patient by being disappointing in association with the patient's need for a basic relationship of care and support. Until the patient's freedom from these fundamental concerns is established within the therapy it is unlikely that a fully productive therapeutic process will occur. The commitment will be too thin and unauthentic. The patient's reflective possibilities process will be handicapped.

As I understand it, therapeutic change is most likely to occur in the network of safety and support I describe. At points, the therapist leads in the development of therapeutic change. He facilitates reengagement, taking his cues from the patient but relying on his own intuition and initiative as well. Engagement and change are then interwoven. As the patient comes to understand and trust the therapist's motives, he revises his entrenched view of himself, the therapist, and relationships in general. With this internal shift, self-reflection becomes less threatening. A reciprocal process also occurs, as illustrated in my work with Brittany, during which the therapist learns to trust and is profoundly affected by the patient. Ironically, by the time a coherent verbal dialogue about these pivotal emotional issues in therapy is in place, much of the reengagement and even desired change may already have taken place.

Elemental changes in therapist and patient are the building blocks of the conjunctive process. Therapy partners get better at hearing and working with each other. Both partners change, even if the sought after clinical result, as in Marty's case, is mainly within the patient. Through a series of shocks, the first of which may affect the therapist most deeply, the patient and therapist are ultimately exposed to an entirely new set of personal and interpersonal possibilities. Marty couldn't believe that I would be interested in understanding my behavior. People, his father, were not like that; they blamed others for problems. There was no precedent in his life for another male being contrite and self-critical. Russell amazed Tom when he took seriously Tom's mandate that their therapy involve bilateral self-revelation and a heartfelt personal connection.

The change that took place in Marty's and my sense of reality qualifies for the designation *creative*. It was not simply that a distortion, based on a transference or deriving from an aberrant developmental experience, was cleared up, returning Marty to a better version of himself. Our experience became, for both of us, the basis of a new line of development, built upon what a previously unfamiliar kind of joining with another person.

At first glance, the development I am talking about may seem uncomplicatedly unidirectional, from the therapist to patient, analogous to that of a mother interacting with her child. Actually, development that has been arrested earlier in life, is always furthered in a constructive therapy relationship, leading to reinstigated, *renewed development*. But it is not that simple: Marty had to distress me, even torment me, to capture my attention. Finally, we entered another zone where my mind became crowded with the perception that he might have a point. I felt humiliated and confused, in unfamiliar territory. I listened to him more carefully and respectfully, and behaved in a way for which he was unprepared. Lest it seem like this activity was not dynamically informed, Marty and I were always exploring the psychology of our interaction, with a full accompaniment of hunches and interpretations. These therapeutic probings helped. However, it was the tenacity of my interest in understanding Marty's objection to my fee raise, as well as my reason for being angry and defensive, that was instrumental in setting the stage for our reconciliation and for the creative development—affecting both of us—that resulted.

As therapists, we often leave climbing partners dangling. Therapist and patient may be great at coconstructing probable maps of the territory they are traversing, but then what? Actually getting deeply into that landscape, the therapeutic crevices and seemingly impassable cliffs, is the trick. The two must make sure neither partner abandons the other, settling for the convenient rationalization that because they both understand something and feel good about it, they have arrived at their destination. Creative change requires arduous climbing, no shortcuts. Therapist and patient need to throw in their lots together, and then be open minded about what they encounter. When I was stuck on a ledge with Marty for several weeks, pierced by the cold winds of his hostility, I shockingly needed him to help me get off; when I had to follow Brittany into the recesses of her stark isolation I found a lovely world buried so deeply that no human being could have entered without submitting to the most uncompromising scrutiny by Brittany. Recognizing the seriousness of my intention to follow them was enough to jolt Marty and Brittany to give human beings another chance. Overall, we induced and forced the other to listen and collaborate, leading to surprising and profoundly creative change.

5

The Patient Leads

While ultimately the therapist is responsible for the repair of the therapy bond, often the patient orchestrates the repair, informing the therapist verbally or nonverbally that there is a disjunction, moving him back toward a therapeutically productive stance. The patient's part in this process is frequently carried out using subtle confrontations and role enactments to alert the therapist about the disjunction. Once the therapist is able to comprehend his failing, he again assumes responsibility for the therapy's progress, redressing any damage his lapse may have caused. The experience of having the patient lead in reworking a therapeutic disjunction, if it succeeds, draws patient and therapist closer. They experience each other in new ways, as people, with the patient first, and then the therapist, making heartfelt efforts to reach and influence the other.

Making sense of the often wrenching emotions that can be generated in therapy may be like reading a map in the middle of an arctic storm. Sometimes the therapist cannot see through the frenzied atmosphere to be sure that his therapy partner is there, or even that he or she is listening. It seems unfair to put this kind of burden on the least well-trained member of the unit, but often there is no real choice because for the moment the other is so blinded.

Although the emphasis in the last chapter was on the therapist's initiative, Marty started our scenario by confronting me with what I did not see, and he kept it up until piercing rays of light reached my brain. In this chapter, we will look more closely at the patient's role in rescuing the therapy as he or she identifies a disjunction and triggers its repair.

According to therapeutic lore, patients are not supposed to take major responsibility for fixing the therapy. After all, the therapist is the sought after authority and is paid to diagnose the patient's pathology and oversee his recovery. This traditional concept seems all very reasonable, but it brings us back to the problem, what does one do in the midst of a vicious storm, anyway? In a storm you may have your life on the line and you had better do what you can to save yourself, including evaluating your companion's skills. In therapy, as a patient, your very life may also feel in jeopardy. Submitting to the therapist's ideas, if they are misguided, could have serious consequences for your welfare and future.

Contemporary psychodynamically oriented theorists leave a lot of room for both partners' subjectivity and authority, but most still preserve some special wisdom for the therapist (e.g., Aron, 1996, pp. 98–100; Grossman, 1999; Hoffman, 1998, pp. 8–10; Mitchell, 1997, pp. 227–230; Seligman, 2003). The therapist's training, whether in classical or modern thinking, usually is invoked creating asymmetry in the therapy situation, according the therapist an edge on the truth.

While I take the position that the therapist ultimately assumes responsibility for the outcome of the therapy, insisting that therapists have a depth of wisdom not available to patients is a seductive setup for therapists. Therapists, even mildly blinded by their authority, may not have to face up to one of several possibilities at critical points: (1) the patient being more perceptive about himself, his own needs, or the requirements of the therapy than the therapist; (2) the patient's theoretical framework, whether stated or implicit, being more accurate than the therapist's; and (3) the therapist being temporarily disadvantaged by his own background, culture, emotional life, or personal circumstances.

The picture of the all-knowing therapist is inherently peculiar, since it is so illogical. How could my patient this morning, a seasoned and successful psychiatrist, not have been dissatisfied when I misdiagnosed as emotional the depression he developed after taking antihypertension medication. In fact, assuming that the role of his perspicacity should be minimized could only harm my credibility and wreak havoc with this patient's sense of agency and self-respect.

Disjunctions initiated by the therapist and patient are ubiquitous in psychotherapy, the breaches ranging from subtle misunderstandings to major disruptions. While Marty could see my waywardness through the complex terrain of our emotions, he insisted I reestablish my credibility before he could trust me to lead again. The patients I talk about in this chapter were more proactive. They did everything they could to make sure the therapy would survive, and did not trust the therapist to take over until they were sure his competence was restored.

Actually, responsibility for keeping the work going shifts back and forth in therapy, although the patient's part is usually more unofficial. Both patient and therapist use interpersonal strategies to reengage and restore rapport. While this activity may be unacknowledged therapeutically, it involves at least two significant interactive strategies, *role enactment* and *confrontation*, which communicate the subject's awareness of a disjunction and his distress.

Shifting Responsibility to the Patient—An Illustration

In the following example, the transfer of responsibility occurred quietly and was congenial. Of interest is that the shift was never discussed, probably in part because the move would have been controversial, not acceptable as standard psychoanalytic operating procedure. Yet for a period, the patient, myself in this case, was clearly in control and both patient and analyst welcomed that rearrangement. That it needed to remain implicit, not openly discussed, is fascinating since that stance is so ultimately limiting for the therapy. Patients need to know that the therapist can face personal and therapeutic matters squarely. Otherwise, the two conspire to protect the therapist, creating an emperor's new clothes type of atmosphere for the therapy. Also, open acknowledgment that a patient's good judgment has changed the course of the therapy can only enhance that individual's sense of competence and agency, bolstering his self-esteem. In fact, the most powerful outcome of the episode to be discussed may have been just that, an affirmation of my capability, accorded to me by a person for whom I had great respect.

Case Illustration—Dr. Mark

My training analysis ended over 15 years ago. One period especially stands out. Throughout our work, my analyst remained conventionally mysterious. He said nothing about himself and showed almost no emotion. When, close to the end of the analysis, I received a call early one morning from his wife to say he'd had a heart attack, the tone was similar. "Dr. Mark will contact you when he can see you again." That was all.

Six weeks later, he and I returned to the analysis. Dr. Mark motioned me to the couch. I stopped midway and hesitantly asked how he was. He looked sad. "Pretty well, I think." His eyes were imploring. I took a risk. "Was this your first heart attack? . . . Are you worried?" He paused long enough that his reassurance seemed hollow. In spite of myself, I looked directly at him. I said I was sorry, and that I had been concerned about him. I then went to the couch.

For months, I dutifully pretended not to notice his distraction, and even that he fell asleep on two occasions. However, privately I became entirely occupied with this new risk to our analytic work. The training analysis already had been interrupted, but far worse, my confidence in Dr. Mark's capacity to continue was shaken.

My solution was to take on both our roles, becoming patient and analyst. I produced most of the energy for the analysis during those ensuing months. I introduced and examined issues. I came up with the few significant insights. Previously, I counted on Dr. Mark to help me tie things together. Instead, I carried the analysis on my own, neither of us saying anything about his detachment.

During this period, there was a paradoxical harmony between us. I would enter the office and sense his emotional absence. Immediately, I reached for all the analytic tools I had accumulated over the 7 years of our work. Typically, I recounted an event or dream from the previous day and associated to it. Dr. Mark might make a comment, usually about guilt, and I would recognize it as timeworn. After acknowledging his statement, I would go further, perhaps returning to the dream or following an already started theme.

Dr. Mark appeared comfortable with our arrangement. So far as I could tell, he seemed relieved that I was doing both our jobs. Imperceptibly, several months later, his involvement returned. We never discussed his lapse.

There was complicity in our not talking. We acted out roles rather than examining them analytically. Judging from the outcome, however, this activity was successful. I was analytically productive during that period and felt stronger afterward.

Earlier in my training, it would have been blasphemous to imagine that I could take over for Dr. Mark. The idea that I could support us both seemed a dangerous corruption of the psychoanalytic process. Yet, in this instance it made perfect sense. The analysis was threatened, and one of us had to do something. We had made real strides together. Too much was invested in completing the analysis for me to sit by and be passive.

Theoretical Considerations

Outside of therapeutic exploration and interpretation, how do therapist and patient influence each other to further their therapeutic work? My particular interest is in the ways therapy partners reenlist one another in order to revive and sustain the therapy during and after a disruption, especially when the patient takes the lead in that process.

Traditional analysts like Dr. Mark keep their distance. Although Dr. Mark clearly cared about me, his "neutral" stance limited the likelihood of directly helpful interactions developing between us (Gerson, 1996; Renik, 1995; Shill, 2004; Stone, 1961).

Against his highly regulated background, I uncomfortably observed that if I did not compensate for Dr. Mark's distraction the training analysis would be crippled. Dr. Mark conveyed his distress to me nonverbally, his imploring glance seemed anguished. I also experienced an inexplicable conviction that he approved, and was even relieved, when I temporarily took over most of his analyzing functions. I am inferring that these experiences reflected a communication from him to me through a nonverbal, interpersonal process similar to, and likely including, projective identification (Gabbard, 1995; Goodman, 1995; Jacobs, 1991; Meyerson, 1994; Ogden, 1986; Tansey and Burke, 1989, pp. 9–37). In his compromised state, Dr. Mark understood my shift and implicitly arranged to have me take over the role of his healthy self. He could reclaim it when he recovered.

In the sequence with Dr. Mark there were, in addition to a mutually caring relationship, at least two other processes at work, both initiated by myself, the patient, to bring us beyond our impasse: my recognizing and indirectly confronting the problem we were having, and role enactment. In the first, confrontation, I made the judgment, in part consciously, that I needed to compensate for Dr. Mark's disability. In the second, role enactment, Dr. Mark responded by supporting an interaction in which I temporarily became the analyst. His silent invitation for me to do so fit well with my understanding of what our analysis required. I nonverbally accepted his invitation and took on the role of analyst for months, without analytic reflection on either of our parts about my having done so. In this chapter I am interested in working with the general topic of the patient's role in repairing a disrupted therapy bond and I will especially focus on the mechanisms of confrontation and role enactment, as used by the patient, for achieving this end.

My term *role enactment* refers to the repetition of internally prescribed roles played out between two people. These roles may be complementary and welcome or conflicting and disjunctive. The interaction is experienced as real, an event in the present. Where there is an active disjunction between the two therapy partners, the role enactment may be orchestrated by one member in order to distress and alert the other that the therapy bond is threatened. Alternatively, the role enactment may provide a missing therapeutic function for one or both members, as it did with Dr. Mark when I took over as analyst.

In role enactment, the roles can originate separately from within each participant and be acted between the two, each member of the couple finding characteristics in the other that makes him or her a fitting subject. Alternatively, both roles can begin within one partner, with an unwanted role transferred to the other person who tacitly accepts that part in the interaction. The transfer may be initiated by a nonverbal request about which the recipient feels friendly, as when Dr. Mark indicated he wanted me to take over as analyst, or through the mechanism of turning passive into active as when Marty insisted I feel as crazy with him as he did with me. The transfer may also involve projective identification, the process probably at work when Brittany forced me to experience her despair as vividly as she did. While, at times, projective identification is implicated in role enactment, I view it as a more one-sided operation than role enactment, involving an exported, usually repudiated, state of mind without requiring a complementary, relationship-based response from the subject. Role enactment is also different from Sandler's (1976) "role responsiveness," because it denotes an interactional scenario between two people that has the specific objective of bringing them closer. Role responsiveness is a more general phenomenon and refers to the way people seek out and test each other's receptivity. It lacks the deliberate character and specific goals of role enactment.

It seems to me that patients regularly initiate the restoration of disrupted or threatened therapeutic work. Patients usually want therapy to succeed regardless of any unconscious, competing need to defeat it. They subtly inform the therapist when he is off. They help him see what he has missed or misinterpreted. They stay with and direct him as he finds his way. This influence by the patient may happen quietly or noisily (Bader, 1996; Blechner, 1995; Casement, 1985; Langs, 1978a, 1978b; Searles, 1975). Often, it is masked by a tacitly agreed upon view that the therapist is the expert, even when the therapist appreciates the intersubjective nature of therapy (Hoffman, 1992). In my opinion, in viable therapies there are always reciprocal restorations of disrupted therapeutic rapport initiated by therapy partners, each attending carefully to the other's needs and communications. At points, the patient becomes a trusted, sometimes brutal guide. He may see most clearly what the therapy needs and where the therapist has failed. In the end, the contributions of both partners, working together, weave an ever stronger interpersonal and therapeutic fabric.

The Patient Actively Seizes Control of the Therapy—An Illustration

To study the role of the therapist and patient, separately and jointly, in restoring disrupted therapeutic rapport, I have again, as in chapter 4, reviewed case material from the clinical project I described in the Introduction. The following case example, drawn from that project, demonstrates how a patient took an active role in reengaging me after I became defensively removed.

While each of us was affecting and responding to the other through a variety of psychological invitations, most often we were unaware of these occurrences, with only the patient, Alison, initially understanding my defection.

Alison

In *Intricate Engagements* (Frankel, 1995), I discussed Alison, a 45-year-old mother of two boys, who as the focus of the final chapter provided lessons about the therapist benefiting from the patient's wisdom. Alison required that we conduct therapy in her way, from a place in the office outside my view. This maneuver was designed to make it easier for her to feel and show her "real self," her more usual way of being with people associated with her less authentic, "false self."

Alison's mother and father were alcoholics, often unable to care for their two children financially or emotionally. During her first 5 or 6 years of life, Alison's drunken grandfather molested her at night when he visited the family for a few months each year, insisting she hide these acts from her parents, his threats insuring she would forget about the molestations as she got older.[1] Alison married a man who in spite of his success as an architect, like her father was emotionally vacant. Both her father and husband allegedly had an insatiable appetite for admiration, Alison's role being to provide that for them.

As a child, Alison desperately wanted her father's attention. Hoping he would be proud of her, she achieved well at school making sure never to get into trouble. During that time, she spent

---

[1] When *Intricate Engagements* (1995) was written, the person Alison at first implicated in the molestations was her father. Further therapy work revealed that the father may have been occasionally involved in some inebriated sexualized play where he treated the child, Alison, like a wife, fondling and inappropriately confiding in her. Later memories and the testimony of an aunt revealed that most or all of the molestations were carried out by her paternal grandfather.

endless hours practicing gymnastic routines, waiting with futility for her father to notice. Between ages 11 and 13, Alison's gymnastics coach filled in for the disappointing father, dedicating himself to the idea that she might eventually qualify for the Olympics. She remembers that part of her life as uniquely harmonious, she and the coach working tirelessly to develop her skills as a world class gymnast. Sadly, that relationship was abruptly terminated at age 14 when Alison's family moved; from that point her disengaged parents neglected her further training.

At age 20, Alison began the first of the three psychotherapies that preceded ours. The initial therapy was arranged through her college counseling service. Ironically, each therapy was brought to an end when Alison had to move, at first to attend graduate school and then twice after she married. In therapy, she wanted to find a guide, someone to help her progress beyond her emotionally devoid past and its legacy, the inauthentic politeness and detachment she experienced when with others. While she felt she had been helped in her therapies, she was disappointed each time by the therapist's "emotional aloofness," an attitude she believes perpetuated what she referred to as her "false self."

The following sequence occurred during the third year of our twice weekly therapy. Alison's life had changed dramatically. At the start of therapy, she struggled to attain social legitimacy through serving others, in that case as a wife and mother. Everyone depended on her. Now she had a doctorate in educational psychology and a diploma from a training program in psychodynamic psychotherapy and had become selective about personal obligations. She credited our therapy with these changes.

Alignment

Alison's initial commitment to our therapy was unwavering, her husband objecting to its importance in her life. In general, she strived to impress me, hoping, I thought, for an experience reminiscent of the one with her gymnastics coach early in her adolescence. At the point of the described sessions, 3 years into treatment, Alison's longings entered the picture. She was disturbed by this development, but faithful to her therapy commitment, reported them all. Now, she thought about me frequently, during the day and had idyllic dreams about the two of us together, walking, talking, at the beach, and sometimes in each other's arms.

Alison talked about the absence of romance in her marriage. She assumed her fantasies about us were a measure of her interest in having a loving relationship in her life, but she had little current desire for one with her husband, appalled by the relentlessness of his demands for attention, as well as his self-involvement and lack of consideration for her needs. She wanted to be more responsive to him, but said she couldn't force herself.

Here I need to make a distinction between Alison's experience of her longing and my interpretation of it. For Alison there was little or no sexual or even romantic content in her desire for closeness with me. Alison's fantasies about me were of caring, being adored, being thought about, as well as reciprocating those feelings. The balance of her interest was in the direction of being cared for, casting me in a fatherlike role. But, it was hard for me to entirely focus on the innocence of her wishes. Alison was a fully grown woman, attractive, feminine, and inclined to use her beauty and feminine wiles to interest men, unselfconscious habits that were repeatedly reinforced culturally. To me, her overtures, her longing, seemed to have a romantic and, at times, sexualized edge. I was careful about these attributions, but they were difficult for me to avoid.

Dissonance

I remember feeling overwhelmed by the swiftness of this new development, Alison suffused with her longing to be closer to me. I found myself wondering what men had done in the past when Alison behaved similarly with them. I had no doubt that they would easily have been hooked, infatuated by her unique combination of beauty and thoughtfulness. The onslaught felt heavy to me, and I speculated to myself that we might be experiencing a reenactment of some aspect of her childhood molestation experiences, in this case, with her husband identified as perpetrator and me as rescuer. I prepared myself to examine this development with her, careful about the impact and timing of my statements because I knew how easily Alison could feel blamed, child sexual abuse victims regularly being made to feel responsible for their own victimization.

Therapeutically, I had to manage two pulls: the first one was for me to tolerate and experience both sets of feelings, Alison's and mine, powerfully enough to fully understand them; the other was to work with Alison to examine these feelings. I did everything I could to keep the momentum of the therapy going. I questioned Alison about her ostensibly romantic thoughts. She talked with animation about her wish for not just a love relationship but an unconditional love relationship and could see that she was imagining me in that role. But peculiarly, and most interesting from a therapeutic perspective, I found myself becoming distracted and defensively disaffected, distancing from her during those therapy hours, a development I hardly noticed at first. In retrospect, I could see how I was misinterpreting as romantic and possibly sexual, Alison's attraction to me as a loving, parentlike figure. At that point, however, the experience was a jumble for me, one that I needed to distance myself from in order to make sense of and use therapeutically.

My withdrawal was painful and confusing for Alison. As she later told me, it amounted to the abandonment she had anticipated if she opened up to me. She had tested me assiduously, concluded she could let down her guard, and now was beginning to feel deserted by me.

In reviewing my notes I could see that Alison's first response to my withdrawal was to do everything she could to rekindle my involvement. She labored at this. She came to sessions with dreams and memories, brought letters and photographs from her childhood. When my distancing did not relent after several weeks, she also began to pull away. However, even as she detached, she continued to warn me that our rapport was failing, hoping I would act to stop the erosion. Ultimately, when I failed to come through, she struck back, vindictively withdrawing.

As I understand it now, my shift from therapeutic awareness to vacuousness was probably orchestrated to some extent by Alison who, in overwhelming me with her childlike infatuation, succeeded in transferring her own trauma-based loss of self to me, making me feel vacuous and confused. Consciously, she intended to embrace me to care for her, draw me closer. The effect of her intensity, however, was the opposite. I felt invaded, unable to integrate the intensity of the onslaught, needing emotional distance to make therapeutic sense out of my experience. The parallel in Alison's childhood was her own confusion when appeals to her father for love were repulsed and misused, resulting in bewilderment and even danger when he was drunk.

In effect, Alison put me to a rigorous test by flooding me with her delight in our relationship. While I intended to explore this development, it also overwhelmed me, I was concerned that I had become too important to her, leading to a blurring of boundaries. From what Alison told me later, she hoped I would not be undone by her needs, as she had been as a child, when, to her dismay, they were met with harshness and molestation rather than kindness.

But to some extent I was flooded, Alison's making me feel the power of her desire for intimacy having a communicative purpose. It imparted to me the intensity of her excited fantasies about our hoped-for union, as well as her conflicting fears of being betrayed and used sexually. I failed the test by becoming disoriented. In the end, my withdrawal, following our stunning success in therapy, seemed as disheartening and hurtful to Alison as her father's detachment after she won medals in gymnastics. Finally, she retaliated against me in a way she could not have done with him at that time.

Still, alongside this reenactment of the enticement–disappointment sequence she experienced with her father, Alison quietly maintained another goal. Even when she finally began to get back at me for my withdrawal, there was always a part of her, rooted solidly in the present, that pushed us toward rapprochement. Her attacks were intended to signal me that something was terribly wrong. She hoped I would join her in repairing our teetering therapy bond.

The sequence of events leading to Alison's ultimate withdrawal was as follows. At first, Alison doubled her commitment to our work. For weeks, she wrote endless notes for me documenting her introspective efforts. Toward the end of this time, she became a presence at postgraduate courses at our psychoanalytic institute. Over the next few months, as she grew disenchanted with me, she used these interests, originally intended to join us, to turn the tables on me by choosing one of the teachers whose ideas conflicted with mine, attending a few of his lectures and extolling the virtues of his thinking in our sessions.

Alison was using several tactics to reenliven our therapy. First, through a role enactment she did what she could to please me, taking on the part of an ideal patient, keeping track of each potentially interesting thought and dream. Then, she inundated me with her invitation to have a special experience with me that would reverse the failed parenting of her childhood. Her intention was to reengage me, but she bewildered me instead. Then, she tried to stir me confrontively through punishment and devaluation. Contrary to her intended effect, I remained a bit remote.

Over the next several sessions, Alison unequivocally withdrew. She discussed an upcoming visit with her brother-in-law, who she claimed took every opportunity to devalue her. She signed up for more analytic lectures. Of immediate relevance, Alison's disaffection with her husband intensified, due she claimed, to his decision to switch architectural firms, possibly requiring a move to a distant city. Alison mentioned critically that her husband had fallen asleep at a party they attended. Her metamessage in that statement and her complaints about her brother-in-law were to warn me about her growing intolerance for my obtuseness.

Then, in a following session, she revealed she had been propositioned by one of her husband's colleagues, saying it excited her. She seemed cold and a bit demonic as she talked, not her usual way of speaking. I recognized that tone of voice from other times when she had been angry at me, and it put me on emotional alert.

Talk of a liason with her husband's colleague grew over the next several weeks, with Alison unable to think about much else. The therapy, and implicitly my relevance in her life, were being cast aside. Noting the intensity of my reaction to her announcement, I did what I could to explore the situation with her. But I was less than straightforward when she asked how I would feel if she had the affair. Rather than responding more vigorously, I asked her to tell me how she might feel, a response she experienced as disinterested and anemic.

Alison was forcefully retaliating for my withdrawal. She was also protecting herself from further humiliation. However, her threat to have an affair had another critical purpose. Most broadly, it was a confrontation and was intended to alarm me, to jolt me. She hoped that, in response, I would stop the therapy from eroding further. And it worked, but not at first.

In effect, Alison's father was alive again, re-created in her idealizations of me and then her plunge into dejection when she felt I failed her. Now he was creating havoc in reverse through Alison's threat to do to me what she felt I, and earlier in her life, her father had done to her. His drinking left Alison and his other children, along with their mother, stranded and tormented. She had wanted to get back at him. Now she was doing that to me in punishment for my withdrawal following her alleged enticements. I had not seen Alison's rage coming. As yet, I did not fully understand it. Certainly, I was not aware of causing it.

What I failed to understand was my actual devaluation of Alison, my misinterpreting her seemingly seductive behavior and withdrawing from her. Alison was accurate when she accused me of abandoning her like her father. She now, as we belatedly took on that subject, began to recall her father's coldness when she lost—or even won—gymnastic competitions. Her current threat to have an affair, and by design leave me feeling anxious and deserted, accurately reversed that experience, this time placing her in the instigating, indifferent role.

I had inadvertently repeated Alison's traumatic experience with her father by encouraging her attachment to me and then failing to follow through consistently. When Alison behaved in a way that in an adult world could be misconstrued as a sexual invitation, it was presumably part of the recapitulation. At first, my abandonment made her want to be close to me again, repair the breach in our connection. Unfortunately, as had happened often in her adult life, I misunderstood her appeal for reconnection as seductive. I was repeating the behavior of other men who read romantic designs or sexuality into her behavior when neither were intended. However, whatever the meaning of her reaction and my response, the experience had meaning in her current life: I actually had marginalized Alison by misjudging her motives and intentions and then becoming distant and distracted.

At the beginning of the next session Alison was again disengaged, claiming she could find nothing to say. After waiting for 10 or so minutes, I found myself feeling bored. In an attempt to lead us out of our stalemate, I asked her how she was feeling. Alison became elusive. I pushed. Was she having feelings about me—perhaps concerning my noncommittal reaction to her possible affair? She immediately agreed, ''You let me down. I needed a stronger response from you, a clear stand against the idea.'' She went on to explain that my response made her wonder whether I cared if her marriage survived; I seemed almost willing to let her do something she would regret.

Looking back, I am impressed by how long it took me to grasp Alison's disappointment in me; it was only Alison who recognized its place in our fading rapport. She had attempted to confront me with it earlier, but I was not able to hear her, my own apprehension causing me to believe that my withdrawal had been reasonable.

The following several sessions were dedicated to my coming to terms with our rift. Alison confirmed that my distancing had been painful. She recalled her father's pleasure in humiliating her at just the moments when she was trying to please him most. He would revile her nightly when her homework was not perfect. He made cruel remarks about mistakes in her gymnastic routines. She remembered losing respect for him when she brought friends home to meet her parents and he arrived inebriated. Disappointed by me, Alison had the thought that it might be better for her to take a break from therapy, even switch to a therapist who would be more emotionally reliable than I was, and perhaps a woman.

Alison held her ground for several sessions, remaining angry and detached. I felt immobilized, my desire to understand and overcome our disjunction stalled. I struggled to both comprehend and assuage her anger. I concentrated on each of her words. I said I was beginning to see she was right, I had withdrawn. I wanted to understand, and hoped to undo any damage to our work I may have caused. I also offered tentative thoughts about how aspects of the abuse by her grandfather and father, as well as abandonment by her parents, had been re-created in our relationship, with my incorrect evaluation of her intentions and my withdrawal repeating that experience with her. My taking responsibility for my role, I hoped, would indicate to her that unlike her detached and blaming father, I was willing to take charge of restoring our connection.

Still, there was little movement for several more sessions. I found myself thinking back to Alison's earlier unconditional commitment to the therapy. Those sessions seemed so distant. As we reached the end of one current therapy session in particular, I mentioned that she had not again brought up the subject of her proposed affair. To my astonishment, she replied that she was now feeling more drawn to her husband. She realized that her becoming enthralled with our relationship, followed by my misinterpretation of her intentions and then my withdrawal, repeated a cycle she had experienced with other men. She now wondered whether she behaved in ways that could be construed as seductive by them, and by extension, by me. Almost always, however, she had no desire to consummate these flirtations. She actually hoped for the opposite.

Alison's father's promiscuity and drinking and her grandfather's molestations were the sources of her greatest pain as a child, and her mother's inability to help her only made matters worse. What she wanted from me was integrity. I needed to be concerned, care about, even treasure her, and be free from sexual designs. Where I failed was that I misconstrued her wishes. I experienced her excitement about our therapy relationship as reflecting her desire to draw me into a romantic liaison. Laboring to comprehend and contain this development, I had become temporarily removed from the job of usefully understanding them. My withdrawal was an impediment to the progress of our work. Still, however, it was part of a therapeutically valuable recapitulation of Alison's experience as a child with her father, as well as a way of showing me what the experience of excitement, desperately wishing for a nonsexual caring relationship, followed by disappointment, was like for her.

Alison's revelation was pivotal in revising my understanding of the events in our therapy. I came to view her apparent enticements as partly designed to create a repetition of her traumatizing experiences with her father and grandfather, this time with the objective of understanding them, not repeating them. Intense involvement had come out quickly in most of her promising relationships with men. There, too, she was apparently seeking an antidote to her failed relationship with her father, wanting devotion, not sex. However, it was my misreading these messages, as they had, that was the problem. Alison wanted me to join her to understand and gain control over these developments, not react as though she wanted to live them out with me. She felt misunderstood and hurt by my limited ability to see beyond her feminine allure, my failure to recognize her wish to reverse the distorted understanding of her needs by men earlier in her life, including her grandfather and father.

Alison began the following session on an entirely different note, talking about Camron, a designer friend of her husband's. She and her husband had been to a seminar with him. His wife was away and it was clear that he was interested in seducing the woman with whom he was seated. He also talked about his wife disparagingly. She wanted my opinion about his behavior; did I think it was as repugnant as she did?

Uncharacteristically, I simply said, "yes." I wondered whether her reaction to him reminded her of the feelings associated with her father's and grandfather's promiscuity.

Only when I reviewed my notes, did I realize why I responded so directly to her question. I was saying in so many words that I finally heard her. Of course, I did not have romantic intentions. I had found her intensity stimulating, joined with her learned seductive behavior (ironically, intended to draw me in as a caring, substitute father), but acting on them was quite another matter. I was there to help, work with her as a therapeutic partner.

She went on to say that what had particularly disturbed her was the impression that I hardly objected to her behaving in a way that would jeopardize her marriage. She wanted me to be the opposite of her father and grandfather, who were sexually crass. Becoming teary, she described how disappointed she had been with my response to the subject of the affair. I said I was beginning to understand.

In the next session, Alison said she was feeling differently about her marriage. In contrast to her earlier description of her husband, she emphasized his stability and loyalty. She was interested in understanding better how her early traumatic experience with her father and grandfather could find its way with such force into her present-day relationships, including those with her husband and me. She also wanted to talk more about her perceived seductiveness, amazed that her invitations were so subtle and effective that, at first, she failed to recognize them, and, as with other men, my misconception had advanced so far.

Discussion

How to understand this therapy sequence? After becoming disconcerted by what I misread as Alison's romantic interest in our relationship, I defensively withdrew from her. She became aware of the gap between her expectation that I would assist her to contain and understand her reactions and my disengagement. After attempting to cautiously reenlist me, she arranged a confrontation, expressing her rage following my withdrawal. During this time our rapport continued to deteriorate. Alison persisted in her assaultive and contemptuous attempts to reengage me, this time making me feel invalidated. When I finally recognized the nature of our disjunction and my part in creating it, she transferred the responsibility for restoring the therapy back to me.

Alison's reparative efforts were of two kinds. The first was direct and confrontational, as she worked planfully to reinvolve me. For example, she made a point of telling me about her excitement about the psychoanalytic lectures she was attending, even mentioning the possibility of seeking psychoanalytic training. She talked about it with some pressure, insisting I listen. Later, to jolt me, she withdrew harshly, repeating with me what she felt I had done to her. Second, she orchestrated role enactments, interpersonal scenarios designed to induce my reinvolvement. For example, in the beginning of this sequence of hours she became imbued with our relationship, forcing me to notice her, inadvertently conveying the sense that she might want to be romantic. Then, when I withdrew further, she confused me, teasingly switching loyalties to my analytic colleague, in effect repudiating me. Finally, she disqualified me entirely, making me feel useless as a therapist, threatening to have an affair that would put her marriage at risk.

Alison and I were mostly unaware of these role enactments as they were occurring. Most were neither understood nor discussed, recapitulating the power and mindlessness of her original traumatizing situation. There, her father and grandfather senselessly victimized Alison while she was forced into a state of dissociated oblivion in order to contain her pain and bewilder-ment. Later, by reflecting on my own distress within these as-cribed roles, I was able to comprehend Alison's disappointment and rage when I failed to understand her desire to be cared for by me, misinterpreted it, and abandoned her instead.

Apart from repeating Alison's original trauma in our ther-apy, each of the described experiences also drew me into her life in a real way. They brought us closer through powerful, shared interpersonal experiences. While they took part of their shape from the past, they were always felt as events in the pres-ent. For example, after I failed to take a clear stand about her threat to have an affair, I had the acutely painful experience of Alison's disapproval, feeling personally chastised by her. I real-ized that I had made a mistake, disappointed Alison in reality. It was up to me to heal the breach I had caused, as well as take the lead in examining it therapeutically.

Alison's warnings succeeded. As I understood her message, I could be more active in restoring the direction of our therapy. I apologized for not being more vigorous in my objection to her having an affair. I acknowledged the value of her assessment of the molestation and disappointment themes. My tone became gentle when I asked how her discomfort with her husband's colleague's flirtation reflected feelings about my defection, and complimented her on her ability to think through her role in having enticed him. We could then discuss her feelings toward me, and her wish for my help in comprehending and managing them.

Understanding this therapy segment with Alison makes my experience with Dr. Mark more comprehensible. In the work with Dr. Mark, I, as the patient, had a major part to play in restoring a troubled therapy. The difference from the segment with Alison was that the resolution of my disjunction with Dr. Mark was instigated by both of us: I was aware that Dr. Mark's heart attack based distraction reflected a personal emergency as well a threat to my training analysis, and I reacted by compensat-ing with extra energy and initiative. At the same time, Dr. Mark seemed to provide a subtle invitation to relieve him of responsibility, communicated through his imploring glance, for example. I responded by becoming both therapist and patient, giving him the rest he needed. We participated in an unacknowledged role reversal. He could be left to heal, while I temporarily took over many of his functions as analyst.

The illustrations I have used in this chapter emphasize the patient informing the therapist of his failings, in particular through confrontation, role enactments, or both, always with the goal of resolving a therapeutic disruption. Looking more closely, listed below are a number of additional steps from detachment to reinvolvement. Also, individual sequences may differ, with one or more of the steps missing; for instance, in my interaction with Dr. Mark, there was no period of confrontation or overt collaboration.

1. The therapist or patient seizes the other's attention directly through interpersonal confrontation and more subtly by arranging role enactments.

2. The therapist becomes disoriented as he realizes he does not understand the events at that point in the therapy.

3. Therapist and patient struggle to comprehend their experience. Much of the exchange is nonverbal. Both participate collaboratively, through transferring the authority to know and lead in the therapy, as well as through reciprocal knowing. As part of this process, as the therapist exists within the role enactment, playing his part in it, he also works to move outside the enactment, attempting to make sense of the confusion he experiences while participating in it.

4. The therapist learns enough about his place in creating the disruption to make his subsequent behavior more constructive. He endeavors to differentiate himself from people who, in the past, had been injurious to the patient.

These last two steps are familiar components of therapeutic intervention (Renik, 1995; Weiss, 1993). On the other hand, interpersonal pressure and role enactments are usually considered sources of distortion in therapy, linked with enactment and projective identification. Missing from this view is that these devices may be used constructively by therapist or patient to reengage each other when they are caught in a therapeutic disjunction.

As we have seen, the patient may be the one to initiate the reengagement. Alison impacted me in ways that made me feel her distress and face up to how I was letting her down, even victimizing her. Then, for the most part it was up to me to put the therapy puzzle together. In an even stranger circumstance, as happened in Tom's and Russell's experience where Tom set the standards overriding Russell's rigidities, the patient does the analyzing and informs the therapist in no uncertain terms about aspects of the therapist's psychology with which he, himself, is unacquainted. I suspect patients are more often able to provide this kind of information than is usually recognized. It can be unnerving for a patient to say you are misguided, mean, or seductive, and be correct. Also, patients tend to be afraid of that kind of stepping forward; they are potentially worried they will offend the therapist or even destroy him, or the therapy.

One more note about dealing with distressing role enactments orchestrated to restore therapeutic rapport, such as those initiated by Alison in response to my withdrawal. It is therapeutically imperative that the therapist be drawn *temporarily* into these enactments. Unless the therapist allows for this level of affective involvement, his appreciation of the patient's experience will lack precision and true empathy. Also, the patient will not feel fully understood, the unresolved disjunction persisting or deepening. The patient has to be sure she has delivered her message—assured she will not be retraumatized by the therapist's too limited comprehension of her needs or experiences—then, collaboration and resolution can proceed.

The Interpersonal Dimension

Psychotherapy is dialectical. What the therapist does for the patient, the patient returns, through his enlivened initiative. The reverse is true when the patient does the initiating. In this intricate trekking expedition where therapist and patient alternately or simultaneously take responsibility for restoring the integrity of the therapy, understanding is only part of the process. The tension caused by rifts in the therapy needs to be tolerated and contained, primarily by the therapist, until he and the patient understand the meaning and work through the consequences of the disjunction. In our sequence, Alison incrementally increased the seriousness of her threat, until I finally heard her. Then I regulated the tone and content of my comments to let her know I understood her and cared. Only when she could trust me again, could we explore the disruption in our work and the opportunity it offered for our shared progress.

According to this view of the therapy process, the patient's contribution to reviving and sustaining the therapy is often as important as the therapist's. In my opinion, the patient's role generally has been underappreciated. This observation appears true even with the current groundswell of psychodynamic literature on symmetry and self-disclosure (Aron, 1992; Gerson, 1996; Beebe, Jaffe, and Lachmann, 1992; Goodman, 1995; Hoffman, 1992; Seligman, 2003).

One outcome of these linked movements between therapist and patient is that each has a profound personal effect upon the other. In part through living out difficult and exacting roles such as parent and child, friend and enemy, imagined lovers, both always work to recognize, comprehend, and resolve their differences. In addition to improving their understanding of the patient, therapist and patient grow more deeply connected as human beings.

In my view, emotionally demanding therapeutic involvements such as these are integral to progress in dynamic psychotherapy and provide the foundations for conjunctions, the peak moments of therapeutic joining. As happened in my work with Alison, the therapist who allows himself to feel the pain the patient inflicts, and then struggles to find out why the patient must do this, will gain a particularly intimate understanding of the patient, as well as of his own failings. He is also likely to discover the personal legitimacy of the patient's experience and communication. He gets to know the human aspect of the patient's struggle, not just his psychopathology. Through a parallel process, the patient discovers a therapist who is different, more complex and fallible, than the one he began with. Therapist and patient together grow in their involvement with one another. Each is deeply influenced and creatively transformed by the other.

The therapy process is a true partnership, rife with challenges when it works well. The requirements of a climbing expedition seem almost tame compared to the sheer fury when patient and therapist lurch into the blinding storm they discover or create together. Finding reliable places into which to sink an emotional ax and become tethered is tricky; earth movements occur unannounced, threatening to wipe away these strongholds. After such an expedition, ending in therapeutic conjunction, the therapy partners invariably launch into a new world of more imposing and exhilarating challenges.

Following the heart attack induced episode with Dr. Mark, I was more confident about my ability to work on my own. It wasn't just the experience I gained by taking over the analytic work while Dr. Mark was convalescing that impacted me, but as much, the confidence and appreciation Dr. Mark showed as I successfully did my part. Alison says that my confirming I mistook her wish to be cared for as seduction, and then going on to understand how that occurred, was a critical therapy experience that helped to establish her sense of competence. Now several years later, she takes more breaks from therapy, enjoying her developing ability to manage on her own. She also trusts I will still be there when she returns. As important as the formal therapy work in these cases, was the sense of agency the patients developed as I heard and respected them for the initiative they took in shaping the therapy. While the therapist is ultimately responsible for the success of the therapy, the patient needs to know he is a full, valued partner if he is to reap its complete benefit.

We have come a long way toward understanding how therapy works. But there still are holes. How did Alison and I actually manage all the details of our interaction so they worked to our benefit? What made Dr. Mark know in the moment of clarity when we decided to transfer his role to me, that I could and should take the lead in our training analysis? Some of what guided these interactions leading to consensus was articulated, much was never verbalized. These factors, embedded in the therapy matrix, and drawing heavily from the nonverbal substrate of psychotherapy, will be the subject of our next chapter.

6

Working Consensus:
How Patient and Therapist
Decide What to Do

In a way, this subject, how decisions are made in psychother-apy, is the toughest with which we will grapple. After all, how do you talk about what, for the most part, you can't hear or see when it is happening? Brittany would say that she is always going for the feel of things, and I know it's the same for me. I go into the consulting room and everything changes. My eyes widen and I go into a staring mode. I hunch forward feeling for the electromagneticlike field Brittany emits, which is differ-ent each day; I monitor how near or far she is, whether she withdraws or relaxes, and follow her as she changes. I talk about her next door neighbor, whether she is interested in a relationship with him, as if those words carry the power between us. Brittany listens for the tension, worry, or softness in my voice and imme-diately registers how present or preoccupied I might be, what could be interfering with or enhancing our potential rapport.

How did I know when to become an advocate for Brittany changing jobs, or to begin to take seriously Marty's arguments that I was illogical about bringing up his lowered fee, or to hear Alison's complaint that my withdrawing from her seemed mean spirited? In each of these cases, I eventually made an internal shift that allowed me to more clearly hear the patient's point of view. The change within me was profound, moving from skepticism to belief, from conditional involvement to passionate commitment. However, on the face of it, in each situation the timing and reasons for the shift seem mysterious: a mystery that only the most microscopic details of the interpersonal therapy transactions can solve. Was I simply worn out and frightened of Brittany's potential for suicide, and forced then to shift to her side? Or did I finally notice how much she was willing to endure in order to solicit my support for her changing jobs? Why did I finally listen to her? Did the words and tone of her irritation with me for not believing that her request was urgent, trigger some old experiences of mine, where I underestimated another person's earnestness and left him or her hanging?

The shifts I am describing are not expectable, and certainly, at the time, were not explicable. In each case they went against my grain at that moment. I was convinced that progressing as a public relations executive in her prestigious company signaled psychological health, progress for Brittany. That was my prejudice. I was disaffected with Marty at the moment he challenged my fee raise, and had reservations about whether we should continue our work, given his criticism of virtually everything I did. With Alison, at first, I was oblivious to the impact of my withdrawal on her, or even that I had withdrawn.

Before further exploring this world of microscopic but strongly felt influences, we turn to Brittany with an example of how well and precisely the nonverbal dialogue between two people can work. Decisions to act in psychotherapy often require one or both partners to invoke an intuitive hunch that has been gestating, bringing the two into previously unmapped, often dangerous seeming, territory. Therapist and patient continually work to establish which topics to address, how forcefully, and in what order; the largely silent agreements they make constitute their *working consensus.* Arriving at points of consensus requires the pair to sample the influences in their therapy field and prioritize their actions according to what they want to change, tame, or accentuate. It seems remarkable, given the complexity and seriousness of the task and its ever changing nature, that much of this effort is carried out intuitively by each and through tacit agreements.

Deciding to Hold Brittany's Hand

The picture of my interaction with Brittany is actually quite complicated. Say I recognized that holding Brittany's hand might make all the difference for our progress in therapy. I am acutely aware of the clinical arguments for and against hugging a patient or holding his or her hand (Maroda, 1999, pp. 141–159, and especially pp. 144–145; Shane, Shane, and Gales, 1997, pp. 53–65; Toronto, 2001), and the ethical arguments concerning these decisions (Gabbard, 1994, 1995). Such considerations call up the critical commentary from a professional reader of a manuscript of mine, about the analyst's role in resolving analytic disjunctions, which I recently submitted to a conservative psychoanalytic journal. He or she alleged that I was too emotionally involved with the patient I used as illustration, and was running the risk of transgressing analytic boundaries. With this thought, my anxiety magnifies. But I am quite sure it is the right thing to do, and I decide to hold her hand. Also, I have confidence that if it is a mistake, the signals would be there: Brittany's body would stiffen, her voice die off—and I would make any necessary corrections.

You know the outcome of this event: Brittany relaxed and by the end of the session was feeling much more hopeful. Given my misgivings, how did we in our mostly nonverbal dialogue, come up with just the right answer and with accurate timing, to boot? My assessment is that Brittany sent a strong signal, letting me know that the only way I could reach her deeply enough would be through some safe form of physical contact.

Later, I also discovered that our rapport became momentarily diluted when I tried too soon to talk about my decision to hold her hand and her history of not being nurtured. Too intellectual for the moment, Steve, I just needed to feel you were there and, also, that the physical contact didn't scare you. If it had I might have concluded that my need to be comforted was repulsive to you, as it was for so many others in my life.

Brittany and I found our way through this sequence, battling our personal misgivings and concerns about propriety, following the complex path of our separate and shared intuitions. Before seeing how these influences work together let us break the decision-making process in psychotherapy into some of its component parts.

Constituents of the Decision-Making Process in Psychotherapy

Of the many global factors influencing how decisions are made in psychotherapy I have chosen six: those with a societal basis, those that tap the mind to discover emergent meaning, ways in which people implant their experiences into others, people's capacity to intuit what others mean and feel, the neurological basis for comprehending other people's experience, and inspiration. Awareness of these categories should be helpful in understanding and guiding decision making in psychotherapy.

Decisions Are Made in a Social Framework, Shared between People

Social, in this context, can refer to any interpersonal situation without necessarily assuming commonly held cultural meanings. Roy Schafer (1997) invokes a wide social perspective with his notion of shared narrative story lines. Schafer (1997) says, "objective simply refers to one's adhering in a reasonable way to social conventions." In this vain in *Tradition and Change in*

Psychoanalysis (1997), he identifies "interpretative efforts . . . [as] story lines that are manifestations of . . . master narratives" (p. 198). Pursuing a similar line of thinking, Jay Greenberg (1999) sees the therapist's authority getting its "support from a broad social network" (p. 29). The view that meanings are developed collaboratively and, at least in part, are culturally based seems accurate to me. Stephen Mitchell (1993) adds that "the accomplishments of social living and culture are testimony to the likelihood that we do seem to understand each other a large portion of the time" (p. 60).

Logically, one way therapist and patient can move beyond their own narrow experiences is to access its wider social connections. By convention, most 30-year-olds aspire to romantic relationships. Brittany, having lived in an austere, sexually devoid world for so many years had not developed these expectations for herself, though she privately longed for a romantic relationship. Perhaps if Brittany had been more able to sense and constructively use the normative expectations of society, her personal goals and current experience would have been more ambitious by the time she reached her current age. She might be poised to launch into romantic involvements.

Meaning Behind Decisions to Act in Therapy Is Emergent

Donnel Stern (1997, pp. 17–20) states, "Over and over again, in conducting an analysis, and in life in general, we have the compelling feeling that meaning is emergent and incomplete, the sense that experience melts and verges into words—and escapes them" (p. 16). Stern is interested in the process through which words become useful, able to represent experience, lose or gain their potential for creativity, and, by extension, their capacity to access and communicate more fundamental states of mind. Christopher Bollas's (1987) notion of the "unthought known" refers to aspects of self that are isolated from consciousness or discovered within others and begin to emerge into one's consciousness under propitious circumstances. He calls the catalyst for this process the "transformational object" (p. 13). In psychotherapy, this person may be the "good enough" (p. 36) therapist-mother who protects "against impingement that might lead him to replace being taken care of with precocious mental process[es] that . . . dissolve being by means of premature thought and vigilance" (p. 34).

This category of nonverbal influence has special relevance to the main topic of this book, conjunction. The experience of conjunction is marked by surprise and discovery. A sense of elation emerges from the pleasure two people experience when one is the container and facilitator of discovery for the other, and then, in the best of circumstances, when the other serves the same purpose for him. There may be similar excitement when emergent meaning is discovered in oneself by oneself, separate entities within the self-communicating process.

Decisions Are Made Through Meaning Transmitted Through Affective Manipulation

Edgar Levenson (1998) emphasizes the limits of what can be translated into words clinically; in his opinion, clinical work consists largely of "tapping into an unconscious flow that is not, in the ordinary sense, intellectual or even linguistic, but [instead] corporeal-bodily" (p. 242). People create feelings in others constantly, making them feel expectant, pleased, tense. These created states represent both linked and disavowed self and other representations, the stuff of transference–countertransference and projective identification. There may be an as-if quality to this experience as in transference, or an absolute quality, where the subject feels possessed, as in projective identification (Ogden, 1982). Attention to these induced thoughts and feelings can potentially increase one's empathic capabilities, and, recognizing others' experience through these transmitted states in psychotherapy, introduces the possibility of usefully transcending one's own subjective reality.

Meaning Is Communicated Affectively
Through Interpersonal Attunement

Attunement, the affective capability to intuit and respond to another accurately, is critical to movement in psychotherapy. Patient and therapist continually, almost without interruption, scan for the right wavelength for reaching each other: the words, tone of voice, cadence that produce emotional resonance. Brittany protested vigorously when I lost our attuned connection, and learned, as we worked together, to report these lapses to me as a prelude to exploring why I might be off on that particular day. In fact, it was this process that led me to decide to share information about my divorce and its impact on me with Brittany.

So much has been written about the intuitive ways that mothers and infants relate and the potential damage when that link is faulty (Beebe, Jaffe, and Lachmann, 1992, 1997; Beebe and Lachmann, 2002, 2003; Charles, 2002; Frankel, 1995, pp. 115–131; Kiersky and Beebe, 1994; Daniel Stern, 2004; Siegel, 1999). Ivri Kumin (1996), using the language of infant researchers, states that "the affect regulating functions provided to the pre-object infant by the mother eventually patterns the later development of affect signaling and affect regulating capacities" (p. 28). The process begins when the "infant's mother, who is attuned to her infant through what Bion calls a state of 'reverie,' senses the nature of her infant's discomfort and responds empathically" (p. 40). The infant reciprocates and is able to match himself to his mother "across sensory modalities" (p. 57). Meltzoff and Moore (1992, 1999) identify imitation and sharing of behavioral states as ways in which infants accurately mold to the environment the mother provides. Schore (1997) adds that the "presymbolic interactive representations [involved in the molding, communicating, and mutual regulating] appear at the end of the first year, and in them the infant represents the expectation of being matched by and being able to match the partner, as well as participating in the state of the other'' (p. 22).

Regarding the mechanism of affect matching and mutual regulation, Schore continues, "It is now very clear that this [ongoing] dialectic with the social environment is mediated by transmission of affect, and that this emotional communication is nonverbal'' (p. 3). Kumin's (1996) thinking is that ''The capacity for intermodal matching does not end in infancy with the development of symbolic mental representations but persists normally throughout life as characteristic of primary process thought. This enables humans to unconsciously transmit and receive affect states without speech'' (p. 60). Using this background, Kumin later describes a technique for how he intuits a patient's preobject based distress, calling the process ''intermodal exchange'' (p. 77). He adds that this preobject communication is generally perceived physically, not cognitively (p. 82).

Some psychodynamic theories incorporate these developmental ideas, usually obliquely. In self psychology empathy is key to the development of a healthy self and its repair when damaged. D. W. Winnicott (1965), whose work has an explicit developmental basis, speaks of the mother's need to be ''good-enough'' (p. 49), neither intrusive nor affectively removed, so the child can discover his or her ''true self'' (p. 140). Melanie Klein (1957/1975b) writes about the destructive wishes a child believes he or she must contain to retain the love of the other. Following Melanie Klein (see for example Ogden, 1982; Spillius, 1992), British writers with an object relations view describe how, beginning in infancy, people defensively stay connected to others in spite of the press to be different, independent, or to act destructively. To accomplish this end, they need to learn to read others well.

To be sure, there is a lot to get in the way of the kind of attuned resonance Kumin describes. Therapy, like life, is rife with affective misattunements. There are the perpetual cycles of disruption and repair (Benjamin, 1992; Frankel, 1995, pp. 89–113) to keep therapist and patient busy, as they continually labor to restore their conjunctive momentum. There is also a lot to go right, as they vigorously inform each other, mostly nonverbally, about the interpersonal resonance required for a conjunction to build.

Meaning Communicated Nonverbally Has a Biological Basis

The biology of communication is relevant for understanding therapeutic work, with people biologically preprogrammed for affiliative behavior (Bowlby, 1969). Theorists have outlined stages of normal attachment behavior for infants and children. Children progress from one stage to the next, ordinarily becoming more secure, gaining safe movement into adulthood with minimal risk of regression. Alicia Lieberman and Gere Pawl (1988) describe attachment as an "emotional relationship with a specific figure that is characterized by feeling safe and protected in the presence of that person and by feelings of longing and the desire to restore proximity and contact when that person is absent" (p. 328). Greenspan and Lieberman (1988) propose a developmental hierarchy of attachment. The first stages include the "achievement of homeostasis" and "the forming of a human attachment" through the development of intentionality. From there the child is progressively able to internalize part of the relationship, at first through imitation and ultimately through "forming mental representations and ideas, such as object permanence," which develops into "the basis of self representation and [becomes] consolidated as object constancy" (pp. 407–408). Clearly, the ease with which people communicate, their affiliative capability, is directly related to the security of their previous attachment experiences. It stands to reason that securely attached people are less likely to distort other people's motivations, and misunderstand their communications.

The neurobiology of how people, therapist and patient included, understand each other's nonverbal communications rests on the notion of pictorial, nonlinguistic communication in part occurring between the right hemisphere of one partner's brain and the right hemisphere of the other (Charles, 2002; Cozolino, 2002; Schore, 2003; Daniel Stern, 2004). There is a great deal of evidence for the validity of these explanations, and for the mutative value of the intuitive, affectively based connections therapists and patients can establish (Beebe & Lachmann, 2002; Siegel, 1999). This research suggests that through the kind of implicit communication described, therapist and patient may reactivate basic affective states, at times reviving the power of mother–child experiences and influencing each other accordingly. Put differently, structural transmutations involving the repair of "structural deficits" may require a "right hemisphere-to-hemisphere interface between therapist and patient [Miller, 1986] . . ." (Schore, 1994, p. 463).

Spirituality, Extrahuman Experiences

As I worked on this chapter, I suddenly became aware of a glaring omission. Left out was the spiritual, the mystical dimension of therapy work; the uncanny ways people seem to know about each other. I actually have thought a lot about this subject in part because my good friend Trevor, who is a well-respected psychiatrist, believes in psychic phenomena, and if you push him he will elaborate in the most scholarly fashion. Such belief systems hold that at least some people can know and influence other people's experience, even when separated by time and space. If one needs inspiration, the suggested direction is to appeal to one's "higher self" or "the universe," and we are told these methods hold the key to unlocking a person's deeper, more fundamental nature.

It would be easiest to simply dismiss this fervor as chicanery; just a bunch of unscientific people frightened by the idea of mortality. But there are so many of them: our often closeted colleagues, enchanted by the world of meaning beyond words.

Asked to reflect on the essence of therapy, my understanding is that these people would generally place inspiration in the center, without putting as much emphasis on the content of formulated communication as many of us would. And what if they know something that the more conventional of us will always miss, since we are so attached to the observable and the logic of Western life?

What if the intuitive factors that allow people to understand each other, and bear much of the responsibility for consensus, go by rules more mysterious than those that make people like myself comfortable? If we allowed for this expansion of consciousness, perhaps we could improve the speed and efficiency with which people come to understand each other, and make the currently unobservable forces more comprehensible in therapy. Perhaps meditation techniques, combined with expressive psychotherapy, would work better than therapy alone. What about consciousness broadening possibilities of Eastern disciplines such as Chi Kung, or techniques developed in the West like biofeedback and eye movement desensitization and reprocessing (EMDR)? Thousands of people have found these techniques useful, but until recently they have usually been discounted as superficial by conventional depth therapists. Until the recent, and now copious, work relating biologically based, affective communication to what happens in psychotherapy (Siegel, 1999), there was scant neurophysiological justification for claims that a meditative or spiritual approach could lead to or facilitate permanent psychotherapeutic change (Schore, 1996, 1997). With this emerging data there is little reason to dismiss my psychotherapist friends to whom spirituality is a key to understanding people and how to help them.

To what do we attribute the depth and mysterious accuracy of observations people sometimes make about each other? I have to admit that there was something uncanny about Brittany's observations concerning my "lack of presence" coming at just the right time, making even clearer to me the personal work I had to do about the effects my divorce had on my mood. As I mentioned earlier, Freud (1913/1955) and Jung (1927/1968), among others, developed extensive theories of a collective unconscious residing deeply within people and consistently communicated. So, in accord with our interest in decision making in psychotherapy, the topic of spirituality, ways in which people get to know about the deeper, more abiding forces influencing their lives, deserves close attention. I am sure that when a true conjunction occurs in therapy the experience transcends the expected and the known, reaching beyond ordinary life and not entirely explicable using our current theories of psychology.

Knowing that decision making in psychotherapy has social, emergent, affectively manipulated, attunement, biological, and even spiritual referents, doesn't solve the question of how a therapist can use awareness of these largely nonverbal areas to move a therapy toward conjunction. Understanding the place of these factors in therapeutic change creates an enhanced awareness and respect for the nondeliberate in therapy transactions. That awareness may encourage the clinician to regularly reposture himself in response to nonverbal cues. Perhaps Brittany's most profound impact on me was in this area. She taught me how to be patient and wait for meaning to emerge in our dialogue, she required me to struggle to find points of attunement between us, and she showed me what experiences of childhood hope, interrupted and distorted by bleak disappointment, felt like. So much of what Brittany and I did consisted of my reorienting myself so that I could be a more attuned participant in the revision of her troubled early experience with attachment figures.

Maintaining Consensus: A Case Illustration, Natalie

When we begin to catalog the forces that steer a therapy and produce conviction on the part of each partner, it becomes clear how much of what is understood is neither explicit nor verbal. The ways in which I came to believe in and understand Brittany, Marty, and Alison provide a framework of parallels as we embark on my experience with Natalie. Believing was the single most important theme in my work with Natalie, and my difficulty in fully trusting her story of childhood molestation both dogged and provided the depth for our ultimate joining. We easily formed the words articulating our therapy goals, and we seemed to agree about how we would achieve these. I was to help her understand and resolve the psychological basis of her depressions and eczema. Our techniques would involve accepted methods of therapeutic exploration, and especially those dealing with trauma. Natalie was sophisticated about psychological matters, and the issues and road to resolution seemed plain enough. Natalie believed in the centrality of the intersubjective and interpersonal in therapy, and was comfortable with the idea that the interpersonal aspect of therapy was not simply a matter of working through transference–countertransference distortions but that the quality and depth of the therapy relationship counted, as much. I don't think any of the other patients I've mentioned approached dynamic therapy with such a clearly articulated notion of how it would work.

The second child in a sibship of three, and now 52 years old, Natalie had endured depressions almost daily and severe, disfiguring eczema attacks from late adolescence. She felt fated to suffer alone, believing that if people really knew her they would run. Her parents belonged to an ultrareligious organization, whose rituals included disciplining children through physical beatings. Despite this background, she did well for herself, becoming a hospital administrator, one of the more respected members of her local medical community, and mother of three successful girls.

Soon after we started our work, Natalie confided that she had a tormenting suspicion she had been repeatedly molested as a child, no memories, just a nagging hunch at first about her father and then one of her uncles when she was 10. All I could do was listen, take more history, and wrestle with my nagging skepticism. At that time, the height of the false memory furor, patients' recollections of childhood molestations were being contested in the media and in court, putting most therapists on alert, making us more vigilant about substantiating our patients' stories.

But Natalie started to produce data: episodes where she had difficulty breathing; the sense of something heavy pressing on her chest at night, and unexplained bouts of nausea. As we worked, these sensations became more coherent, nausea and breathing difficulties becoming nightmarish impressions that something large was being crammed down her throat, the heaviness on her chest now feeling like a large male body. Her dreaming increased and became more vivid, sometimes memorylike. Most of the dreams had sexual content; in several she and her daughters were raped. Her productions were convincing enough, but created problems for both of us.

If we seized on the sensations and dreams as evidence that she was molested, if Natalie believed her evolving story, she felt clear that she would have to confront both her father and her mother for overlooking and tolerating the sexual abuse. Further, according to Natalie, maintaining any sense of integrity would require her to cut herself off from the implicated family members. The family policed all its members rigorously, each keeping close tabs on the others, with the mother overseeing this operation.

For me, the issue was corruption: Natalie's influence was moving me from a more traditional stance in which vague memories and bodily sensations at first needed to be evaluated and treated as possible deflections from other disturbing issues, to one that would raise family eyebrows because of allegations of incest. My training in developmental psychology was to be discriminating about patients' claims of childhood recollections, especially when these involved blame.

So, I went to a consultant and described the case in detail. She furrowed her brow, concerned for the future of my work with Natalie. She said I had no choice about whether to believe her. If I didn't take Natalie seriously, we'd both fail: she'd see herself as hiding a secret and me as afraid of coming along with her. If I believed her, and we didn't find clear evidence of molestation at first, we still would be better prepared to recognize it if it turned up later; this kind of abuse being so alarming that everyone from the perpetrator to the child victim, her parents, and society conspire in perpetuating disbelief (Herman, 1992; van der Kolk, 2002).

As I write these words now, I feel a bit dismayed about my skepticism because it slowed our work, and at the time, disappointed Natalie. In my defense, however, in order for Natalie and I to work successfully, I needed to be authentic, honest about my uncertainty about the alleged molestations. I hold that it was my conversion to believing Natalie's story, its stark contrast with my initial skepticism, which proved to be one of the most potent factors in our ultimate conjunctive success.

The next step was for us to dive fearlessly into the underworld of Natalie's barely formed impressions and her suffering, bringing all our therapeutic tools with us and adding more. Natalie carefully logged dreams and impressions. We followed bodily sensations as some led to probable memories. In session after session, we also attempted to recover the details of Natalie's traumatic experiences using a "regression" method recommended by my consultant. With this technique, the therapist, supported by a relaxation protocol, accompanies the patient through imagery to the scenes of the molestations, exploring them in great detail. Incidentally, EMDR, one of the most effective contemporary techniques for working with trauma, had not yet become widely known and was only marginally accepted when we did this work. By this point in our work, Natalie also began to dig for factual information, in part by questioning family members.

Together, we moved inexorably into the grotesque, emotionally violent world where three children slept in a small basement room and had to watch for family marauders at night. Going was slow at first, with Natalie fighting against reexperiencing the traumatizing events, inclined to leave them in their dissociated hiding places. But one by one these demonic experiences began to reemerge, key players like Natalie's uncle finding their way back, repeatedly. Reassuring by now, was the repetition of these impressions as they took shape and the graphic dreams which themselves had a memorylike feeling about them.

The problem was with the snipers, family members who Natalie and I believed threatened to assault us for building a major case on hearsay. In part, our fears were anticipatory, based on our concern that through these revelations Natalie would be censured by her family, members of which could actually be hurt. In part, they also reflected my awareness of the false memory controversy, which was at its height at that point, with lawsuits abounding.

Natalie was, indeed, besieged by her parents and three siblings. They became acutely aware of Natalie's quest through the questions she was asking about incest and her growing alienation from those she was beginning to implicate. In retaliation, family members plotted how to punish their dissident member and Natalie's trusted husband began, for the first time, to express doubts; all a warning to me, since I felt that I, as therapist, could be responsible both for "misleading" Natalie and for a failed therapy and broken family relationships.

We were now 3 years into this story, Natalie and I clear we were onto something real. When either one of us threatened to abandon ship, temporarily uncertain about the validity of our quest, the other insisted he or she get back on. Our growing conviction about the molestations had become life sustaining for Natalie, my role becoming that of preserving the integrity of her recollections of her past, bearing witness to her trauma (Auerhahn & Peskin, 2003). We were getting to know that the other was there for keeps, and the challenge of believing what we were finding was getting less shaky for both of us.

Here is when Natalie remembered that at about 10 years of age her uncle demanded special favors for playing with her.

Clear recollections of the payment, putting his penis in her mouth, floated back; then there were his threats to tell her parents, and on a few occasions to hurt her, if she told. The feelings associated with these memories and those in her molestation dreams were similar. The rage was almost too brutal for her to bear.

"You do believe me *now*, Steve, don't you? I almost believe myself. But what do I do, confront my parents, or just never speak to them again?" "Good questions, Natalie. In spite of the gravity of their likely violations, the answers will take time." "Well, for the moment Steve, I intend at some point to publicly confront them; after that, we'll see what happens."

Because of her persistent confrontations and questioning, family members began to confirm her suspicions about the molestations. An aunt confided that she knew that as a teenager, her brother, Natalie's uncle, had molested young girls and was sent to a counselor to get help with the problem. During those years, he had tried to fondle Natalie's aunt also but she resisted. A cousin nearly Natalie's age described a series of episodes where he gained her confidence and then forced her to perform fellatio.

Natalie's depressions began to mitigate, as did the severity of the eczema outbreaks. With these developments the question of my ongoing commitment to her came to the fore. "You, Dr. Frankel, are the only one who knows. My husband is wonderful and protective, but it's reflexive for the most part. In contrast, you really know. If I lose you, I'm cut loose from the part of my reality that now makes life comprehensible." Behind this request were two principles. First, we did not want to lose touch with Natalie's painful memories of sexual abuse even after therapy stopped. These memories were as much a part of her as her cherished memories of her children when they were young, and we needed never to minimize or forget them. Second, I was her witness, her connection to the steamy, putrid childhood world we had discovered. And so I made it clear that for as long as it was in my power, I would never abandon my post.

Natalie had to be taken seriously. As I worked methodically to do that, she encountered and tolerated my imperfections: ways I did not empathize well, my difficulty in believing her. We have little trouble finding our way when we are together now. Reconnecting, reviving the dialogue, can relieve her depressions in record time; she no longer has to induce anxiety and confusion in me to alert me to her distress. We rapidly arrive at an explicit consensus about Natalie's current issues and what to do about them.

However, this is not the full story. It is a bit of a contrivance. The molestations and the memory of them were indeed foremost in Natalie's mind during this part of our work. They clearly had occurred and left their hideous mark. From the perspective of resolving her depressions and mitigating the anxiety component of her eczema our work on the molestations was invaluable, and served us admirably as the basis for our working consensus. However, further developments, as we began to terminate our work in therapy, suggested even more fundamental issues to explain Natalie's suffering. From this point, betrayal, Natalie's disappointment in both parents for allowing the molestations, for acting as if they never existed, but more critically, for neglecting her as she cried out for attention, became increasingly implicated.

The point of this illustration is that it is often an error to rely on manifest dialogue to discover how people understand each other and what they find out. Regardless of the topic we were dealing with, Natalie and I were building a powerful bond, one made of her innumerable disappointments with me, my disbelief about her claims, and our ceaseless work to reconcile these disjunctions. Our unfailing commitment to our molestation project spoke for itself, and progressively drew us toward points of consensus about the molestations and their relationship to her depressions and anxiety. But, as I have said, there was more, the strata of experience we could always feel, but that were hidden from us.

My experience with Natalie illustrates the process through which consensus, in both its overt and silent forms, firms and deepens in therapy. When Natalie and I talked recently after she had a serious automobile accident, reinforcing the trauma-shape feeling that she is undeserving, I understood. I had seen Natalie crash into the glass shards of despondency time and time again. Hatred for her arrogant, always violent father and indifferent mother welled up; she could see in my eyes that I understood and cared, and she was satisfied. The language of our communication was our passion, her rage and my empathy, deriving in part from my own terrors based on my early exposure to my mother's depression and father's angry vehemence.

Our spoken language created a frame to contain and direct our experience and help us move from point to point in our formal exploration of Natalie's trauma, but much of our experience of coming to believe one another and becoming committed to our project was inexplicable. Points of agreement, verbal and nonverbal, disrupted by episodes of disaffection, progressively grew into shared, tightly held convictions. The atmosphere that developed to contain our agreements, our ever-deepening connection to one another, was the conjunctive process. Natalie's expressed wish for me to guard the sanctity of her past, and my decision to participate, was our conjunction.

Research on the early childhood sources of nonverbal communication and its counterpart in adult life (Beebe and Lachmann, 2002, 2003; La Barre, 2001), as well as observations of the power and specificity of nonverbal processes in therapy, for example, as illustrated by the handholding incident with Brittany, suggest to me that people frequently understand each other with remarkable accuracy, whether or not this understanding is put into words and in spite of the slipperiness of their individual subjectivities. People have enormous nonverbal vocabularies, made up of nuances, actions, and tones of voices. They are often good at cueing each other so their responses are progressively in sync, leading them in the direction of conjunction. They can even be hatching a plan for working together, while lost in overt disagreement. Brittany and I did that when, as she was constantly finding fault with my empathic skills, she and I were positioning ourselves to address her deepest sense of betrayal and disappointment within her original family.

The opposite may be true as well, with neither therapy member able to accurately cue the other nonverbally. That is what happened with Marty when I did not want to face my irritation at him and privately blamed him for disrupting the treatment. My anger and defensiveness made shared understanding temporarily impossible. I both did not understand Marty's view of life, and, for that moment, did not really want to understand it. In addition to the subjectivity of each partner and the intersubjectivity of the couple, the list of potential impediments to consensus, that is, factors leading to disjunction, is quite long. Maintaining a consensus in the conjunctive process is actually daunting. It is a shared experience, usually uneven, but when it succeeds the result is the dense matrix of a hard won conjunction.

What Actually Happened with Natalie: The Value of a Relational Configuration Analysis

Why did it take me so long to trust Natalie's allegation that she may have been molested? Even my consultant was clear that for the therapy to succeed, Natalie would have to be certain I believed her. I concurred with that view. Somehow, rather than seizing on the reversal of dissociation as the critical step in her resolution of trauma, I kept remembering Van der Kolk's warning (1988) that a trauma victim tends to set up a reenactment of the traumatizing situation with his or her therapist. In brief, according to this principle, therapists need to be especially careful about regulating the intensity of involvement with their traumatized patients to make sure their patients' transferences, their expectations of love and exploitation, do not become too real so that the trauma is re-created.

Other factors were at work as well, moving me to distance myself from Natalie. I have already mentioned my concern about family retaliation and the issue of my professional stature. Natalie was a member of my extended professional community, and I automatically may have become extra cautious, wanting to avoid professional censure, in this case connected with the false memory controversy.

Further complicating this picture was my awareness of Natalie's husband, a respected lawyer, who by reputation, tended to be unemotional and judgmental. Of course, I did my best to resist being concerned about his opinion, but sometimes it was impossible for me not to picture him objecting to the direction of my work with Natalie, our searching for evidence of molestation, or, worse yet, his censure if I failed to help her. My concern about his judgment was pitted against another attitude of which I was vaguely aware. My influence in Natalie's life, paired with Natalie's intermittent complaint about her husband's excessive pragmatism, alerted me to the possibility of therapy creating problems for the marriage. It seemed conceivable that Natalie could split her ambivalence about the marriage between the two of us, her husband becoming the devalued partner in the process.

Added to the above was a level of our interaction that included "music" and few words. Natalie liked the intensity of our encounter. She liked the words; but even more, she liked their sound, meter, and fervor. So long as we were talking about feelings in the transference and how they might recapitulate aspects of the molestations, for example, there was always intensity between us, and Natalie never got lonely. We had a project that was intimate in itself, all ours, and it kept going and going. Every so often I stepped back far enough to notice that this intensity might reflect as an yet unappreciated therapy theme, possibly transference or countertransference based; but it was so integrated with the rest of our work that the new perspective always seemed to evaporate.

At the same time, my heart went out to Natalie. I liked and respected her. She was suffering terribly. In spite of periods of remission, her depression and eczema had been getting worse over the years. I fervently wanted to help her. Also, as another factor encouraging our work, I liked the promise of working in therapy with a dedicated, sophisticated patient.

In summary, from my side the relational configurations picture included: (1) the belief based on my training that I should initially regard Natalie's allegation of molestation with "reasonable" caution (my "cautious" configuration); (2) my concern that as a repetition of her trauma Natalie might move me into the role of perceived perpetrator (my "dangerous" configuration); (3) my worry about censure in my professional community (my "fear of being judged" configuration); (4) competition with her husband, encouraged by Natalie (my "male competitive" configuration); and finally; (5) my growing suspicion that the existence and pace of the therapy was meeting some powerful, as yet unformulated, need of Natalie's (my "responsive" configuration).

All these relational configurations were balanced against configurations drawing me toward Natalie and the therapy, including (6) my empathy for Natalie (my "empathic" configuration), as well as (7) my eagerness to undertake an interesting therapy (my "self-serving" configuration). And, further, both of these configurations were mitigated by other (8) self-regulatory configurations, which served to govern the propriety of my work, always helping me to maintain safe boundaries, impelling me not to use patients for my own needs; for example, for the pleasure of working with an interesting patient.

A main point here is that I was only subliminally aware of most of these forces, although they were all operating, with different valances most of the time, always influencing the decisions Natalie and I made. Of course, Natalie had her own set of relational configurations at work, interacting with mine. Natalie liked my comfort with emotions and interest in understanding them. At times, uncomfortably, Natalie imagined sexual involvement with me. Like me, Natalie was preoccupied with the possibility that her claim of having been molested might be contrived, perhaps to punish her self-serving parents. She was as aware as I, but less worried about, the potential for censure from her husband and colleagues about her search for evidence of molestation. Also, like me, she was concerned that the therapy could compete with and erode her marriage.

Natalie wanted to be helped and was eager to be in therapy. But unlike me, she had no interest in it as an academic exercise. Stylistically, she was more reserved than I, less likely to spontaneously offer information about her feelings about her husband, for example.

In relational configuration terms, in the beginning Natalie was (1) uncertain like me about having been molested, and worried that we would collude to convert false memories into convictions (her "cautious" configuration, precisely matched to my own). (2) At times, Natalie was attracted to me, yet uncomfortable with any sexual feelings she experienced (her "sensuality" configuration). (3) Intermittantly, Natalie pitted me against her husband, sometimes making me the more admirable of the two of us (her "disloyal wife" configuration). (4) Unlike me, Natalie's motivation for therapy was not contaminated with concerns about humiliation if we failed or with an attraction to the technical or intellectual challenge of therapy (her "work" configuration). (5) Natalie was a fervent therapy partner, ceaselessly working to understand and reverse the traumas of her childhood (her "stalwart" configuration). This configuration was hard to distinguish from her part in our facilitating and analyzing relational configurations, those that supported and provided essential fuel for the therapy. Yet, the intensity of her commitment to our therapy suggested there was something more, motivation beyond the goal of reworking her trauma. However, the meaning of this configuration was not revealed until we started to finish our therapy.

It is striking to contrast the issues revealed in this assessment of relational configuration states to the conscious experience Natalie and I had in therapy. Most of the time we were aware of a powerful, shared drive to resolve Natalie's depressions and mitigate her eczema attacks, our matched concerns about fictionalizing her claimed molestations, and her periodic complaints that I was too removed to really comprehend the personal agony she experienced, all arrayed around our shared desire to help Natalie. In brief, within this segment of our experience we were involved in a dedicated therapy effort with a few relatively obvious disjunctions to work out.

Here is where the relational configuration analysis needs to include a measure of magnitude, identifying the relative influence of each configuration, in addition to categorizing them. Omitted from our awareness was the intensity of Natalie's "sensuality" and "disloyal wife" configurations. As we worked on the molestation themes Natalie experienced genital sensations, arousal that seemed sexual on the surface but was fundamentally humiliating and physically uncomfortable for her. Natalie had a history of reckless sexual involvements prior to marriage, always ending in painful loss of dignity and humiliation. Reports of these episodes foreshadowed occasional suggestive invitations to me, made compulsively and always followed by insightful retractions. She was well aware of the likely association between these compulsions and her childhood molestations.

In short, potentially contaminating our stated commitment to work together and not fictionalize Natalie's molestations, was a clash of passion and restraint. To a degree neither of us always recognized, Natalie was beset by an unwelcome compulsion to draw me into a sexual liaison; at each point both of us were affected, resisted and always adhered to our work in therapy. For Natalie this interest was entirely unwelcome, sexual ideas and feelings invading her mind and body, Natalie unable to dispel them. The technical challenge was complex. When it came, the sexual arousal seemed real and pressing to Natalie. Her subsequent embarrassment was also intense, made worse for her by my awareness of her professional stature in the medical community. With these episodes, she became confused and defensive, at times lashing out at me, accusing me of pushing her unnecessarily to discuss them. Periodically, she even wondered whether it was damaging to submit herself to that kind of indignity, thinking for that moment about ending the therapy. Each such experience had to be explored and managed delicately, a slow and sometimes tortuous process.

Judged from a distance, Natalie and I were clearly handling and pacing each other, convinced we were onto the solution of Natalie's depressions but intuitively aware we had to be slow in getting there. Some topics, like Natalie's sensuality, had to be handled tactfully. Others, like the unexplored force making Natalie so fervent about our therapy project, simply weren't yet available to be understood. In retrospect, I would describe our 3 years of work to that point as labored emotionally, with Natalie being pushed by her posttraumatic sexuality and her sometimes petulant demands for confirmation of my dedication. Nonetheless, the therapy was remarkably sophisticated, Natalie producing an unending sequence of memories, dreams, and useful associations. Our progress was steady and unremitting, attesting to the powerful trust we were developing in discovering and unpacking Natalie's traumatic memories.

In summary, this relational configuration analysis suggests that the most important implicit therapeutic transactions between Natalie and me were, first, dealing with a potential reiteration of her sexual trauma detectable especially in the erotic thoughts and the genital sensations that seemed to invade her; and second, comprehending Natalie's zealous commitment to our therapy project, a topic powerfully influencing our work but not yet understood. Natalie's marriage was honored and strengthened, her physical symptoms, including her depression, were exposed as somatic relics of the abuse she had experienced in childhood, and in the end the person who accompanied her in exposing the abuses of her past, myself, promised to remain on guard to preserve the recovered memories and support her commitment to a new kind of future.

Here, unveiled, is the therapy field with *working consensus* continually reformulated by the therapy partners, nonverbal aspects juxtaposed with the verbal. As in all human transactions, much of the action is directed unseen from the wings. That which is verbal and conceptual, such as the frequent exchanges Natalie and I had about the details of the molestations and a related assessment of the dynamics of the family, may be organizing and useful, but it is often off the mark, out of sync with the more powerful, nonverbal therapy dialogue. In fact, in the end, the topic of Natalie's molestations faded and was replaced by a new, even more influential issue, her betrayal and abandonment by her parents, and its potential repetition as she lost me in therapy. That was the topic, as we discovered, that provided the fuel for her almost fanatical involvement in therapy, the one that caused her mind to be in such constant motion.

It is interesting to see, using an relational configuration analysis, how many conversations are going on at once, adding up to a therapeutic moment. Over and above our formal therapy explorations of the traumatic component of her eczema and depressions, Natalie and I talked most easily with each other about the risk of perpetrating false memories. However, our most critical dialogues for most of our work, the ones about repetition of sexual trauma and her continued need for restraint from me and the others about Natalie's intensity in therapy, were almost entirely nonverbal.

There were the other conversations. For example, in my anxiety about professional censure, I was mainly conversing with those who held the keys to my professional reputation, from my early teachers to current colleagues. That Natalie's husband and her parents' and siblings' censure concerned me, suggested that I needed to assuage them for my potential trespasses against them based on my power as Natalie's therapist. The point here, once again, is to highlight the complexity and power of the underlying nonverbal currents in the therapy field, and to begin to consider their ultimate relationship to therapeutic consensus.

Return, for a moment, to the six global influences on decision making in therapy I introduced earlier in this chapter. (1) Natalie and I were always aware of the social setting in which our work occurred. Natalie's professional dignity constantly entered the picture as we discussed issues involving sexuality; I was often occupied with how I would be judged by my colleagues. (2) The themes we successively treated were not available all at once. Rather they *emerged*, one following the other over time. (3) My reticence and Natalie's drive to repeat her trauma were felt, *affectively*, by both of us, coloring and directing our work. (4) The issue of *attunement* was everywhere, determining how well Natalie and I worked together, even when we were feeling antagonistic. (5) Similarly, Natalie and I depended heavily on our intuitive ability to follow each other, an activity in part *neurologically* based, supported by communication between the right cerebral hemispheres of both partners. (6) Finally, we always believed in each other, adding what might be construed as a *spiritual* dimension to our work. All six categories, in different amounts, are operative in the development of working consensus, bringing the therapy couple ever closer to their conjunctive goal.

In retrospect, it is worth noting that even when Natalie and I were most affected by the clash of her passion and restraint, as well as other issues, such as the potential censure about our molestation theme that worried us, the conjunctive process was always alive and well. The field was rife with disjunctions, but we nonetheless worked well together. Illustrated here is the centrality of relational configurations involved in maintaining a constructive atmosphere in therapy, allowing patient and therapist to use disjunctions, including their personal stylistic differences, constructively. In fact, it stands to reason that real progress in therapy is dependent on the existence of differences in belief, comprehension, and vision between therapist and patient, and how these differences are handled by them. The relational configurations that support this productive atmosphere include (1) shared "facilitating" configurations, connoting that significant trust and good will exist between the two; (2) shared reflective, "analyzing" configurations; (3) major shared goals, providing content for the therapist's and patient's "work configurations," dedicated to maintaining and furthering the therapy.

My guess is that there are other imponderables contributing to this kind of successful collaboration leading to conjunction. It helps for therapist and patient to have successfully weathered difficult storms together, leading to improvement in the therapy. Cultural, gender, and age similarities may make for easier understanding between the two. Common background experiences may help, and finally, similar temperamental characteristics that aid each in recognizing what the other intends may contribute. Natalie and I come from New York City, are reasonably close in age, and work in the medical community, a strong set of similarities that may have made our differences more bearable and enhanced our skills for working them out collaboratively. Note that the same could not be said of my match with Brittany. Her parents, as I have said, are fourth generation New Englanders; she is very intelligent but temperamental in ways consistent with her artistic talents; and also, she is considerably younger than I am.

Working Consensus

Did Natalie and I reach a consensus about our therapy goals and how did we achieve it? This is a more complicated question than perhaps it seems. Reflexively, my inclination would be to say, of course we did. We discussed and agreed on our manifest goals, the resolution of Natalie's depressions and eczema attacks. At the beginning of our work we were also in agreement about the dangers of indiscriminately accepting her thoughts about molestation. But, what then to say about our differences? The minor ones were our levels of concern about censure from the professional community and Natalie's husband, and the major one originally concerned sensuality. Where is the consensus here, if consensus is defined as points of agreement, accord, harmony, or mutually acceptable compromise? Also, we don't want to limit consensus to verbalized matters. Tricky stuff.

Omitted from this picture, and profoundly influencing our assessment of her difficulties, was our mystery configuration, the one associated with Natalie's fervent commitment to our therapy. That one turned out to be the most elusive and yet perhaps the most fundamental. Expressed in the most powerful ways but never articulated was the legacy of Natalie's experience of abandonment by her parents. Everything was okay for Natalie in therapy as long as we had a riveting project and she was constantly occupied by the roller-coaster ride of therapy. There was no need for her to feel empty under those circumstances. It was when our common purpose disappeared for even a moment that everything changed. Natalie's unremitting dedication then gave way to the most awful sense of emptiness, so overwhelming that her mind shifted to frenetic activity to avoid experiencing it.

Most revealing of the abandonment theme, were developments as we began to discuss the end of our therapy. Then, suddenly, shockingly, Natalie's sense of purpose shattered. She found herself worrying, obsessed with fear for her future. She was flooded by memories of being left alone in the care of her sister at age 7, her parents gone for hours or even days, and tormenting recollections of parents who didn't get out of bed until 2 in the afternoon, and even then, only wanted to argue with and criticize each other. As a child, Natalie desperately needed someone to reassure her, even just be there when she was frightened and upset. And so Natalie and I added these final memories to our collection, as well as an additional year and a half of treatment, as we continued to sharply revise our working consensus about the nature of Natalie's problems.

I believe the definition of consensus needs to be practical (Renik, 1993; Rorty, 1991; Strenger, 1991); the idea of consensus needs to be useful and clear, not vague and general. Consensus about unspoken matters seems like a helpful notion to me, providing that there is some operational marker to follow revisions of the consensus. Our relational configuration analysis highlights yet another principle associated with consensus: the judgment of whether Natalie and I were working in consensus depends on one's frame of reference. Judging from whether we agreed about manifest therapy goals and were committed to achieving these, we were in consensus. Looking at the matter from the point of view of our initially different opinions about the certainty of the molestation, we weren't then in consensus. Still, both positions were at play in the therapy field, at the same time. What one can glean from this appraisal is that when two people have a consensus about some matters, they may disagree about others. Ideally, these agreements and areas of difference will become explicit in therapy. Also, an articulated consensus or disagreement may occur alongside the opposite stance about the same issue, the latter position not articulated by either therapist or patient. Finally, the idea of consensus is not necessarily equated with truth. Rather, the consensus two people arrive at usually needs to serve several purposes in addition to reflecting a meeting of minds, and in so doing it minimizes or even fictionalizes some issues while emphasizing and accurately representing others.

Natalie and I arrived at an unspoken agreement supporting some of my skepticism about the molestations as we first worked together, since doing that privately assisted Natalie in downplaying her sensual feelings and reduced the likelihood of her husband's criticism of our work. For a time, also, we both treated my position about the molestations as if it were the agreed upon truth because it gave her time to decide what to do about the hostility of her family members to her claim that she had been molested. Reciprocally, I was tolerant of Natalie's need to minimize her compulsion to repeat her sexual history in the therapy, waiting until Natalie could reflect on that subject. Until she became comfortable with it, the topic of her genital sensations was acutely embarrassing for Natalie and there was no pushing her to talk about them. Nonetheless, at each of these points, Natalie and I generally worked well together, maintaining a practical consensus that directed our work and kept us feeling united.

Given the complexities in the use of the concept *consensus* and the practical way I have been framing it, I believe the notion of *working consensus* is the more useful concept. It captures the ever changing, compromise nature of the consensus process, making it applicable to the type of interpersonal direction finding that continually occurs in psychotherapy.

My claim is that, when viewed from a distance, Natalie and I would almost always have been judged to be in consensus. That is what I meant when I referred earlier to our progress being "steady and unremitting." In our therapy work we were on target most of the time. How to explain this observation, given the coexisting differences revealed by the relational configuration analysis? To do so I need to again invoke the notion of relational configurations that provide management, that is, executive functions, overseeing other relational configurations and keeping the therapy work in synchrony. People guard their valued relationships, regulating them to make sure they remain healthy, a concept roughly analogous to the way a mother and child regulate one another. The mother, who in this example may temporarily be the therapist or the patient, always makes plenty of room for manageable disruptions and keeps her eye on repair.

Here I am referring to relational configurations involved in collaboration, relational configurations partially shared between the two participants, including "work configurations" where both members agree on goals and pursue them jointly. For example, Natalie and I labored to understand the psychological component of her depressions. These relational configurations set the themes for a particular interaction, such as the task of reviewing the timing and character of Natalie's symptoms when she came into therapy and reported retreating to bed, depressed, on the previous morning. Critical in this collaborative operation are also strong, partly shared, "facilitating configurations," both members of the couple committed to supporting each other. Then, of special significance are the relational configurations involved in the assessment and implementation of a task, "analyzing" configurations. Consensus, articulated or not, requires ongoing evaluation by both parties for repeatedly formulating and maintaining their agreements. Clearly, the kind of working consensus I describe involves a complicated, dedicated operation with several threads of content, commitment, and appraisal from each contributor coming together, at its backbone.

As a contrast, I had a much easier time maintaining consensus with Natalie than I did with Brittany, even though both therapies were stormy when viewed from the surface. I had to labor to understand Brittany's latent goals for our therapy. Brittany had limited interest in supporting my role when she felt I was being unempathic and at these points became distant and inarticulate, unable to reflect on our therapy experience. The intermittent nature of our working consensus predicted that the kind of core commitment characterizing my work with Natalie, an unfailing gyroscope guiding our work, would be much slower to develop with Brittany.

I am not using the term *working consensus* as synonymous with agreement. There were always significant places of disagreement, disjunction, between Natalie, Brittany, and myself. Ultimately, these disjunctions were generative in both cases, fueling discovery about the forces at work in each therapy. Instead, the consensus I am referring to is the overriding sense of unity that makes a therapy productive, regardless of coexisting mismatches and schisms. *Working consensus,* as I use this term, is a practical concept referring to the compromise action plan therapist and patient agree upon at each point in their work. The agreement is usually made nonverbally with verbal components contributing, and factors like intuition, empathy, and societal influences automatically shape the process.

Conjunction Revisited

At this point, there should be no question about the complexity of the nonverbal dimension of the conjunctive process. To effect conjunction there is no need for the therapy pair to be in close agreement about all, or even most, issues. The critical factor is whether they can use their disagreements and agreements, verbal and nonverbal, to move penetratingly beyond the interpersonal world they previously inhabited.

Unexplored by us thus far is the question of how closely the two members can draw to each other, what factors, explicable and nonarticulated, make clear the depth to which they can open up and unite. These criteria set a kind of interpersonal ceiling on the process. Despite the power of our work, the air between Natalie and me is at times still slightly prickly, as if she is on guard that I might vacate my sentry post. Brittany regularly slips back to worrying that I may be critical like her father, and reciprocally, finds herself questioning whether I am sensitive enough for her to safely entrust with her well-being. The barriers I am describing with both Natalie and Brittany exist in spite of our having had some of the most emotionally intimate experiences I can imagine with each other. What, then, is this subtle glass wall that separates us? How much further can we go as we work toward coupling conjunctively?

The next two chapters are devoted to this subject, as measured through the lenses of authenticity and self-revelation. The chemistry of authenticity is anything but straightforward. All components, both participants, have to pull toward the center to assure ultimate cohesion, while individual parts, oriented in different directions, may repel each other. When all combines correctly, however, enormous energy may be released propelling the two people involved into the uncanny universe of their combined subjectivities.

7

Finding the Balance between
the Disjunctive and
Conjunctive: Authenticity

A major requirement for promoting therapeutic conjunction is that therapist and patient strive toward authenticity, while at the same time they clear away their contaminating personal agendas. Eradicating distorting scenarios, such as those incorporated into transference and countertransference themes, is the time honored task of analytical therapies. This principle accepted, what more comprises authenticity in therapy? Is authenticity the same as honesty? To what extent is authenticity the uncomplicated product of self-examination and openness by therapist and patient working cooperatively? With all the conflicting factors at work in a therapy, how can therapeutic communication be fully authentic? Required is a practical orientation involving the notion that honesty in psychotherapy needs to evolve with therapist and even patient not exposing their personal lives all at once, the therapy dialogue fitted to the patient's tolerance so he can be retained as a collaborator. In this version of authenticity, concern for the therapy's survival and the patient's needs and goals are in the forefront.

Authenticity is not a state that can be forced. Neither patient nor therapist may know at the outset whether each is being guarded about what he or she "really" means or feels (Frie,

2002; Schafer, 1976). Either or both may hold that they are being open, and undoubtedly believe they are, each wanting to encourage the most open therapy possible. However, there are always factors discouraging openness, including the limitations of each person's capacity for self-understanding, and the other's inadvertent judgments and feelings of competition, to name a few. On the helpful side, partners constantly evaluate the other's genuineness, monitoring the authenticity of the dialogue, and provide clues for how it can be improved, aiding the other to emerge more authentically.

Being Authentic: About What and How Much?

I have told you about Russell, the nonanalyst therapist who had the good sense to tell my colleague Tom he was "feeling better," after Tom, his patient, came into his office and asked him how he was doing. Tom was amazed that Russell too was capable of feeling down, like he sometimes was. On another occasion, Tom reports, he was grateful when Russell said he often thought of retiring but wasn't sure he could afford to. The effect of Russell's candor was that Tom wanted to open up more, his faith building that Russell could hear him, Tom feeling more connected to Russell as a human being.

Authenticity is a trait that is generally considered a great virtue by contemporary, nontraditional dynamic therapists (Hoffman, 1998, pp. 83–84; Maroda, 2002; Slavin and Kriegman, 1998). In contrast, the blank screen ideal of old did a lot to cut the patient off from the person of the therapist. Elevating authenticity in therapy is a reaction against this overrigid standard. In discussing authenticity, I am referring mainly to the therapist's emotional honesty. Cognitive honesty counts too, but it mainly consists of manifest themes in a person's life, while latent, unappreciated, emotionally based agendas are expressed nonverbally and frequently are experienced as riskier.

Obviously, at any point a person will feel and communicate about many different, often conflicting issues. He or she continually makes choices among these items, always creating a unique interpersonal moment. Authenticity, then, is a matter of choice, deciding whether or not to pull more closely with your partner through selecting what to reveal and what to withhold. As I will illustrate, some people associate authenticity with frankness, others with empathy and tact. Yet, there are few subjects as critical to psychotherapy as authenticity. The value and depth of a therapeutic connection are closely tied to its authenticity, in part a function of the extent to which the two people involved have shared their deepest thoughts and feelings. Clearly, then interpersonal considerations about the level of authenticity two people can and want to tolerate impose a critical, sensitive limit on the depth of their relationship, and in the case of psychotherapy, on the therapy.

But authenticity can be a problem. Back to Russell: He got Tom excited about methodically looking for patterns in his "family of origin," something his training analyst had never done. They discovered subtle ways that Tom believes his all-but-flawless mother probably kept him enslaved for the purpose of adding vitality to her flagging life. Russell said it would be good for Tom to formalize the project, retrieving and recording all the information he could. Tom liked the exercise; he was making discoveries at an astronomical rate. He wanted to share each one with Russell. Tom assumed Russell would be as excited as he was and wouldn't mind if Tom used a bit of Russell's time outside the formal boundaries of the therapy to leave phone messages for him. Of course, from a different perspective, Tom could be seen as insisting on being special, gleaning favors from Russell, and taking advantage of his and Russell's professional identities as colleagues.

According to Tom, he left two phone messages for Russell, certain it would be fine with Russell to receive the calls. In a return message from Russell, he was shocked to detect no such excitement, hearing instead, "Tom, there are three reasons why I don't want you to leave messages like that: it uses up my answering machine time, it is inappropriate, and if I go to use the bathroom I may inadvertently have the speaker of the machine on while a patient is in my office."

Tom answered by machine: "Russell, that's pretty harsh. Couldn't you soften it a bit, after all you don't want to stage a rerun of my father's constant disapproval of almost anything I ever did as a kid?" No answer. No return phone call. Tom found himself burning up inside, feeling decimated and angry. There is no question about whether Russell was being authentic. In a way, he was being too authentic for Tom's blood at that moment. He was being authentically confrontational and honestly moody, but in so doing he ran the risk of retraumatizing Tom.

There are other kinds of authenticity that can be troubling for patients. Think of the blank screen conviction of traditional analytic therapists. No practitioner could be more earnest, following the rules with almost religious fervor. Beyond that, there are also cultural authenticities, as well as gender-related, stylistic, personality, or historically based particularities that can be emphasized in an interaction. How does a therapist navigate between being authentically helpful to the patient and devastatingly straightforward, when these attitudes contradict one another? One kind of integrity can cancel out the therapeutic benefit of another. Russell's moodiness made Tom forget how grateful he was for Russell's being forthcoming about his life.

The objective of all this authenticity, the final common pathway, is connection, or more accurately, conjunction. You can not connect unless you are open and honest with each other. Yet, obviously, some kinds of honesty produce alienation, not closeness. These authenticities are an impediment to conjunction, even if they provide openings for understanding the complexity of the other person and exposing disjunctions.

When Authenticity Is Problematic

Authenticity That Suppresses

Tom's experience with Russell identifies one class of authenticity that is particularly problematic. Russell probably sees himself as a very open, even uniquely straightforward therapist. The therapist has the right, probably duty, to be open, even bold with the patient when the patient needs to hear something important. But what does this kind of unbridled openness accomplish? In Tom's case, it made it harder for Tom to work with Russell. Clearly, Russell could not always be counted on to accommodate to Tom's needs, even when they were heartfelt.

Rather than setting the stage for a conjunction, Russell's authenticity generated a disjunction between Tom and himself: Tom felt disillusioned and less enthusiastic about their work. And, after the damage was done, Tom was not ready to initiate the repair aspect of the disruption–repair cycle I have described.

One side of this disruption was the unfortunate effect of Russell's behavior: his crowding Tom with his insistence that Tom do things his way. Here, authenticity refers to direct revelation of one's mind to another in a way that squelches the other's ability to make himself known or felt. The other side was Russell's impact on Tom, his apparent lack of concern about how his behavior would affect Tom. In the first, the focus is the extent of the subject's openness, in the second, the impact of that openness on the other. In both views, the result was suppression, forcing Tom more inward.

Inauthenticity

Contrasting with the situation where the therapist's openness is oppressive, is the more usual case of the therapist sharing too little of his thinking. At issue is whether the information being withheld is germane to the treatment, if only because the inclination to withhold relates primarily to the therapist's mood and behavior. Of course, the therapist will often be unaware that he is impeding treatment and believe that he is using a correct therapy technique. It may be up to the patient to inform him of its effect. The fact that this situation arises more frequently than we might like as therapists, makes a strong argument for the therapist being open to the patient's feedback, soliciting it, and using techniques like mind clearing and controlled disorientation to enhance his receptivity.

The following examples from Brittany and Natalie are to the point. They both made it perfectly clear that I had to come clean about my feelings or the personal value of our dialogue would be compromised.

Brittany

Brittany could tell that something was bothering me. Beneath my affability was seething anger she said I could not see. I seemed closed off to her in a subtle but powerful way, not really there. She had left her job a few months previously and had been feeling upbeat for weeks. In a message over the weekend, though, she said she was depressed again, having a hard time writing that morning. Rather than listening, I planted my feet, and in the nicest way said I was sure her mood was temporary; I hoped it would not stop her from creating. Perhaps her discouragement had to do with guilt about feeling so pleased she could now devote herself to writing. Later, Brittany told me that in that moment an abyss opened between us. I could not have been more obtuse as, in effect, through my apparently insufferable upbeat mood I criticized her for again complaining about her life. At work here was my reluctance to admit the truth that my divorce was bothering me, I was in no mood on that day to listen to her troubles. I had not even considered telling her about the divorce.

Natalie

Well into treatment, Natalie once again needed to be sure I fully believed her about the molestations and was dedicated to uncovering everything we could about them. Apparently, I was less tuned-in than usual, maybe a bit oppositional. As she questioned me, probing my commitment, I found myself squirming but did not want her to know.

The colleague with whom I consulted periodically, questioned me as to why I was again having difficulty with the molestation issue. In response, I worked harder to be supportive of Natalie while she grew more distant, subliminally aware of my partial detachment. In a dream, she represented me as leaving her. When we worked with the dream, she said I had seemed preoccupied for several weeks. I asked what she noticed. As she described me as more disengaged, I found myself feeling irritated. She was right though; I had the page proofs of my new book to do and was overwhelmed by other professional demands. However, what I mainly did not want to admit was that Natalie's requirements that I be the sole witness of the molestations distressed me; the responsibility seemed daunting. At this late date, I was not sure I had the desire to take on such a role. However, I bent the truth, in the service of convincing Natalie and myself that I was as committed as ever to our common project of uncovering and working with the memories of the molestations and abandonments.

With Natalie and Brittany, I set out to be helpful. When both these women confronted me with my failures, initially I faked it, attempting to reassure both myself and them that I was as present as ever. I wanted each to see me as a fully committed ally, a dedicated therapist. Instead, they saw my efforts as labored, inauthentic.

So, we have a dilemma. Where conjunction is the goal, as in psychotherapy, too much honesty may have its downside just as much as too little. To further a conjunction, both members of the therapeutic couple have to be not only open about their feelings but empathic, aware of the other's needs and feelings and interested in honoring these. Both ways of being have to do with authenticity: authentic openness and authentic caring.

The balance I am describing between self and other, gauging how much openness is constructive for treatment, is my version of a therapeutic attitude, or, more traditionally, an analytic attitude. I am referring to a reciprocally authentic encounter, which is consistent with therapy goals and allows for the mutual examination of needs and motives, moving the participants closer to a creative therapeutic experience, one that will force each of their lives in distinctly new directions. Authenticity, without the balance I am describing, like Russell's initial version when he bristled at Tom, may be seductive in the permission it gives for the therapist to emote, but it has limited value so far as the objectives of two people struggling to understand and help the patient is concerned.

Working with Authenticity

As Therapists, When Do We Hold or Discard Revelations of Feelings and Opinions to the Patient?

How to think about Russell's straightforwardness? Was it better or worse than the traditional blank screen, which encouraged idealization of the essentially nonhuman analytic therapist, while allowing the patient plenty of space to look inward, minimizing interpersonal risk? Was Russell's position similar to the blank screen in its focus on boundaries, but different in his willingness to expose his irritation? His straightforwardness satisfied Russell's own need to be personally authentic but not his charge to guard his therapeutic bond with Tom.

Brittany would choose Russell over a conventional therapist and also give him a chance on the empathy side. At least he would let her know where he stood, something I did not do when I broke from my usual mining of her subjective experience and encouraged her to keep writing rather than admit that her discouragement bothered me. She might have been glad that Russell could tell her about his irritation.[1] Then Brittany might talk about her needs: Did he really care about them and was he truly capable of altering his mood to include them? If not, she might conclude they were a bad match, one in which Russell absolutely could not go further with her in their work. But still they would know more about the real structure of their bond and the therapy than Brittany and I did that morning when she could not write and I was being inadvertently disingenuous about my dismissive mood.

From this discussion, I hope it is clear that I believe authenticity is the bedrock of conjunctive therapy. What do we have without it? But when we have it, we need to take a hard look and make sure we have the right variety. Here also is where all of the repair-directed maneuvers of partners come in (such as *confrontations* and *role enactments* used in the service of rescuing a disrupted therapy bond, as described in chapter 5), each partner informing the other where he or she is off, indicating that a disjunction is lurking. The techniques the more aware partner uses range from verbal to nonverbal, but require that one partner takes the initiative whenever the other is therapeutically "asleep." The unsettling implication of this exposing of one's position by the other is that the two partners become cognizant for the moment of a glaring incompatibility between themselves.

Authenticity and Conjunction: Dr. Mark

At this point we return to Dr. Mark, my training analyst, and our post heart attack dilemma. My claim is that the critical moment was when he looked at me imploringly, and I knew to take

---

[1] Safron and Muran's (2000) discussion of how the therapist can help "disembed" a patient and himself from participating in an enactment and work out the distortion contained in the patient's interpretation of the therapist's action, is relevant here (pp. 156–164).

over the analysis for a while. I see this event as a moment of nonverbal conjunction based on years of hard-won confidence in the other's commitment.

The truth is that my formal analysis with Dr. Mark was kind of mediocre. I think by the time I started my analysis, Dr. Mark was already old enough to think about retiring, and that he just wasn't up for the methodical historical and personal exploration psychoanalysis requires. But he did have plenty of compassion. I could tell from the first minute I entered his office that he liked me and was "for me." For example, our psychoanalytic institute required the training analyst's approval before control cases could be undertaken. Dr. Mark sent his in early. Reports trickled back to me that he told other professionals to refer their cases to me because I knew what I was doing. His interventions tended to be about how I could be easier on myself, less burdened. Altogether, the atmosphere he created provided a shocking contrast to my first stab at a personal analysis, where I felt my "flaws," called "impulses" in those days, were always being dug at and exposed, exploited as "grist-for-the-analytic-mill."

Though I was fond of Dr. Mark, as I inferred he was of me, I have to admit that there was something distinctly inauthentic in our training analysis, at least until after the first 6½ years when he was forced by his post heart attack debilitation to hand the reigns to me. I was a captive audience as an analytic candidate; to graduate I had to finish the training analysis. His brand of psychoanalysis was a great relief after the 3 years of oppression with my first analyst during my psychiatric residency, so that tolerating the thinness of our dialogue wasn't particularly trying, just unconvincing. Dr. Mark did his job and I did mine, but there was little about the analysis itself that was moving or mutative. Of course, I was entirely unaware of these limitations during those years. I figured that Dr. Mark, whose reputation was impeccable, knew what he was doing. I thought I knew what my job was. And it was a bit blasphemous to question the substance of the analysis anyway; in a traditional analytic frame you are always looking for what the patient brings to the pathological table.

In retrospect, it appears that for those 6 years Dr. Mark and I were doing something quite useful, however. We were getting to know and trust each other and accumulating good will. These developments came in handy when we needed them following his heart attack. Our crisis gave us, at last, no choice but to be present as two human beings, both with needs and competencies. In the sterile formality of our past cooperation, consensus was possible, but *not conjunction.* Suddenly, though, in the heat of Dr. Mark's post heart attack turmoil, we both needed each other. I looked for his permission to take over the analysis, and he my help to carry it on. The contract was fixed in an eyeblink, all without words.

I learned later from Dr. Mark that this experience was entirely unnerving, and then groundbreaking for him. While shaking up the foundation on which he based his behavior as an analyst for 40-odd years, our collaboration also set the stage for a friendship between us after the analysis. For the next 8 years until his death, we got to know each other personally and confided in each other. Before our incident, he said, he was perfectly comfortable doing analysis the old way. He never shared his personal feelings with patients, and, if he could help it, he never talked outside the office with them. He never anticipated having a heart attack, nor imagined being seen by others as vulnerable or needing their help, then. He cared for his analysands like a queen bee, directing and protecting them when necessary. The heart attack, the months following it when for a while he was expected to die, and the 2 or so years of recuperation put an end to all that. Soon thereafter, he retired, and became a world renowned connoisseur of food and wine. He made "more friends during that period than during the previous 50 years." Our revelatory incident leading to our conjunction came at the beginning of his metamorphosis, and he told me it was partially responsible for initiating it. The authenticity we were forced to embrace changed us both.

I have already charted the course Dr. Mark took. For me, the experience was a prelude to my owning and frequently again directing my training analysis, and then, as I am doing now, writing about my analytic experiences and opinions with a clear sense of independence.

How Much Authenticity:
Theoretical Considerations

The Place of Authenticity in the
Conjunctive Process

A conjunction is the evolved version of a process where patient and therapist strive for profound relatedness, and work to identify and eradicate each one's distorting effect on the other. The distortions I am referring to result from one partner, mostly nondeliberately, attempting to influence the other through the lens of his developmental deficits, needs, or pathogenic agendas. In the conjunctive process, therapist and patient are thoroughly dedicated to attaining the authentic connectedness I have described, each tolerating enormous personal exposure. That exposure may occur as partners confide their personal thoughts and feelings to one another, their anger or affection, for example. The two may enter even more sensitive territory if the therapist offers information about his personal reactions, or even about his personal life. The timing of these revelations, of course, counts heavily, at some points the risk of exposure being distinctly greater for either or both partners than at others.

Therapist and patient need to see who the other is, his or her needs and motivations, whether he or she is capable of and interested in sweeping self-modification through a process of personal scrutiny and feedback. Their experience determines whether they like, even come to cherish, one another, and how motivated they are to listen to each other. Tom was certain he trusted Russell until he experienced Russell's harsh response to his phone message; I liked Dr. Mark but had little sense of who he was until 6½ years into the analysis when a serendipitous event forced us to depend on each other. With Russell and Tom, the conjunctive process came to a screeching halt as a disjunction intervened; with Dr. Mark the conjunctive process took 6½ years to get started.

I believe that therapy situations missing the arduous, bilateral striving I describe are fated to be inadequately authentic, lacking the depth required for fundamental, sustained therapeutic change. The authenticity I refer to cannot occur without candid self-revelation from both therapy participants. Yet, no one can know in advance what level of verbal or affective disclosure will bring them closer to one another. There is always the problem of distinguishing feigned or forced exposure, which has limited personal value, from that which is authentic (Schafer, 1976). The validity of a newly consummated connection will have to be tested and confirmed, the belief that it is profound often fading for one or both partners over time.

Limits of Authenticity Imposed by the Patient

A view emphasizing mutuality assumes first that the patient's pathology is not so severe that he misreads the therapist's motives for self-exposure and is overwhelmed by the level of emotional openness that results. He needs not to see the therapist's openness as surreptitiously malevolent, regularly mistaking his own motives for the therapist's intentions via projection. With patients like these, the therapist has to be self-contained, sorting between the patient's allegations about the therapist's intentions and his own motivations, working to dispel the patient's projections. Here, the limits to authenticity are imposed by the necessity of the therapist maintaining for the patient a constant and reliable distinction between his world and the patient's. Except for Karen's (chapter 1) projected terror that I could destroy her when she wasn't rigidly controlling me, none of the patients I have described in the book to this point fit this description. While Brittany had a tendency to believe I was critical of her and that I was deliberately withholding my support, she was readily dissuaded from those beliefs when I was forthcoming, as happened, for example, when I finally told her about the effect of the divorce on my current mood.

There are several categories of other, less disturbed, patients who place restrictions, at least initially, on the therapist's ability to be forthcoming, not ready or able to know him accurately. Some patients, for example, insist that the therapist fill the role of an idealized or fantasized parent, resisting the therapist's efforts to disclaim those wished-for traits. Others, with an ''as if'' character style (American Psychiatric Association, 2000), support most anything the therapist does, insisting on the perfection of the therapist and therapy. Another group is characterologically averse to experiencing the troubling feelings that arise from introspection or in intimate relationships, and prefer to remain on the surface. Among the many other categories of patients for whom authenticity is an issue, blocking conjunctive possibilities, there are those who are simply dishonest, unable to feel or introspect because by temperament or as a response to early trauma they learned not to trust anyone. Most interesting about this group is that some of these people can read others' emotions and motives with razor sharp accuracy; what is missing is their capacity to join, care about, and be empathic with another person.

Limits of Authenticity Imposed by the Therapist

Therapists committed to therapeutic authenticity cannot find the technical challenge simple. They are beset with choices, such as whose authenticity should be given priority, the patient's, the therapist's, or the therapy couple's? Which standards should take priority, the therapist's personal standards or those advocated by his professional community and theoretical commitments? Are he and the patient capable of collaboratively evolving a standard of authenticity that will best suit their particular therapy? These are real choices and judgments, faced repeatedly by therapists as they sit with a patient. The patient is likely to have similar questions. Multiply the number of choices for one partner by the choices facing the other, and you have a sense of the complexity and ambiguity created by the authenticity question in psychotherapy.

There are further dilemmas. Should therapists reveal personal information about themselves, such as their actual reactions to their patients, as Russell did with Tom in response to Tom's return phone message? In that case being authentic was about Russell's disapproval, hurting Tom. What about the facts of the therapist's life, the therapist even mentioning his personal habits or political leanings? After all, if a patient knows these details he will understand the therapist more accurately, matching what the therapist knows about him. Add to this list, the therapist's personal preferences, the question of where the therapist draws the line about how much he wants the patient or his practice to encroach on his personal life. Below I review the ways others have decided to deal with the issue of authenticity in psychotherapy and compare it to my own position.

Lewis Aron (1996) and Stephen Mitchell (1997), as representative of modern relational psychotherapy, do not endorse a picture of the therapist being as affectively involved and revealing as I do. They argue that the justifiable asymmetry of the therapy situation would be undermined by assuming so much parity between therapist and patient. They certainly champion the view that patient and therapist mutually influence each other and are limited by their subjectivity in what they can reliably know. Yet, in the interest of keeping the therapy ''analytical'' (Mitchell, 1998, p. 228), they accord the therapist an edge in knowledge and control, even if this advantage is understood to be arbitrary or perhaps irrational (Hoffman, 1998), or it is mainly used to offer the patient a new kind of experience (Mitchell, 1998, p. 52).

Why the seeming inconsistency between Aron's and Mitchell's belief in mutuality and their treatment philosophy? In part, I think, because, given the awesome nature of his charge, it is natural for the therapist momentarily to invoke the authority of his knowledge and experience, even while defending mutuality. After all, someone needs to be there to lead, especially when the going gets rough. But, returning to the topic of subjectivity again, what to do about the limitations it places on the therapist's ability to know anything about the other partner and the therapy with certainty, a condition that, in my view, mandates a fully collaborative therapy?

In my model of psychotherapy, after an arduous, at times years long reciprocal process of verbal and nonverbal knowledge gathering, the therapist—in consultation with the patient—develops a reasonably clear view of who the patient is and what he needs. The therapist then acts. He may make a laserlike statement through words or action, a *leap of inference,* probing to see if the patient's response supports his insight. His move is often bold, creating asymmetry, while protected by trust from the patient. His action forces the therapy in new, sometimes radical, directions. By virtue of his training and experience with therapy, the therapist is especially suited to this function, managing the therapy in a way that supports the conjunctive process. The productive asymmetry I describe, however, is always preceded by a dedicated collaboration emphasizing the wisdom of the patient. Apart from the therapist orchestrating this collaboration and making sure the therapy is progressing, it is the symmetry of my model of therapy that makes it distinctive.

On the other hand, I think tolerating the emotional storms and attaining the degree of authenticity that I believe are required in the therapy sequences leading to the leap of inference, may be so disorienting and stressful for the therapist, and the patient and therapist working together, that it seems almost unrealistic to insist that all therapists practice in this way. Required is that the therapist be able to face the limitations of his capacity to understand and work in a fully authentic way with another person. This recognition is almost always disconcerting, and at times challenges the therapist's confidence. These discoveries are made only slowly, often through a series of disorienting surprises, all testing the therapist's capacity to absorb the unexpected. After all, the authenticity and depth of the relationship Dr. Mark and I ultimately developed, in which we could each discuss our experience of my analysis, and both grew as a result, would be hard to replicate and required a heart attack to get off the ground. Russell's finally coming through for Tom was not a given, because he had a preference for privacy.

Even Karen Maroda (1999), who represents the therapy interaction as open and scruffy, doesn't seem to conceptualize authenticity as a therapeutic objective to the same extent I do. In Maroda's view, no therapist has unlimited patience, or wants a patient to intrude too much into her life. Maroda might not think that the end I advocate is either fully achievable or desirable. She paints the therapeutic situation as open and honest, giving the partners permission for emotions and fallibility. She writes, "Caution against being seduced into the patient's pathological re-creations has been replaced with even-handed discussions of role-responsiveness . . . (Sandler, 1976) . . ." (p. 50). "Of particular interest to me is that the patient must *perceive* that the analyst has given over in order to achieve the therapeutic benefit" (p. 51). Note that while consonant with my own ideas, the emphasis here is on the therapist's, not the patient's role in mutual responsivity, half of the therapeutic picture I would like to create. Also, Maroda qualifies her position by saying: "Equally vital to defining the new psychoanalysis is a reminder of the importance of maintaining the boundaries and exercising appropriate control over the analytic situation" (p. 51). From this statement it seems to me that Maroda's goals became conditional; expressiveness and, by extension, authenticity has its limits. Yet, when Russell disappointed Tom by reprimanding him about leaving his long phone message, he had a patient much less committed to unconditional self-exposure, and Dr. Mark required my full interest and initiative for, my analysis to break free from its heart attack created paralysis.

Taken alone Hoffman's (1998) idea that the therapist's "power" is likely to be used for "affirmation of the patient . . . in an authentic way" (pp. 82–83), could also subtly diminish the patient's contribution to authentic engagement. Hoffman adds, "the ongoing dialectic . . . must emerge from an authentic kind of participation by the analyst rather than from adherence to some technical formulation. The patient may benefit, however, simply from his or her recognition of the sincerity of the analyst's personal struggle with the issue" (p. 84). Hoffman's focus here, like Maroda's, is on the *therapist's* authenticity. The therapist is the one pulling the strings, making the authentic therapy situation possible or not. Or take Lewis Aron (1996): "I believe that it is the emotionally responsive aspects of the analyst's subjectivity that are communicated to the patient through the interventions that lead to its effectiveness" (p. 93). In the same vein, interpretations for Winnicott (1971) have the purpose of offering the patient spontaneous and authentic responsiveness, as well as showing the patient that the therapist is alive and imperfect, thereby emphasizing the therapist's role in that process.

Clearly, but confusingly, the current watchword in modern analytic therapy is *authenticity*. Mitchell (1998) states, "The standard for [relational analysts] is not objectivity or rationality, but candor, oneness and authenticity. The goal is not to circumvent influence, but continually to deconstruct or reflect on it. The analyst's contribution is important not for its transcendent correctness, but for the genuineness of its self-reflective reports on the interaction with the patient . . . [It is the] consensual validation provided by the analyst as an agreed on version of the truth that is useful" (p. 99). However, as I read Mitchell, the therapist is the *ultimate* arbiter of the truth, even if that truth at best has uncertain objective value. When the idea of authenticity is used by Mitchell, Hoffman, Aron, and even Maroda, it indeed refers to the mutuality inherent in a two-person therapy model. On further scrutiny, however, I infer that the mutuality they each advocate has limitations which come from the extent of the control they still accord to the therapist.

My Model: Bilateral Authenticity

In stating that most other authors describe a mutuality that is limited, I want to distinguish my version of the active, involved therapist from the therapist described by these theorists. I advocate extensive bilaterality, the therapist feeling his way into the patient's reality by submitting to and living with enormous amounts of disorientation, engendered in part by repeated shifts of authority between himself and the patient. The therapist also continually checks with the patient to validate his, the therapist's impressions and the usefulness of his actions. In this effort, both the patient's and the therapist's willingness to be authentically self-reflective determines the quality of their final conjunctive process.

W. W. Meissner (1996, p. 214) is the only author I have read so far who carefully defines authenticity. He includes a long list of factors identified with authenticity, among which are wishes, goals, inhibitions, and aspects of internal organization. However, he talks about the patient's, not the therapist's authenticity ("authentic self"). He works within a one-person model, with his emphasis being self-integration through resolution of inner conflict. His use of the term *authenticity* allows for exposure of unattractive parts of the patient, which, when revealed, the patient may fear will limit or put an end to the therapeutic relationship. Note, in addition to authenticity, he talks about a second "value" in therapy, the "quest for the truth" (p. 215). Again, while he ties this goal to the patient's self-understanding, this kind of search for honesty is the one-person counterpart of my emphasis on reciprocal depth probings, creating shared authenticity in the therapeutic process.

Judith Kantrowitz (1996, pp. 207–215) brings the subject of authenticity in psychotherapy full circle. From her Boston Psychoanalytic Institute study, she creates a picture of the typical therapy situation as restricted by the facts that the therapist: (1) idiosyncratically picks areas to work on that he understands and resonates to, excluding other areas for psychological reasons; (2) can become increasingly dependent on the patient for feedback about his irrational contribution to the therapy; (3) benefits, if he can trust the patient; (4) profits, if he can see, respect, and use in the therapy the patient's healthy side and skills, which often exceed his own. In effect, she makes the responsibility for authenticity bilateral. Darlene Ehrenberg's (1992) focus is compatible with Kantrowitz's, when she identifies the authentic interface of therapeutic activity as the "intimate edge" where the therapist and patient influence and transform one another.

Most discussions of authenticity in the literature are implicitly one-sided in their focus, dealing especially with the therapist's authenticity, with Meissner's interest in the patient's authenticity an exception. The progressive attention authors now give to authenticity is a powerful correction to the blank-screen position of traditional psychoanalysis. However, even the contemporary dynamically informed literature describes a greater overriding asymmetry than I think characterizes a therapy that is likely to impact the patient most personally. I hold that unless a state as interpersonally riveting as the one I describe for therapy is attained, the most vital aspects of the patient's subjective world will not be engaged fully and cannot be expected to yield to creative development. The process I am advocating is vitally bilateral, even if there is a conditional division of labor resulting from the therapist's training and experience, as well as the authority deriving from the patient having sought psychotherapy and paying the therapist.

Finding the Balance:
Russell and Dr. Mark

Putting Dr. Mark up against Russell in this chapter makes the essential point about authenticity and how it works in the therapeutic conjunctive process. Authenticity is almost always a good thing. Sometimes it will point to and facilitate the demise of a therapy gone awry; at other times, it is the basic ingredient for a conjunction. When that is the case, it may initiate a long, arduous, and thrilling process of self-examination, or, more exactly, reciprocal self-examinations. It is not the authenticity itself but what is done with it that creates the nuclear level energy release associated with a true therapeutic conjunction. My struggle to understand Brittany and Natalie, and then myself, learning how to depend on them for wisdom and help, and recognizing how, to the detriment of our work, I hid my feelings when I was personally distressed, began our conjunctive processes.

Russell came through powerfully for Tom. He not only tolerated Tom's reaction to his, Russell's, phone message, he encouraged Tom to talk about it. Then, rather than simply apologizing for his insensitivity, he welcomed Tom into his life in a different way. Long after the telephone event, after Tom stopped seeing him regularly, Russell invited Tom for coffee. No fanfare, just a confirmation of his regard for Tom. Still, ironically, Tom waited for a week before returning the call, inadvertently repeating the theme of the therapy sequence described in chapter 4. Tom had invited connection, but when it was offered he balked, draining power from the growing conjunction. With Dr. Mark, all those years of tolerating and getting to know and like each other provided us with a solid foundation on which to build our remarkable transformation, occurring in response to a heart attack that threatened to ruin the analysis. Then, our collaboration and friendship could finally flourish.

Authenticity was a requirement for potential conjunction in all of these cases, the energy that made the power plant generate and ignited the lights, determining how well the therapist and patient could read each other and whether they were interested in building on their developing conjunction. Russell has done his part; the burden, clearly now falls on Tom to understand and rectify his own withdrawal. To do so he will have to unpack the ghosts of early, disappointing relationships, those that failed at just the point he expected the most from them, dropping him into a free fall.

In all these cases, the therapist's willingness to eradicate his preconceptions, therapist and patient entering fearlessly into each other's world, never abandoning the goal of understanding the other for the purpose of helping the patient, led to the personal transformation I advocate, associated with creative development. In Dr. Mark's case, his breaking the rules and ultimately inviting me into his life, at times sharing his celebrations with me, at others confiding his disappointments, provided the fission. The shift began when he signaled me to take over the treatment after he became disabled. When I saw him there, fully exposed, I gathered the courage to disrobe emotionally, also, and grow.

8

Self-Revelation

Self-revelation, judiciously deployed, is a requirement for authentic engagement in psychotherapy. Neither member of the therapy pair can hope to get to know the other very accurately when too much information about that person is held back. Still, what to reveal, how much, and when requires the therapist's dedicated self-scrutiny, part of an exploratory process involving collaboration between the two. Therapist or patient on his or her own may not be able to recognize when their impressions about the need for and the risks of a particular type and level of disclosure are faulty.

One-sided revelation in therapy, when the disclosing partner is the patient alone, is a formula for limited authenticity. True, the patient interacting with a relatively anonymous therapist, the traditional psychoanalytic standard for practice, is for the most part left with his subjective—albeit interactively created—responses, highlighting his internal psychological world for use in therapeutic exploration. But this concept, so far as it goes, fails to take into consideration the vast amount of nonverbal as well as verbal information exchanged between therapy partners. The anonymous therapist can unwittingly represent himself in endless ways: careful, erudite, brave, even a bit reckless, for example, creating a world mainly according to that therapist. No matter how hard a therapist tries to prevent it, that world is likely to be defensively constructed. Dr. Mark, in spite of his attempts to disguise his personal identity, left me with a picture of him as matchless in his sophistication about fine art and books. In part, information about his expertise in these areas was public knowledge, but also these accomplishments inadvertently influenced his demeanor in analysis. Whenever we came close to one of these topics, Dr. Mark became a bit aloof, and I felt foolish about broaching it. The result of these experiences, because of Dr. Mark's injunction against direct self-revelation, was to shut me out from directly knowing about his actual attitudes about these subjects and inhibit me from commenting on them.

The disclosure process in psychotherapy evolves collaboratively. Partners begin by being curious to know one another. Each is blocked by preconceptions about the other partner, as well as by his own projections onto that person. Repeated revelations occur through experience and commentary by the other therapy partner, challenging those impressions. Working in the opposite direction, against full disclosure, is each partner's awareness of the requirements for keeping the other person engaged. The disclosure process then consists of two basic types of considerations: one working in the direction of increased frankness, the other of diplomacy, governing when and how much honesty can be tolerated by the two at any point in time.

The terms *reciprocity, mutuality,* and *authenticity* each apply to the character of the therapy process, as I understand it. Unlike self-revelation, however, reciprocity and mutuality describe conditions under which a therapy occurs, patient and therapist trading initiative in the case of reciprocity and sharing influence with mutuality. Authenticity is a standard of openness and integrity to which therapist and patient commit. Self-revelation, in contrast, refers to a technique, communication used in the service of achieving the other three.

Self-revelation is the most specific and controversial of these categories. It is more meaningful to talk about the degree and type of self-revelation than of authenticity, for example. The potential pitfalls of unregulated self-revelation are easier to picture than those of liberally dosed reciprocity. Technically, for all four categories, the criteria for understanding when and how to apply them are the consideration of the patient's welfare and the success of the therapy. For example, as was illustrated in chapter 7 by the irritation Russell expressed about Tom's phone message, authenticity, when carried to an extreme by therapist, might serve the therapist's needs but not the patient's.

Overall, the subject at this point is still, as it was in chapter 7, how close the therapy pair can and should come to a genuinely open relationship. To what extent are they willing to engage in mutual probing to achieve this end? When all is said and done, what will they have then? My opinion, of course, is that with this probing the two will test to what extent openness can be established in their therapy. If they discover that dedicated openness cannot be tolerated by even one of them, their restricted dialogue, verbal and nonverbal, will lead to limited therapeutic results.

Why Self-Revelation?

Authenticity and self-revelation are givens in modern expressive psychotherapy. According to Freud's (1933/1964) cardinal rule, we expect patients to be as open as possible with us. To parody the subject, I will begin with you as the patient and ask you to tell me anything that comes to mind about your inner life: embarrassment that you are sometimes incontinent, your noticing that my shirt has several coffee stains, a passing thought deriding the fact that I am Jewish. Never mind the content, telling may provide a chute for us to slide into your unconscious.

Perhaps, as the therapist, I should promise that the image of your incontinence won't trouble me, and certainly that I won't make any private judgments about you. But, that would be disingenuous since the thought actually repels me a bit, and when it is mentioned I can't help but think about my uncle Larry who as an Alzheimer's patient progressively lost control of his bodily functions. He was placed in a nursing home where the sounds and stench were almost intolerable, leaving me with hideous memories. So, how revealing should I be about my visceral reactions to your report of incontinence?

To extend my argument, what if I were the one making the judgments, and I had disdainful feelings about coffee stains on your shirt or your religion? When I picture myself being as revealing about my inner thoughts as I expect of you, the imaginary patient I just created, I'm appalled. How often would I ever spontaneously tell a patient he has coffee stains on his shirt, or that I had thoughts about poking fun at his religion?

Add to this argument, the issue of tact. As the therapist who is making these kinds of judgments, the only topics from the selection that I might consider bringing up, and then with great care, are the coffee stains and possibly religion, not my personal reaction to your report of incontinence. For me to even raise these topics with a patient, without disrupting the therapy rapport, would require us to be engrossed in understanding how the therapy relationship affected both of us, and for you, the patient, to be interested in and canny about psychological phenomena.

There is, indeed, a double standard when it comes to self-revelation. Because of the therapist's mandate to keep his revelations useful to the therapy, the subject matter of his revelations to the patient are likely to be a good deal more circumscribed than those he expects from the patient. This situation prevails even if the therapist is revelation-friendly and is committed to the principle of encouraging parity with the patient, actively fostering respect for his wisdom and judgments.

In the created example, the therapist's relative immunity from revelation is based on the requirement that he keep the subject of his revelations meaningful for the treatment, and nonprovocative when the provocation is extraneous to therapy goals. Note also that openness in psychotherapy occurs in ways other than just by the therapist telling details about his inner and outer life. Rather, the communication may be affective, via content, tone, and pace, for example. Even "anonymous" therapists like

Dr. Mark reveal a great deal more about themselves than they may think they do.

From the patient's side, the term *meaningful* generally refers to anything communicated to the therapist: thoughts, feelings, actions, which further the goal of therapeutic exploration and change. Hostile and sexual fantasies also qualify, except when they are used repeatedly to create an atmosphere in which productive therapy is stifled because the therapist or patient feels too much under siege. Marty's constant complaints about his always failing life and my deficiencies eventually affected me like that, at times making it difficult for me to be helpful to him. While generally not acknowledged in the literature, the patient, too, not just the therapist, has responsibility for keeping his or her hostility or sexuality in bounds, and to a degree contributing to a productive-enough atmosphere in therapy.

The therapist's role, though, is more deliberate than the patient's. He needs to make sure the patient can become and remain reflective, the therapist regulating the intensity and flow of the therapy interaction for this purpose. He also assures the interpersonal depth of the work by monitoring its authenticity. As we have seen, authenticity includes the therapist's recognition of when and how his personal limitations, needs, or psychological agendas enter into the therapy, when these factors are generated from within himself or as a response to a role the patient engages him in, and how they affect the therapy rapport. The therapist also needs to monitor when he is unsure of his perceptions and requires feedback from the patient. In all of these situations, revelation of personal experience by the therapist is appropriate, so long as it deepens and enhances the therapy dialogue. Either the therapist or patient, for example, may notice that something is diverting the therapy, moving it from its focus. On examination, the two might discover the therapist has been distracted, as I was with Natalie when I became uneasy with my proposed role of keeping her molestation memories alive after therapy was over. At first, it was clear to Natalie, and then to me, how important my willingness to disclose my distraction was in that situation.

As with the patient, authenticity mandates that the therapist may need to share his inner reactions, aspects of his actual life, and past life, *as these affect the therapy*—but not everything nor all at one time. The reason for self-revelation by the therapist is to clear away rubble from the therapy field and assure depth; for the patient, it is mostly to further the ends of the therapy by making himself known. Both share responsibility for keeping the other engaged, but obviously the therapist carries the larger load here.

Self-revelation, as I understand it, is one means through which the emotional intimacy of the therapy relationship can be achieved and conjunction developed. Used in the service of authenticity, the two partners expose themselves cognitively and affectively in ways that involve interpersonal risk. Therapeutically relevant self-revelation needs to be mutual, one partner signaling the other that he has been felt and heard. This mutual self-revelation begins with the assumption that the other person, as unknown and unfamiliar, needs to be encountered and embraced as fully as possible. That experience always involves confusion and surprise. Each partner must be honest and may have to be blatant enough in his or her delivery so the other person is alerted into seeing who the partner really is.

Telling Alison I cared for her after she began to withdraw was okay but not very powerful. Telling her she had really gotten to me was different and made me see how susceptible I was to believing she was being seductive. She turned my reality upside down and made me pay for the false accusation that she was enticing me, requiring me to appeal for reacceptance. In this sequence, I was compelled to recognize and admit to Alison that I was confused, then that I had been uncomfortable in response to mistaking her attempts to please me for seduction. This is self-revelation with a bite; it affects patient and therapist deeply. The exchange is one that two emotionally sophisticated people would call deeply meaningful. The alternative is cheap confession, providing the semblance but not the substance of depth.

As therapists, we have gone for so many years doing depth therapy with a minimum of self-revelation, why do we need it now? When two climbers died in Yosemite, a husband and a wife, apparently, the husband was being careless. He attached his wife's rope to himself but failed to clamp his own rope to a secure piton. His wife slipped off her ledge and her husband followed, pulled down by the rope. In contrast, the process of tying myself authentically to Alison provided a secure connection for us, because of the multiple places where I painstakingly tied myself to her. Included was thoughtful self-revelation fueling collaboration with Alison, based on our shared process of self-examination. We were bolstered by the substantial granite of my education, training, and my own analysis, and then the solid rock of our commitment to Alison's therapy, with Alison often directing the connecting effort.

Who Is the Therapist, Really?

At times, it may be easier for the patient to guess at the true identity of the therapist than to get him to confirm who he is. Withholding my opinion that Dr. Mark was too preoccupied and depleted to carry on with my training analysis is a case in point. When I asked, several sessions before he actually fell asleep, whether he was dozing, he queried how that thought made me feel, warning I was asking too much. Similar was Russell's message to Tom when he let Tom know that he was overstepping his bounds, and Russell didn't respond specifically to the content of Tom's message about their topic of family of origin. Even in cases like Russell's and Tom's where the therapist is by conviction open to self-revelation, the therapist gets to decide what and how much he tells.

Subtle, seemingly benign withholding by the therapist occurs all the time. A review of clinical examples used so far in this book illustrates my point. I kept to myself initially my real thoughts about Brittany quitting her job. Then, in subsequent sessions, Brittany saw that I had a personal crisis that made it hard for me to be emotionally present. Even after accepting Marty's point about my irritation with him, I continued to shift our focus away from my angry thoughts about his taking advantage of me. With Alison, I withdrew after finding her appealing and seemingly seductive, but not saying anything to her about these feelings, not understanding then why she became so impatient with me. Natalie was initially dismayed about my tentativeness in believing she had been molested as a child and my initial reluctance to yield that position. I have already mentioned my problems, as the patient, in having Dr. Mark not discuss his disability with me. In each instance, where I was the therapist, I initially was reluctant to fully acknowledge my reactions. Even as I began to understand them, I often, in effect, invoked the therapist's "privilege" to be anonymous. Dr. Mark frequently did the same with me in my training analysis, restricting its effectiveness.

Of course, the fact that the therapist has personal needs and reactions creates a predicament for him. From one point of view, the therapist has only agreed to work in therapy with the patient, not be the subject of the therapy. The patient depends on the therapist to be reliable and insightful; at least that is the expectation most patients have when they enter therapy. If the therapist insists on revealing much of what the therapy situation and the patient elicits for him, the patient has cause to worry that the emphasis will shift to the therapist, and the therapy pair will be distracted from their work for the patient. The asymmetry inherent in the picture of the not-very-revealing therapist makes sense when viewed from a one-person therapy model and in that framework can seem quite defensible, as if the therapist is the only rock to which the piton is attached.

The problem, of course, is that the partners are often not completely aware of what is going on in the therapy. Seeing the part contributed by the therapist is seldom completely possible without a reliable collaboration, where patient and therapist provide incisive feedback to each other. Yes, a therapist needs to be professional, trained, self-reflective, as safe a climbing partner as possible. Unfortunately, this role is fraught with pitfalls, the most basic of which is that no human being can ever be certain that he or she has an accurate view of his or her own inner life, or the interpersonal situation in which they are embroiled. To deal with this problem, the therapeutic duo is forced to develop their hypotheses and see if they work. Irwin Hoffman (1998), Donnel Stern (1997), and Christopher Bollas (1991), for example, describe the use of the patient's and therapist's associations and subjective experiences to develop these hypotheses. But the heart of the matter is what the therapist knows about his own needs and reactions, and when and how he shares this information with the patient. If the pair does not develop a storehouse of information about the therapist, as well as the patient, I contend they will become progressively lost from each other. And the problem is that therapists, including myself, frequently do not like the idea of being so self-revealing; it is uncomfortable, to say the least.

Judith Kantrowitz (1996), in her study of the "patient's impact on the analysis" at the Boston Psychoanalytic Institute, demonstrates how frequently the wish for anonymity determines an analyst's behavior and the benefits to the analysis of overcoming this preference. Kantrowtiz's observations are so central to our subject, they are worth an extended quotation:

> The sense of safety is, of course, much higher for the analyst, since the patient's material, not the analyst's, is the focus. The analyst is also less vulnerable because he or she is not expected to reveal thoughts, affects, fantasies, and reactions to the patient . . . the first jolt of recognition of being caught in an emotional reaction causes [the analyst] distress. The analyst sees that he or she is not in conscious control of his or her affective reaction to the patient. . . . The patient, however, unlike the analyst, has no reason to be empathically attuned or responsive to the personal meanings stirred in the analyst in reaction to him or her. . . . Potentially, however, the process of working through is [also] available to the analyst . . . the

actual experience of work is not so different [for the analyst from the work with the patient] once the analyst becomes aware of what has been rekindled. . . . Yet, if the analysis goes well, a rapport develops between patient and analyst in which the analyst can, and does, increasingly count on the patient with his or her ever-increasing capacities to be reliable and trustworthy. . . . This kind of person . . . has a great impact on the analyst. . . . The analytic situation is potentially one of great intimacy. (pp. 214–219)

Kantrowitz's view, like mine, is that the analyst (the study involved only psychoanalysts), in part through self-revelation, may usefully become the subject of the analytic dialogue and be legitimately helped within the analysis, ultimately, for the sake of the patient. Kantrowitz's notion of the two becoming important to each other, as well as developing great intimacy, reflects her interest in the forces joining therapist and patient as they work together therapeutically.

Of course, not everybody feels as passionate about the value of symmetry between patient and therapist as Kantrowitz and myself. The debate among modern dynamic therapists about authority and influence in the therapy process is heated. The following citations concern authority. To Irwin Hoffman (1996, 1998), overvaluing the analyst's authority is "ironic," because of the analyst's participation in the analytic interaction; he adds that analytic authority is altogether losing its traditional sanction. Owen Renik (1998, 1999) sees no theoretical justification for according analysts sagelike status. In contrast, Stephen Mitchell (1998) says, "One of the central features of the analyst's role is his or her function in preserving the relationship as analytic and conducting and protecting the inquiry. While the analysand's role entails a giving oneself over to the experience of the analytic process, the analyst . . . must also pay attention to holding and protecting the process" (p. 27). "For many patients, the most difficult thing about the analytic relationship is precisely the differential importance analyst and analysand have in each other's lives" (p. 29).

The issue of self-revelation is very much tied to one's point of view about symmetry in the therapy situation. The current debate is reminiscent of the older one between blank screen traditionalists and more interactive analysts, but with some differences. Today, almost all analytic therapists advocate some degree of mutuality, but they are divided as to how much authority should remain in the analyst's hands and how open the analyst should be, how mutual the analysis. My own position is to question the value of a therapy, and even a formal psychoanalysis, in which the therapist or analyst is not, *within the scope of the therapeutic objectives,* subject to the kind of probing the patient experiences. The potential for developing mutual understanding and respect is then likely to be circumscribed, and hence the scope and depth of the therapeutic procedure becomes limited.

The Debate about Self-Revelation

Returning to the observation that most modern therapists champion the idea of mutuality in therapy, it is interesting that the topic of self-revelation by the therapist is so controversial. I am offering a brief literature review to make clear how this debate seems to rise and fall on apparently small distinctions, and to reveal these differences as potentially reflecting wide variations in the way therapists work.

Last week when speaking to my analyst friend Jessica about self-revelation, I discovered that she consistently considers how direct information about herself will affect each patient in the therapy, relying heavily on the "vast amount of information exchanged effectively" to make her determinations. There are some patients who "learn a good deal" about her for reasons particular to that individual. There are others who "need to know little or nothing and who would find such knowledge a burden." As well, whenever I think it will encourage mutual disclosure, make myself and the patient better acquainted, I do give information about myself: my age, marital status, information about my children or my parenting, for example. I provide this information carefully, testing to make sure that the therapy process will be furthered, not inhibited by making it available. As I selectively review the literature in the following paragraphs it is important to recognize that while the way therapists describe their philosophy and techniques may make them sound similar, the differences in the way they practice may be substantial. Worth noting, also, is that there are a wide range of opinions about how freely self-revelation should be used, even on the part of those who are revelation-friendly. On the contrary, the asserted differences may be trivial, while the picture they give of their positions on self-revelation may nonetheless be confusing and inconsistent and thus hard to quantify.

Lewis Aron (1996) regards self-revelation in dynamic therapy as "an inevitability, . . . not an option" (p. 84). However, his point of view about self-revelation is consistent with his ideas about asymmetry. He and Stephen Mitchell (1998) see the analyst as fundamentally having the responsibility of maintaining the analytic situation. They believe this kind of asymmetry is appropriate and helpful and, therefore, needs to be preserved. The analyst decides how much to tell about himself, not wanting to focus analytic attention unduly on himself.

Aron's position seems somewhat ambivalent to me: He embraces mutuality and intimacy in analysis, while defending limited asymmetry in revelation. He agrees with Hoffman (1994) that, "It is precisely the protection offered the analyst by the asymmetric position of relative anonymity that allows the analyst to function at his or her best as an analyst . . ." (p. 247). At the same time he says, "I am suggesting that one way of thinking about the quality of our 'expertise' is that it is part of our function as analysts to allow ourselves to be and (through our own 'training analysis') to prepare ourselves to be emotionally vulnerable with our patients."

Aron contrasts his point of view with Karen Maroda's (1991, 1999), whose writing on self-disclosure he calls the "most thoughtful . . . and thoroughgoing of any analytic theorist's to date'' (p. 243). However, he sees Maroda's goal as gaining information about the patient, identifying influences unknown to her, rather than about the analyst's participation in the process. According to Aron, Maroda's recommendations are to wait with disclosure until finding out its meaning to the patient. Disclosure begins with the analyst's countertransference, that is, her ''immediate affective experience,'' with the analyst revealing only later in the analysis ''the origin of these feelings in their own personal life.'' Aron believes, instead, in discovering the meaning of disclosures after they are spontaneously offered to and processed by the patient.

Indeed, Maroda's more recent writings (1999) continue to reflect her differences with Aron and Mitchell. Consistent with her views in her earlier book, *The Power of Countertransference* (1991), she advocates, ''self-disclosure when done at the patient's initiative'' (p. 26). However, like Aron, she complicates this picture. Maroda also describes the analytic process as an ''emotional giving over or surrender . . . the heart of the exchange [being in] . . . the mutual expression of deep feeling, and in the experience of shared vulnerability—not in the accumulation of personal information'' (p. 28). But in speaking about the limits she believes need to be set on self-disclosure, she further says, the analyst requires some privacy (p. 29), ''[or] patients can very quickly begin to wonder if you are reversing roles with them'' (p. 59).

Others who write from a position similar to Aron's and Mitchell's, but seem somewhat more self-revelation friendly, include Kenneth Frank (1997) who describes the constant flow of the analyst's inadvertent self-revelations and the value of dealing with them collaboratively. Samuel Gerson's (1996) observations, similar to Frank's, are that the analyst is always communicating about himself through his actions, mood, and errors.

Even more committed to self-revelation, Owen Renik (1995) takes the position that anonymity in analysis is altogether impossible, that any attempt to maintain the role of an "anonymous" analyst invites idealization and a subsequent fall from grace. He is skeptical that analysts can devise a stance that can deconstruct the analyst's undeserved authority. He therefore proposes that, "it is useful for the analyst consistently to try to make sure that his or her analytic activity is understood as fully as possible by the patient. . . . I am not advocating imposing one's thinking upon a patient, but I am suggesting that one's thinking would be made available" (p. 482). He describes his kind of self-revelation as "basic to an attitude in which the clinical enterprise is conceived of as a true collaboration between peers" (p. 492).

References to Renik's work are curiously absent from Hoffman's (1998) and Mitchell's (1997) books, perhaps reflecting their differences with him. Aron criticizes Renik for not adequately respecting the need for "an optimal degree of" (p. 239) analytic anonymity and for asymmetry. He says Renik advocates that we "not only disregard the principle of analytic anonymity, but that we must actively and forcefully contradict it" (p. 236).

I am firmly aligned with Renik's view regarding anonymity. Ideally, I see every reason for the therapist to be as fully self-revealing as can be used therapeutically by the patient. Also, I concur with Maroda and Renik, that the therapist should not indiscriminately reveal everything and needs to be thoroughly vigilant about the effects of revelation on the patient and therapy. In this vein, I somewhat prefer Maroda's "wait and see the effect of the revelation" stance to Aron's more nonspecific emphasis on spontaneity. Yet I agree with Aron that a major use of revelation by the therapist is to understand the therapist's impact on the therapy process.

Overall, in spite of points of agreement with them, my goal in using self-revelation is somewhat different from most of the other authors I have named. All, like me, are interested in achieving what they call an authentic mutuality between patient and therapist. Perhaps Maroda is most passionate about that end.

However, in many cases that mutuality is limited by the therapist's prerogatives to withhold information and in other ways regulate the therapy process. While called by the same name, *mutual* or *collaborative,* for example, the procedure may be quite different in different hands. Some therapists tell a lot about their lives and are chatty, others show little affect, some are flexible about time and payment, others not.

In my view, apart from providing valuable information about the psychology of each participant, the primary purpose of self-revelation by the therapist is to clear away interpersonal debris, the anxieties and blind spots that prevent the development of a committed, trusting relationship. Therapy with Alison might have come to a halt had I not been willing to talk about my misreading her behavior as seductive. Marty would never have continued his work with me if I had not acknowledged my error in bringing up his reduced fee, and the irritation behind my making that statement. Consistent with my picture of the revelation process, this relationship, and the personal growth and change that goes into building it, is powerfully bilateral. The flow of information, care, and indeed, inspiration is solidly in both directions, between therapist and patient.

When I can be, I am very real with my patients. I like the idea of their getting to know who I am and hope they will come to organize their therapy experiences around realistic notions about me as a human being. I trust that we will still be able to collaboratively work out a productive exploratory process under these conditions, the patient's needs and fantasies potentially being robust enough to become manifest as clearly as they might otherwise. In the end, exposed to the principles of revelation associated with the conjunctive method of therapy, the patient has a real life ally in the therapist, not just a technical one.

What Is the Therapist to Do?

Back to incontinence and derisive thoughts about religion. If my patient's provocative words or behavior contributes to my thinking, do I have to let him know that has happened? If I don't tell him, how might the therapy suffer or even benefit? The answer, so far as I can tell, starts out as simple and becomes complex. Try to imagine a serious friendship or a marriage fraught with thousands of little deceptions, ways of avoiding your partner getting to know the attractions and rages you feel throughout the day, especially when they relate to the partner. The relationship, while polite, rests on illusion. Neither partner yet knows what it would be like if he and the partner really got to know each other, and they will not unless they engage in the demanding developmental task of understanding each other.

Now, step up to psychotherapy, the singular relationship in one's experience where the ground rules begin with the assumption that the two will *strive* toward total honesty. What happens when the anchorperson in that relationship maintains a veil of secrecy, while the other is required to be thoroughly self-revealing? The whole situation begins to feel shabby, at least to me. I'm not sure I would want such an unknown person anchoring the rope that controls my safety. I wonder how I could even guess about the risks of slipping off the ledge in that situation. Relationships, therapy, are precarious enough, given their subjective nature.

A major part of therapy, then, is like a shared rock-climbing course: getting the right equipment, learning how and where to anchor your pitons, understanding risks and responsibility for identifying and overcoming hazards, and mainly working together on the most difficult technical project you may ever undertake. In the process both grow, in part because of the trials that are constantly encountered, working ever more intuitively and smoothly together.

One source of complexity, a way that self-revelation can backfire, is when it leads to the Russell-like situation described in chapter 4, the discovery that the other is fallible, even unappealing or dangerous to you. Here, a seemingly promising relationship may crash on the rock pile of a near-fatal disjunction. Or, the discovery of such a disjunction may, as was the case with Alison, signal the beginning of a much deeper reaching, transformative process. As I discussed earlier, the requirement of committed self-revelation might be too much for the therapist or patient to bear. It may feel weird, wrong, shabby, self-effacing, burdensome—in sum, unprofessional—to be that open, especially as a therapist. Yet, in my opinion, the larger risk often comes when the therapist is not forthcoming at the precise moment the patient needs him to be, because the omission is certain to put distance between them, thereby cutting into the honesty of the relationship.

Having said that, I do contend, without contradicting my position, that there are situations where self-revelation by the therapist is clearly contraindicated. Examples include work with patients who are in danger of feeling invaded by the therapist as intimacy builds, and who risk becoming confused about the difference between the therapist's needs and opinions and their own. There are also times when a patient is in so much psychic pain that all attention should be exclusively on him. Actually, moments when all the attention is in one direction and self-revelation is inappropriate arise microscopically and frequently in almost every therapy hour. At these points, the therapist (and at other times the patient) takes over and leads, at least until he has some indication that his certainty is ill-founded. I have already talked about the different tolerance people have for paying attention to another. Brittany thrived by hearing about my inner processes. It reoriented her and reduced her own self-criticism; speaking on that level also matched her remarkable capability for thinking psychologically. In contrast, if I spoke about my inner life or countertransference response for more than a few minutes Marty concluded I had grown tired of him and became irritable.

Finally, there is the traditional admonition that the therapist not bring his life directly into the therapy dialogue, except perhaps to reflect on his subjective experiences as they provide information about the patient's inner processes (Racker, 1968; Tansey & Burke, 1989). So much has been written about how such a stance itself involves a communication (Gerson, 1996; Stone, 1961), as well as the epistemological problems it may create (Spence, 1987, 1993), making the case that there is something powerfully restrictive in the notion of an analytic attitude "protecting" the therapy or analysis (Aron, 1996; Mitchell, 1998). In my view, the decision of how disclosing a therapist should be is the end product of a dialectical exchange between patient and therapist, where each is informed by the other about therapeutic matters as they arrive at points of consensus.

Once the relevant information is exchanged, the therapist and patient are prepared to move forward, with the therapist usually able to comment, and as often, to act, advancing the newly established direction of the therapy through a leap of inference. Over time, the process of reciprocal information gathering brings the therapist to the point where he feels relatively certain about what the patient needs, what the patient's latent goals in therapy are. The therapist formulates his insight into words or action. By action, I am referring to the persuasion with which the therapist makes his comments, as well as a range of behaviors from inquiries to giving advice, all with the objective of furthering the therapy goals. The leap of inference is creative in that it goes beyond the edge of what is known, taking advantage of all the latent information gleaned to that point. Implicit in the idea of the leap of inference is another nontraditional notion: the belief that the therapist should take responsibility for actively moving the therapy forward.

When the Therapist Says Too Little

The overarching problem in conducting an authentic therapy, as I see it, is in the natural reluctance of therapists to tell much of what they really think and who they are. The subject of self-revelation is made more complex by the need to strive for a depth of connection unequaled in other professional activities, while at the same time keeping to the goals of the therapy as they are continually revised. Also, in psychotherapy, the professional is a major actor in the drama, *required* to reflect on his own thinking and behavior. These challenges are compounded when therapists who are willing to talk about themselves stop questioning whether they are telling enough. In all of the therapies I have reported in this book, I felt I was being honest with the patient from the start. Frequently, I did not recognize that I was withholding information, only to be informed later by the patient that I was. Brittany and Alison, for example, became aware of my distancing before I did; Marty sensed my irritation, informing me about it; and Natalie became impatient with my slowness to believe fully in her claim she had been molested.

In the following two examples, I eventually discovered how I failed to confide information required to deepen the therapy. In the first case, people other than the patient and myself facilitated my progress. In each case, I, as the therapist, had to tolerate a substantial degree of controlled disorientation, and an exploratory process in which I was likely to learn something personal about myself that I would find embarrassing or even shocking.

Case Illustration—Max

Max, at age 68, came to me for help with his inability to speak in public. He was impressively successful as a businessman and the parent of grown children. In March 1999, a psychologist colleague and I presented our work with Max to a seminar made up of experienced therapists. I prepared the case presentation meticulously: Max's background of neglect because of his family's poverty, having to flee from Romania to Central Russia and then further east prior to age 16, the events following the killing of his family, and his joining the underground to fight the invading Nazis. I went over and over the details to be sure that I would not have difficulties with the presentation.

The setting was benign: lunch with an old friend who was part of the group, as well as meeting up with my 24-year-old graduate school bound daughter who had decided to attend the seminar. My colleague, who had consulted with Max and myself, presented first. His talk was elegant. When my turn came I began my well-rehearsed presentation without the use of notes. I decided not to use my carefully constructed notes at the last minute because something about the presentation I was to give felt inauthentic to me. I started out well, remembering all I had to say. However, the moment I noticed I was doing well, I mysteriously lost my place in the talk, and forgot everything I planned to say.

I had no choice but to reach out to the group and ask them for help. A friend, Gaye, suggested I might be feeling too empathic with Max and guilty about talking about him in public. I discounted that suggestion, but progressively, the consensus grew: I was talking about someone who had been through the horrors of the Holocaust, and the power of the memories was perhaps too big for me or him to handle in public. The group's consensus was that I was much more important to Max than I realized, and he to me, and that the kinds of experiences we were talking about were inexpressible. They suggested that the "inauthenticity" I felt, and later my blocking, related to my wish to protect Max's previously well-guarded privacy. I began to think the group members might have a point, even though I was not yet able to comprehend the extent to which Max's memories and his sharing them with me had affected me.

At the end of the talk, I felt thoroughly confused. Several people said it was one of the best presentations they had ever heard, citing the way I had revealed my helplessness to the group's members and then used them to discover the power of my involvement with Max and his dependence on me. I still felt humiliated, as if I should have been in better control. Months later, I was still somewhat embarrassed about my having become disabled at that meeting, in spite of the acclamation of so many group members.

A week or so after the conference, Max came back from his vacation. I found myself sinking into a style I had developed in my work with him, best described as impassioned encouragement, always something like "Max, you're smart, you can do it." This time, however, I stopped myself. I remembered what I had learned in my presentation before the group. Max needs me to be constant and thoroughly reliable. His parents underestimated the Nazis, with the entire family, except for Max, being killed as a result. Max keeps me on edge—it's always as if it's our last session—in order to warn me that he cannot risk my making a mistake. His trauma, part of which he has exported to me through projective identification, was horrible, inexplicable. In turn, everything rides on my coming through for him.

Max talked extensively about the Serbian crisis. Max said Milosevic had planned it all in order to get rid of non-Serbians, right up to provoking the Americans to bomb Kosovo. I was impressed by Max's discernment. No one else speaking on the subject even came close to suggesting such a powerful explanation. Max's thinking seemed profound.

Drawing on the discussion from the conference, I said, "Max, I think you can make sense out of things that none of us can; we can't know them, we weren't through the kind of horror you experienced." Max became somber. "No, none of you can understand it." He then proceeded to analyze the whole Serbian situation in horrifying detail for the first time, referring back to all the atrocities he personally witnessed during World War II: "In war, that is what you do, anything to win, but the experience with Milosevic is not like it was with the Nazis. Think about what it's like to know that people are going to come to your village and kill all the people. In Serbia, they are mostly forcing them to leave their homes." He was disqualifying my attempt to "empathically" compare the current Balkan situation with his experience with the Nazis.

Suddenly, I could see it all. I knew now why Max had been so successful, rarely making a mistake in business and amassing a huge fortune. On the business front, he was as unemotional and clear about people's motives as he had been in the war. I also could see the cause of his shyness, especially his anxiety about speaking in public. "Max, if you said, or even thought, what you know about people—in any of these situations—you would be so condemning, so misfitted to the excessively polite society in which we live, that you would always feel in danger of being misunderstood by an outsider. The truth, Max, is that you are one of the toughest guys around; and you can't help it, you can't go back to being naive."

"Okay, if I'm so wise, then why are my kids so soft, choosing weak mates?"

I answered, "You wanted to spare them the horror that you knew—to make their lives tolerable. We all do that, Max. Who would want to see the world the way you were forced to?"

The experience in the group, enabling me to discover the extent of my involvement with Max, required two major steps. First, the group showed me what I was missing: the critical role I played protecting Max from making mistakes in his life and, thus, how I was designated by him to be the father who finally would not let him down. In Max's mind, each error, like his family's miscalculation in not fleeing the Nazis, could be lethal. Second, to prepare me for my function in his life, Max imbued me with anxiety equivalent to his own. When I worked with him, I always felt like I was on the verge of failing. He kept switching topics, making our work seem random and trivial; he repeatedly told me that he did not know why he kept coming to therapy. At the end of each session, he would simply get up and leave. All emotion would disappear from his voice; he never said good-bye. I would feel stunned, wondering whether I would ever see him again.

In parallel with the role I played for Max, the group became my protector and facilitator, although I originally reacted to them as if they were my deadliest enemy. I revealed my dilemma to the group, at first nonverbally, through losing my place, and then verbally, asking them to reorient me. In so doing, I played out my own experience with Max. I first showed them how he made me feel on the edge of disaster, and then risked talking with them about it. Together, we inferred that the tense atmosphere I at first created in the lecture hall on that day was a replay of Max's experience: always about to lose his bearings when placing his welfare in someone else's hands. Also, he was frightened to speak out loud since he had seen so much horror, and was uncertain whether he and I could handle this experience. Revealing my dilemma to the group, needing to make sure that in speaking about Max I was in safe hands, turning the trust he placed in me over to potential enemies who could misuse it, as well as recounting memories that had been placed in my safe keeping, gave the group the information they needed to help me find words for my experience with Max. Then, in our therapy sessions, I was able to give Max permission to be who he really was underneath his anxiety and reticence: tough, having learned to survive in the face of extreme risk, and riddled with memories that were too much for him to bear.

Natalie after Termination of Therapy

By the end of therapy, Natalie and I had developed a powerful bond. We had struggled to understand and accept her history of sexual molestation, though for a long time each of us failed to comprehend the weight of what happened to her. We agreed to communicate regularly, with me continuing as witness to her molestation revelations. People who have been traumatized need a witness to feel authentic. They need to believe they haven't misrepresented the events that have caused them so much pain (Auerhahn & Peskin, 2003). Natalie would continue to keep a diary and record her dreams, these activities together with her connection to me potentially mediating future periods when she might have feelings of aloneness and despair.

At termination all went smoothly, at first. Several months after therapy ended, however, I became preoccupied by my divorce. Natalie already knew my wife and I had separated, but I judiciously kept my turmoil to myself. Without realizing it, I

became less regular in my posttherapy contacts with her. I minimized the significance of my change, rationalizing that our past
accomplishment, our shared knowledge of her experience, would
suffice to maintain the integrity of our connection for the time
being.

Privately, Natalie wasn't satisfied. Of course, like with Brittany, the fact of a past consensus wasn't an acceptable substitute
for a present vital connection. But overtly, when I became less
regular in my contacts with her, even by phone, she did her best
to be tolerant. As she told me later, she stopped leaving messages
for me and just waited for my periodic calls. Although I had
become a passionate advocate for ongoing witnessing for victims
of trauma, I had lost sight of recognizing that I was not carrying
through with my own conviction. As you might guess, initially
things got worse for Natalie. A year after we stopped regular
sessions, one of Natalie's daughters was seriously, but not permanently, injured in a car accident, more bad luck in a life that
already seemed cursed. Then there was a recrudescence of Natalie's same affective cycle, periods of normalcy followed by depressions and new outbreaks of eczema, unexplained episodes
of discouragement where all she wanted to do was sleep. Yet for
her, I would learn, there was no clear evidence of what exactly
was provoking these symptoms. Her daughter's car accident and
then one of her own were adequate short-term explanations, but
not sufficient, from her point of view, to explain how precisely
the new symptoms replicated the old. She was thrown back on
the possibility that it was hormonal, a precipitous fall of estrogen
associated with perimenopause, wreaking emotional havoc.
Since at that point even intermittent contact had become temporarily burdensome for me, I too readily accepted her explanation.

Even though the frequency of our contacts declined, I remained minimally dutiful, calling Natalie periodically and leaving messages knowing she would not answer her phone
personally. One more phone conversation after 8:00 P.M. would
be enough to destroy a rare night of peace for me, generous
enough from me because I did not charge for these phone calls.

Strange, how distance developed so efficiently following the closest and most elevating moments only a year or so earlier. I was preoccupied with my own difficulties, not really aware of my shift.

Natalie, of course, figured it out. She suggested that something was wrong. She was concerned about me, so she did not want to push. So far as she knew, nothing had changed conceptually. We had agreed I would maintain a vigil, guarding the scene of a child's rape, making sure no one could post a sign pretending this was simply a scenic vista. She realized my current pain was in some way equivalent to her own and tried her best to leave me alone. Yet, she was in anguish, and I was inaccessible.

Here is where I did not call Natalie for about a month, even though I knew, intuitively, she was suffering. My sense of self-preservation kept me from calling her. I needed a private space to manage my own turmoil. When we eventually talked, Natalie was quite clear; she was depressed, seized with an inexplicable episode of despair. Still she made no pointed demand, no pressing inquiry.

"Steve, I'm awfully sorry. I know you've been honest with me up to this point, but I think something is missing. You're not entirely there. I know by now you don't mean to do that, but I believe it's true. It helps enough to know a bit about your nonprofessional life, so I don't take it personally."

Of course, she was right. I had convinced myself that I was being authentic in two directions: committed to our agreement that I would stand watch over her experience, while, at the same time, dealing with my own personal crisis. In a brief message from Natalie a few days later, her suffering finally reached me. I could feel the bleakness that was developing between us. At this point I pushed; I understood something was very wrong. I said I realized I had drifted away from the connection I had promised her.

"Sorry, Steve. I know your life is anything but easy, but I don't know how to understand or deal with my depressions. I'm surprised that you haven't told me more about your own situation, since obviously it is getting in the way.''

I shouldn't have been surprised by Natalie's clarity. Working at that depth doesn't allow for pullbacks. Depth equals depth, and nothing less. Unfortunately, I had pulled back, my life at that time seeming to depend on that kind of privacy. Natalie, in turn, was as lost to me emotionally as she had been connected to me earlier.

Here was the perfect opportunity for me to be open with Natalie. With a modicum of empathy and initiative and enough honesty, I could have easily put us back on target. But, while I returned at once to calling her more regularly, it took longer for me to reveal to her even scant details of what was happening to me. At first, I was as uncomfortable being honest with Natalie as I am being open with you the reader.

The end of this story is comforting, but ironical, a lesson to me about the potential importance of a therapist being open with patients when he experiences a life crisis. Of course, I told Natalie more about my divorce situation and its current effect on me, and she breathed a powerful sigh of relief. At least you wanted to be there for me, and you've returned, she said. We met several times, renewing our connection, and deepening it as a result of my being judiciously candid about my own torment, based on the reinforced requirement of authentic and necessary self-revelation. Before many months went by, however, Natalie grew paradoxically less needful of my calling regularly. She was finding that she liked her growing ability to run her own life, with me receding to the ''background.''

Two years after this period, contacts have been regular but have decreased to approximately one every few months. At the same time she has moved closer to friends, creating several tight relationships with other women for the first time in her life. She has found ways to make her work situation, which had been oppressive because of a hard to please hospital board, more manageable, regulating her professional time more carefully than ever before. Her older daughter, whose unsociable behavior worried her, began to do better. And Natalie's depressions became even less debilitating and fewer. These changes, we agree, were predicated on shifts in my behavior, but otherwise were a bit magical seeming since they did not occur according to any therapeutic plan. Because as a hospital administrator Natalie is a member of my extended professional community, I have evidence that the changes I have catalogued are as real as she claims they are, and I know they have been sustained. Also, they do not seem to be a product of her simply pulling herself together under the pressure of forced autonomy, based on my temporary abandonment, as she is still quite willing to call me when she needs to talk and checks in with me informally.

The magic, as we both understand it now, was my willingness to reconnect and then reveal private information about my personal struggles, restoring Natalie's faith in the depth of our connection and my commitment to our pacts, the preservation of her memories of molestation and attention to her abandonment fears. From that point in our work, her progress can be explained by my trusting Natalie to move on, in spite of the decline in our anticipated contacts deriving from my partial disablement. Natalie already felt acknowledged. Meaningfully, she was convinced that simply by being tolerant of my reduced availability, she was a support to me, a role opposite to the passive victimized one she had known from childhood. Even being a psychotherapy patient had some sense of victimization attached for her. Interestingly, during this part of our story, Natalie found herself in an interaction with me that in ways mirrored mine with the afflicted Dr. Mark. She took over her life and proved to herself that she could be in control. Even better, she did not lose me during that process; rather our rapport deepened, based on my eventual willingness to discuss my temporary debilitation with her and then my return, supported by our growing conviction that she could succeed.

Why Self-Revelation?

Revealing my experiences with Max and Natalie to the reader is, at the least, risky and uncomfortable for me. I find myself in a dilemma similar to the one I am often in clinically. If I am truly open with my patient, I may be breaking the rules by which I was trained; if I am not, my patient will know for certain, and will feel deceived, and then limit what he or she shares with me.

Max is now writing a book about his life, an idea we came up with a few years ago but that went nowhere until my experience in the conference gave me the courage to insist that he get started. Natalie is usually symptom free. How did we arrive at such points? In both cases, there were powerful, overriding pulls for conjunction, with Max wanting me to succeed in helping him overcome his pessimism about depending on someone, and Natalie progressively showing me the details of her trauma. There were also massive disruptions, with Max nearly firing me every hour and Natalie incessantly testing my loyalty, even before I emotionally abandoned her. In the end, with each of them, I needed to embrace and then acknowledge my part in our disturbance receiving feedback before I and they could move on.

In Max's case, I used the group to tell me what Max could not. At first, Natalie gently cornered me, until I could see how I was deceiving myself into thinking I was being a loyal and fully engaged, ongoing witness to her trauma, as well as adequately meeting her abandonment concerns. Only then could I begin to tell her how the divorce was sapping the attention I promised to pay to our pacts, setting her free to progress. Max will write his book, opening his justifiably obscured past to others as long as he has a personal connection in his current life that feels unequivocally authentic to him. In some ways, Natalie's requirements are similar to Max's, as she continues to test the authenticity of my commitment to bearing witness to her traumatic childhood and remaining vigorously committed to her welfare, to not abandoning her as her parents did. But in Natalie's case, authenticity also now means my trusting her to conduct her own life competently and placing myself on a more equal footing with her, a human being who is fallible and subject to life disruptions not different from her own. Also extremely important to Natalie was that I accepted her attention to my need for relief from her clinical demands and benefited from her support, just as Dr. Mark had with me.

The End Point of Therapy, a Process

So, here we are, Max, Natalie, and I, evolving. The most far-reaching goal therapist and patient are striving for is creative change eventuating in creative development, in directions entirely unique to each member of the therapy pair. The end point of therapy is a process, not a fixed set of ideas or attitudes. Being secured to yourself and another person as conjunction kindles is a thrilling experience that is continually demanding, and frequently transformative.

Putting the past in perspective and seeing how it relates to the present invariably helps. Finding ways that the patient has been self-defeating realigns the pieces so they work more precisely together. The question most therapists I know are left with after 10 or 20 years in practice is why some therapies go so far and others remain limited, or, God forbid, affect the patient negatively. When therapy works, when patient and therapist are conjunctive, therapists may not be able to articulate exactly what made the difference, but they are aware of an experience that affected them and their patients deeply and immutably.

Research, my own projects included, has something to offer (Frankel, 1995, pp. xvi–xvii, 30–37). Results from the many studies assessing therapeutic process put the quality of the therapeutic relationship first in explaining a therapy's success (Bachrach, Galatzer-Levy, Skolnikoff, & Waldron, 1991; Bergin & Garfield, 1994; Roth & Fonagy, 1996). According to Robert Wallerstein's (1986) summary of the Menninger project, both supportive and expressive therapies were shown to be effective, complementing the research on the psychotherapy process. For me, common features of a successful therapy experience include both participants striving to know and understand each other, the integrity of reporting and self-representation by the two, the constant struggle to find, understand, and mutually resolve disjunctions, and a commitment to strive continually to go beyond the edge of one's experience.

Self-revelation by both people is integral to this activity. How else, other than through shared experience, intuition, and perhaps clues from underground, like dreams and associations, can they get to know each other? Ideas about where the two are in their work are constructed, believed, and discarded regularly, but in a forum, where self-revelation leading to consensus ultimately rules. Authority changes hands frequently, even if the therapist generally has the edge in deciding when shifts might occur. These moves are the result of a potent flow of verbal and nonverbal cues. To compensate for the therapist's technical authority, the patient is generally the expert on the subject at hand, his inner life and most pressing desires. The end product is a pair of better functioning human beings, both internally and in the world, with the two growing together creatively, and a therapeutic partnership capable of supporting an open verbal and nonverbal dialogue.

The process I am referring to, the state of mind that is the hallmark of a successful therapy and its end point, provide the conditions for ongoing personal development. In the next chapter, I will organize the steps in the conjunctive process leading to its most desired result, creative change and creative development.

9

Toward Creative Change and Development: The Conjunctive Sequence

The hallmarks of the conjunctive process, uniting therapist and patient, are struggle and discovery. The therapy partners strive to maintain and improve the authenticity of the therapy bond, find and mitigate their psychological agendas and personal limitations, as well as embrace the resources each partner brings to the therapy. Together, they hope to learn what the patient actually needs at each point in treatment. Therapist and patient are always working not to let the integrity of their connection deteriorate. Discovery through therapy is not just of a self and partner different from the one each thought was there, but of a way of being, an entirely new subjective experience created together with the other person, one which may be startling, whether it is upsetting or reassuring.

We have explored ways therapist and patient lose each other in disjunctions and then reconnect conjunctively. In this chapter the conjunctive sequence is spelled out, leading to its quintessence in conjunction proper and its most sought after goals, creative change and creative development. One factor making my views unusual is the legitimacy I accord to the therapist's measured requirements for encouragement and authenticity from the patient. Traditionally, dynamic therapists have been taught to analyze away these needs, at best making them a subject for the therapy. I expand these ideas to include the therapist's needs and biases as inevitable constituents of an interpersonally alive therapy experience. Pretending these personal requirements are not there, and that therapists and patients alike have no legitimate needs to be gratified in the therapy, amounts to taking the life out of the therapy, pushing it in the direction of an academic exercise.

The atmosphere I am describing for psychotherapy, then, is one of evolving intimacy, each partner learning the other's biases and failings and having a role in addressing them. Required is the partners' growing trust, a quality mandating the conviction that one will not deliberately hurt or humiliate the other and that the therapist will advocate effectively for the patient's welfare. In therapeutic success, both partners develop a clear sense of the other's everlasting presence in their inner world; both know they have changed indelibly through the influence of the other and are enriched by it.

The Conjunctive Sequence

While the elements making up the conjunctive process have been named and illustrated throughout the book, they deserve our final look. In therapy, they tend to appear sequentially, steps I call the *Conjunctive Sequence* that can be identified macroscopically over months or years of treatment and microscopically within any therapy hour. At its core, the conjunctive process requires a critical mass of trust, which, as it develops, galvanizes the therapy partners. Change occurs in accord with the patient's manifest and progressively revealed, latent therapy goals, often with therapist and patient having little exact understanding of how and when the change happened. Optimally, both partners, therapist and patient, find they have influenced each other and have been permanently changed by the process. Both appreciate the place of the other's credibility, personal commitment, intuition, and willingness to acknowledge his or her human failings in creating these changes.

The conjunctive sequence describes the pathway to interpersonal intimacy in therapy. Except for the requirement that it incorporate a two-person view of therapy, virtually any dynamic psychology can be used with my model to provide a blueprint for how the patient and his therapeutic needs can be understood and met. My ideas about therapeutic action describe how two people connect and meaningfully influence each other. Using them draws the therapist's and patient's attention to the cyclically disjunctive and conjunctive aspects of their experience, legitimizing the notion that change takes place as two people struggle to know and understand one another, tolerating disorientation and surprise, willing to reach well beyond their familiar interpersonal world to discover and know each other, and thus mandating an emphasis then on collaboration and reciprocation.

The Incipient Conjunctive Process

Therapist and patient begin therapy enthusiastically, imagining the other can understand and work straightforwardly toward the agreed-upon goals. This hope is regenerated repeatedly in any viable therapy. There is seldom a time during therapy, even in the depths of the worst disjunction, when a conjunctive process, facilitating change and personal development, cannot be discerned by one or the other of the partners. Without some expectation of being helped and understood, the patient's therapy experience would do little more than sustain his current level of functioning.

Illustration, Karen

In chapter 1, I introduced you to my early experience with Karen, referring to our almost flawless rapport, she telling me that I "usually was right in tune with her." The description of our later work emphasized her disillusionment with me, my alleged faults in not anticipating Carl's abusiveness becoming the center of our attention for that time. This major disjunction between us was preceded by minor disappointments where trust careened into uncertainty about whether she could trust me not to betray her, by defending in Carl someone whose character she questioned.

In these segments of our work, when our field was shrouded and the original elation of our bond was nowhere to be found, I often thought I had lost her, or at least these were my conscious thoughts. These concerns proved never true, however. As described in the detailed session at the end of chapter 1, incubating below the surface, as robust as it was in the beginning of our work and even more seasoned, was the legacy of our incipient conjunction. The truth is that Karen had never given up faith that we would make it; her belief that we would arrive at the point she preplotted for us was based on her fundamental conviction about the durability of our relationship, as opposed to those who had vanished from her life after the slightest frustration.

So, as is true in all therapies that survive, our incipient conjunction never disappeared, but was meticulously integrated into the fabric of our work, supporting and facilitating it. It initiated our conjunctive process and was the earliest precursor of our ultimate conjunction.

The Discovery of Illusion

Patient and therapist begin to discover a partner who in increasing ways is different from the person each thought was there. The disjunctions that develop are of two sorts: external disjunctions, based, for example, on temperament, style, and culture, and internal disjunctions, understood theoretically as deriving either from intrapsychic conflict over unacceptable feelings and needs or from interpersonal, including intersubjectively experienced, conflict between therapy partners. These disjunctions need to be acknowledged and worked through if movement toward authentic engagement is to occur. Either patient or therapist can initiate the process of recognizing and resolving a disjunction (Frankel, 2000).

Illustration, Brittany

I will briefly illustrate a therapeutic disjunction encountered after an ostensibly good start to a therapy sequence, using an episode from the work with Brittany that I present in more detail later in this chapter. It all begins with Brittany and myself in conjunction; as she put it, we were simply "flying." Suddenly she becomes depressed and I respond by trying to be encouraging, initiating a blatant disjunction. Brittany's good opinion of me evaporates, and to an extent, privately, so does mine of her. She confronts me with what she calls my anger, citing a phone message I left for her. I am dismayed, look for information, and finally give the floor to her so she can help me to see what I'm missing. To rid myself of my confusion I do what I can to clear my mind, hoping to let in a new perspective so I can begin to understand what she and I are contributing to this misunderstanding. That disjunctive scenario repeats itself a bit later when she feels I am not helpful enough in a crisis around the discovery of a critical diary note she wrote to herself about her stepmother. Developing knowledge in this situation is difficult, because Brittany is critical of me both times. In each case my infraction looks small, but Brittany's intolerance for me is unyielding, suggesting that there is more than meets the eye in each instance.

Controlled Disorientation

Confronted by disjunction, confounded by his own and the patient's subjectivity, the therapist becomes aware that he has misapprehended the patient and no longer understands him. The therapist allows disorientation to overtake him, but in a controlled way, with the goal of attending carefully to the nature and source of his confusion. The objective is to discover by whom and how the ground rules for therapy have been changed.

If the patient is communicating a new need or agenda, the therapist uses himself as a sensing device for understanding the patient's communication, which may be occurring, for example, through projective identification. If the therapist's transference to the patient, his countertransference, or personal limitations are the source of confusion, he appeals to the patient for help in understanding these. If the problem is limited emotional depth in the therapy relationship, then the therapist uses himself as an instrument to reattune and reenliven the process. In all cases, the therapist's humility and willingness to tolerate disorientation, provides a model for a dedicated, shared introspective process. As the patient witnesses the therapist's open willingness to ''not know'' he is likely to be reassured that he can join the therapist in doing the same.

Watching the therapist honestly acknowledge disorientation, and painstakingly struggle to bring the therapy relationship back on track, may surprise the patient, usually in positive ways. This discovery creates a radical but productive discontinuity, revising the patient's assumptions about who the therapist is, even about people in general. Radical discontinuities represent a usually unanticipated, fundamental shift in perspective and experience for the patient, challenging his beliefs, expectations, or modes of interpersonal relating. Ordinarily, a parallel process takes place for the therapist, powerfully affecting him as he discovers a patient now starkly different from the one he had come to know.

Being forced to examine himself and receive blunt feedback brings the therapist, and one hopes the patient as well, closer to seeing and then becoming congruent with themselves, ultimately making it possible for the therapist to align with the patient, at a level of more authentic and profound emotional depth.

Controlled disorientation requires that the therapist (and ideally, the patient) wipes his mind clear of stereotypes and agendas. *Mind clearing,* as I call this process, may have the subjective effect of making the therapist feel vacuous, lost, inept, or humiliated. However, the subsequent, metered filling of the created void contributes to building the authenticity of the therapy connection and eradicating distortions each member introduces. Both therapist and patient change as the result of the unsettling discontinuity that has developed in their experience, causing shifts for each. They fill that vacuum with revised views about self and other, and at the same time enhance their interpersonal skills, for example, in the areas of listening and empathizing.

Illustration, Marty

The example of Marty in chapter 4 is almost all about my use of controlled disorientation to understand Marty's criticism that I charged him for a missed hour and attempted, inappropriately, to justify myself by pointing to the reduced fee I originally set for him. Months later, his mood in therapy again began to deteriorate. He complained about being depressed, and in spite of several professional successes could only see blackness. Concluding a deal to sell his subdivision didn't matter, he still was probably being ripped off, and, given the depressed economy, could someday be poor. Then things got worse, with Marty wondering whether suicide might make sense.

Life for Marty was bleak, and once again I was being worn out. I questioned, suggested, even had a few visits with Marty and his wife together, but oddly none of these efforts was to any avail. Then, I made a last ditch attempt and told Marty how much I cared for him, and how personally upsetting this change of events was for me. That was it. The last straw. Marty lost his temper, accusing me of simply wanting to assuage him, not really empathizing with his despair. And, finally, since it was too much for me to bear, I also lost my temper. I looked squarely at Marty and insisted that I did not know what he wanted from me. His suffering and accusations were brutal, and paradoxically no matter what I did to help, he balked. He even refused hospitalization when his wife and I encouraged it to deal with his suicidal feelings.

That time Marty actually stalked out of the office. Then there were letters, long, convoluted ones in which Marty at first made the case that, like others, I clearly didn't like him. I thought, talked to a colleague, and wrote back initiating one or two letters myself. Then we talked, and I started to get it. First, I began to understand because of the communication in Marty's leaving my office. I got it more clearly as he sent the letters he took hours to write. And, finally, I really got it when, to my astonishment, Marty told me how grateful he was for my letters. In vocabulary Marty had never used earlier he said he now knew I was trying to be ''nice'' and that he felt ''understood,'' this time in a way that was different from ever before.

In this case, the entire sequence, leavings, letters, and calls, constituted a framework to allow the controlled disorientation required for me to understand Marty's exquisite sensitivity to betrayal. Each of these steps was also necessary to get Marty to take a chance on continuing to seek the commitment he craved from me. Instigating this episode was the beginning of Marty's becoming attached to me, setting off an alarm that the relationship had progressed past the danger point, exposing him to the possibility of annihilation if I disappointed him. Required on my part was forbearance well beyond what I could bring to our therapy hours, necessitating separation, letters, phone calls, and finally face-to-face review.

Transferring Authority to Know and Lead, and Reciprocal Knowing

At those points where the therapist recognizes his limitations in understanding what the patient needs, or what influences are at work in the therapy room, he transfers to the patient the authority to know what the therapy requires and to lead. Exchanging roles in this way happens regularly, back and forth, deliberately and also inadvertently.

One process that contributes to the transfer of authority to know is reciprocal knowing, a basic activity of therapy. Therapist and patient constantly check their impressions with the other and modify the way they see the other, themselves, and the therapy. While reciprocal knowing refers to a broad set of *collaborative* activities almost always at work in therapy, the act of transferring authority to know is more specific and is often invoked in response to discoveries using the controlled disorientation technique. Reciprocal knowing is an almost automatic process, guided by the principles of collaboration. Transfers of authority to know and lead are more deliberate, preceded by reciprocal knowing, with the therapist usually in charge of initiating and supporting the transfers.

That the therapist in my model is so committed to parity with the patient, placing special value on the patient's wisdom and feedback, may seem paradoxical when at the same time he or she is responsible for monitoring and furthering the success of the therapy through painstakingly formulated understanding and actions eventually constituting a leap of inference. Accomplishing this juggling act requires that the areas in which the therapist is accorded authority not conflict with his capacity to defer thoughtfully to the patient's wisdom. Both of these ends can be achieved if the therapist generally limits his prerogatives to orchestrating transfers of authority, while also monitoring and fostering progress in the work of therapy, in part by attending to its authenticity. In addition, while guarding the therapy collaboration, its reciprocal knowing and transfers of authority to know and lead, the therapist collects data to formulate and execute the leap of inference, invoking the leap only when he has become relatively certain of the validity of his impressions.

Illustration, Alison

Alison's decision to create and work from the place she called "the sanctuary" in my office is described in detail in *Intricate Engagements* (1995), and is a graphic example of the potential power of the therapist to transfer the authority to know and lead to the patient. The "sanctuary" was a place in my office where I could not see Alison, and from which she felt she could talk most freely. She requested this arrangement believing it would assist in our effort to overcome her inhibitions, especially those protected by her "false self." I resisted Alison's request for this procedural change for months, only reluctantly agreeing to it as our working rapport deteriorated. Still, Alison insisted that I was in danger of repeating the mistakes of her previous therapists by perpetuating rather than mitigating her "false self."

Alison was right, of course. The move to the sanctuary was only the first of a number of devices she introduced to enliven our work. She wrote searchingly about the therapy experience, left messages for me on my voice mail, and had me speak to her son several times when he was in emotional trouble, convinced that my knowing and helping another member of the family would strengthen our work. In each case, I was a bit skeptical at first and reluctant to implement the new therapeutic device; each time the pace and depth of the therapy was improved after it was introduced.

In contrast to the more intentional character of transfers of authority to know and lead, reciprocal knowing is simply the moment by moment exchange of information that occurs between two collaborating therapy partners. With Alison, it was the method through which we gained most of our information about why she wanted to use the "sanctuary" in our work, and through which she monitored my progress in understanding and accepting the "sanctuary" as it became one of our main therapy tools. In the conjunctive sequence, reciprocal knowing has the status of a separate technique because its use entails a level of collaborative reciprocity that is more microscopic and spontaneous than transfer of authority to know and lead.

Nonverbal Relating and Radical Discontinuity

Much of the activity in therapy is not understood cognitively; it is nonverbal. Therapeutic change, eventually becoming developmental change, is frequently disconnected chronologically from the formal structure of the therapy, even if it is assisted by it. In my system, the guiding principles of the therapy, and the type and quality of the connection between therapist and patient, radically change at points through verbal, but most especially nonverbal reevaluation. Put differently, at each of these junctures, there is a therapeutically productive discontinuity.

Steps in the conjunctive sequence including disjunction, mind clearing, controlled disorientation, and the leap of inference actually create just some of these points of generative discontinuity. Therapy is most effective when the patient and therapist see these discontinuities strategically, as opportunities to deepen and propel the therapy forward. By definition, these are points that allow therapist and patient to move beyond the kinds of experience they expect to occur between them, into new, unanticipated areas.

Illustration, Natalie

When you reread the case illustration describing my work with Natalie in chapter 7, you may be impressed by how well we got along. I don't mean to be glib when I say this, just to make a point. In truth, however, the situation was complicated, full of pitfalls. For example, Natalie and I did not initially agree about the molestations, with me being the more skeptical. Natalie had everything at stake personally, potentially inciting her entire family's wrath; I had little to lose, or at least so I thought. Natalie always felt at least somewhat humiliated in therapy with me as relics of her molestations intruded into her life. The point is that there were always so many issues with which to misunderstand each other and disagree about, so many ways we could have been at loggerheads; yet, we never were. This fact suggests that the picture I am painting is incomplete. Something significant, a force or factor guiding us, is missing.

As I describe our experience I am impressed by the power and significance of this missing factor, our nonverbal dialogue. I have been trained to look for the complexities, the problems besetting interpersonal situations. But in this, as in so many other successful clinical experiences, there was a guardian angel, technically in the background but effectively taking care of things. In this case, guarding and supporting our work, was our nonverbal dialogue, as sophisticated and helpful as any verbal therapeutic exchange.

The Leap of Inference

Over time, the process of reciprocal knowing brings the therapist to a point where he feels mostly certain about what the patient needs; that is, about the patient's latent goals within the therapy. The therapist delivers his insight as the leap of inference. This activity, while it may incorporate an interpretative statement, is actually a strategically formulated action, designed to move the therapy forward. The leap of inference is creative in that it goes beyond the edge of what has been experienced and is known by the therapy couple, taking advantage of all the information gleaned to that point, verbally and nonverbally. Implicit in the idea of the leap of inference is the principle that the therapist should take responsibility for actively moving the therapy work forward.

The patient's (and therapist's) discovered latent goals are frequently, if not always, dramatically different from his manifest, articulated goals. Only through mind clearing, controlled disorientation, and reciprocal knowing can the therapist discern these previously unappreciated desires and objectives. This developing awareness is one of the most critical activities of therapy.

When personal change and its evolution into bilateral, creative development occurs, it frequently has a mysterious quality. Often, the change is not chronologically correlated with the leap of inference, even though the therapist's initiative in providing the leap is clearly associated with the patient's change. That is, the timing, magnitude, and character of the change are frequently not predictable. Also, the aspects of the therapist's controlled disorientation, struggle to facilitate authenticity, and leap of inference associated with the change are often obscured, working for the most part nonverbally, even out of awareness. These observations suggest that many theoretical explanations invoked to explain change in therapy are unsupported constructions. Their purpose is to give form to a poorly understood process, and they mainly serve to make the therapist feel he understands how the therapy is working.

Illustration, Brittany

In the beginning of my work with the adult Brittany, neither she nor I had any idea that her depression was associated with a desire to change her job and ultimately her vocation. Our growing comprehension and consensus that she should make this change powerfully reoriented our work. As a shift in vocation became immanent, Brittany's inner life became more available to us for scrutiny. It was possible to see then the extraordinary level of emotional focus she required from me, and how vulnerable she became when I couldn't grasp her needs, repeating the trauma of her childhood disappointment with her inaccessible parents. Equally impressive was how Brittany's insistence on being understood became matched by her brilliance and generosity in empathizing with others. Brittany's fundamental goal in therapy was to create and explore just such a reciprocal relationship with me as a prelude to finding it in the world. Eventually, as I understood her latent goals for therapy, I was able to act accordingly and formulate what I discovered into both words and action, effecting a series of leaps of inference, revitalizing our work.

Authenticity and Self-Revelation

Authenticity requires finding a way of being with someone in a way that is entirely unique. Such authenticity is a state entirely dependent upon a reciprocal response in the moment, and this response needs to be distinctive in content, tone, and meter, uniquely felt and put.

Attaining authenticity requires the therapist to be in connection with a fully alive part of the patient, as well as himself. Even if the therapist is dealing with a stereotyped or emotionally dead part of the patient, the therapist's task is to find another, more vital point of contact.

Critically important in understanding authentic connection in therapy is the concept of interpersonal creativity. In seeking authenticity, patient and therapist arrive, in effect, at a deep level of affective disturbance. This state can be achieved only if the partners experience each other as profoundly open and honest. Felt and spoken self-revelation by the therapist cannot be avoided. At points where self-revelation is needed for informing the patient or assuring him of reciprocity, it needs to extend to topics that are personal to the therapist, but selected thoughtfully so they do not burden the patient or otherwise impede the therapy.

Illustration, Marty

Marty was a stickler for authenticity, always believing it was lacking, not only in our work but in all his personal relationships. Over the course of therapy, he made a number of innovative suggestions to make it more authentic, culminating in the most monumental one from the point of view of therapy practice. Marty insisted that a therapist could never really know a patient strictly from office contact. He believed real life was just so different from therapy life that the therapist who never saw the patient outside of the office would always have a distorted picture of the patient. So I followed Marty's lead and visited him in his home several times, met his wife, and read several books he felt were particularly important. These measures were beneficial, in part enabling me to see Marty as culturally more sophisticated and interesting than he appeared in the office. But it was his last suggestion that was particularly fascinating.

Marty came to the conclusion that for a therapy to get off the ground, most promisingly, the therapist and patient should spend several days together, perhaps nonstop. He never insisted on doing this with me and the notion came up when we were well into our therapy, but he presented his idea cogently, making me think about and acknowledge it. Especially through our trying times together, I have wondered with Marty whether some of our misunderstandings could have been avoided if this model had been available to us earlier in our work. Used or not, Marty says it is important to him that I have treated his idea with so much interest and respect.

Conjunction

When therapist and patient become disjunctive, using "not knowing" to understand and then make shared discoveries, the process leading to conjunction is initiated. Ascending to conjunction requires for the therapist the startling discovery of the latent goals and the hidden identity of the patient, and for the patient, to the extent relevant, of the therapist.

The dramatic reorientations that occur in therapy, conducted along the lines of my conjunctive model, that is, the patient and therapist following each other through these discontinuities (not all of which are disjunctions), are the foundation of conjunction proper. Through not knowing, disorientation is converted to knowing and joining at a deeper, more enduring level. In this process, the therapist's and patient's limitations and distortions are revealed, their commitment tested, and a progressively more authentic connection is achieved. By definition, the experience of conjunction is ecstatic, while intermittently wrenching. It is affectively profound, and on the whole remarkably different from anything the patient and therapist have experienced or imagined they could experience together.

Illustration, Alison

It may seem odd that a conjunction can come as a result of a profound misunderstanding. Yet, that was certainly what happened between me and Alison, following the painful months when I misconstrued her desire for a caring, trusting experience as a possible seduction.

The more affected of the two of us, however, was me. To that point, I would have characterized myself as a staunch feminist. After all, my mother was jailed several times in her 20s for marching for women's rights, and it would not be an overstatement to say that she, as a social worker, taught me the basics about people, their most personal needs and motivations. Yet, there I was, exposed. According to Alison, my error was basic and it was "male." Seduction couldn't have been further from her mind. What she was thinking about was care and loving, often wishing I could be a replacement for her failed experience with her father.

I was moved. As I expressed in the last pages of *Intricate Engagements* (1995, pp. 232–238), when I talked about how much I learned from Alison about the experience of childhood molestation, this further experience with her was transforming for me. My blind spots about how women feel and think were being further mined, and new views were quickly filling in. And she was changed, too. She said that none of her therapists, all of whom had been male, or friends had ever taken so much time to understand her so fairly. She felt that her hope for a truly reciprocal relationship had been restored, and she was now ready and eager to reinvest in her marriage.

Creative Change and Creative Development

Through controlled disorientation and reciprocal knowing, patient and therapist are exposed to new versions of each other, getting to know the patient's latent wishes and goals. The therapist ultimately incorporates this new perspective through word or action into a leap of inference. Each partner is then seen more accurately by the other. Both change in ways not expected, a tribute to their making good use of the radical discontinuity that has occurred.

The described creative change (Frankel, 2001) in the patient presupposes analogous change in the therapist. Creative change consolidates into creative development over time as the change in each partner becomes more reliable and the two transform each other interactively. The patient cannot develop in creative ways unilaterally. Without a partner struggling to understand and know that experience, the patient is not likely to be affected deeply enough to give up entrenched, seemingly safe, psychological habits. Further, change in the therapist is the only authentic outcome of an experience where the therapist's misconceptions and distorting contributions to the therapy are bared.

Creative change evolves into creative development, when the personal transformations are unequivocally bilateral, change occurring in each partner through a powerfully experienced conjunctive process. An additional category of change through psychotherapy is the kind of personal growth I call *renewed development*. In that case, as a result of a nurturing relationship, not necessarily requiring profound change in the giving partner, arrested areas of the patient's development are reengaged. Change associated with renewed development can, nonetheless, be dramatic; abandoned lines of development, such as the capacity to have intimate relationships, are given new life. However, these developmental attainments are normative and expectable, not surprising and novel for the patient or the therapist, as in the case with creative change and creative development.

Illustration, Natalie

Unfortunately, it is impossible to thoroughly illustrate creative change and creative development in such a small space. To a degree this entire book is about these subjects. Suffice it to say here that Natalie was shocked by my interest in following her to the depths of her molestation and abandonment based despair, and by my willingness to maintain a committed, humane stance as the bodily relics of her childhood molestation experience tormented her. She says that during our formal therapy, if I had been even a bit more tentative about my dedication, she would never have continued it. Here, she was referring to my basic commitment, not my more superficial skepticism about the molestations. She tells me that the intensity of her involvement in our work, while undoubtedly linked to her fear of abandonment and of my later repeating her disappointment in her parents, was more basically a response to knowing how earnest I was about our work. I made that clear to her by accepting phone calls and messages and arranging for extra sessions whenever she needed them, as well as by repeatedly seeking consultation when we were dealing with issues I did not yet understand.

At first, Natalie was the more affected of the two of us, discovering a world of commitment she had not known before. Over time, however, it went the other way, too. The relatively unconditional dedication I offered Natalie set a standard that made my later abdication during my divorce especially obvious. As described in detail in chapters 7 and 8, it ultimately became Natalie's job to teach me about the fine points of commitment. She did so thoughtfully and tactfully, ushering me into nuances of loyalty that became my practice in other relationships. Creative development brings a person forward in new, at times, remarkable ways, making him or her a different and more complete human being. That is certainly what happened to me over the years of my work with Natalie, and during those that followed, Natalie confirming that it happened to her as well.

The Conjunctive Process

The observation that fundamental personal change and development take place outside the framework of the deliberate therapy work suggests that powerful forces, of which the therapy partners are often unaware, are operating in the therapy. I use the term *conjunctive process* to refer to the general pull toward conjunction that always exists in a viable therapy. The powerful, centripetal joining that is at the core of the conjunctive process supports the centrifugal, differentiating aspects of creative change and development, patient and therapist evolving in surprising ways, often outside their field of observation. The personal transformations involved lead the therapy partners into new and often unprecedented ways of being. The binding force at the core of the conjunctive process then joins the therapist and patient inexorably, even while the two are influencing each other to evolve creatively in their own directions.

Illustration, Karen

Almost through the end of the therapy hour with Karen, presented in detail at the end of chapter 1, the conjunctive process
seemed absent. But in my opinion it was always very much
present, only obscured, communicated through tones and gestures. My reticence with Karen as she struggled with Carl's betrayals and accused me of failing to prepare her for his death,
wasn't simply a technical maneuver; it reflected forbearance deriving from my heartfelt commitment to Karen and our treatment. Further, it was instigated by nonverbal cues from Karen
making me thoughtful, in contrast to the way her always raging
father acted in response to her distress. I was interested in making
considerate moves and so was Karen, though you would not have
known it judging by the tension in the therapy office.

There was also the challenge of finding our way. I felt
stunned and confused by the starkness of Karen's censure of
me, and she by my reticence. To explain her behavior the easiest
choice for me would have been to fall back on my past experience with her, combining that with a theory-bound explanation.
In that case, the problem would be Karen's intolerance of her
disappointment and rage with her dying husband, displacing the
responsibility for her anguish to me. But what about the possibility, as she claimed, that Carl's progressively abusive behavior
touched on her early trauma, her father's abuse? And what about
the contribution of my own psychology and mood? It is always
there, something to be mindful of. Also, the stakes were high:
Karen's rage at me seemed lethal. I had the sense that she had
murderous thoughts and could feel the alarm that engendered me.

The events here are important to disentangle. The ''cocoon'' I pulled into was controlled disorientation. Moment by
moment, Karen and I probed each other to get small bits of
information; for example, about betrayal, commitment, disinterest. These communications, instances of reciprocal knowing,
helped us build a consensus about what each of us meant and
intended, with Karen catching on, at first tentatively, to the fact

that her intense distress about Carl's immanent demise was unavoidable, and that I would be available to help her, not torment her.

A careful look at our interaction reveals numerous points at which I gave over control to Karen, transferring authority to know and lead to her, letting her pace our confrontation. There was something she needed from me, and our emotions, most especially Karen's rage and my anxiety, were obscuring it. That the answer came to both of us, Karen probably conveying it to me first, nonverbally, was apparent through the conjunctive breakthrough at the end of the hour. The point here is that the procedure was complex and precise, anything but straightforward. It included innumerable microscopic encounters, each partially with a communicative intent. We reached our consensus covertly, mainly through feel not words.

At some point in this intense collaborative interaction I made the decision to act in a way that allowed Karen to see me differently. Perhaps that decisive step, the action constituting my leap of inference, was my purposeful willingness to return temporarily to my cocoon and tolerate Karen not letting me off the hook, even after I had detected a sweet melody of reprieve from her.

Notice how elusive the process is that I am describing, its actual structure barely clear in the moment. There is Karen nonverbally imploring me to take seriously the agony beneath her blaming, and to learn the pacing she needed for a response useful to her. There is Karen raging at me, yet hoping I will try even harder to reach and comfort her. And beneath all that activity there was more, a tenacious, silent bond between us that had developed over years. These were the years of experiencing each other, of solving Karen's problems and those that developed between us, of knowing each other and working hard together. In other settings that core connection is called by such names as: love, caring, and attachment, all words that express its fundamental nature. Illustrated here, then, is the conjunctive process in both its differentiating and joining aspects.

Where Angels Fear to Tread

Where angels fear to tread is the inner sanctum of dynamic psychotherapy, both fascinating and dreaded. I have no question about the rest: reciprocal knowing, searching for explanations of experiences that trouble the patient, struggling for perspective about what is happening in the therapy using controlled disorientation, and extra support for the patient and therapist when called for through additional contact, underscoring the authenticity of their connection. The therapist and the patient do have to find their way, after all, and often succeed, regardless of how slippery their private and shared impressions may be. They manage even though much of what goes on in therapy is inferential, inexplicable, the therapist as fallible as the patient, even if his training helps him blaze the therapy's particular trail.

So much, of course, can and will go wrong in any therapy, with the two partners missing each other by light years. And so much can go right, guided powerfully and largely nonverbally by the conjunctive process. The place even angels most want to avoid at times is the most *authentic* one, because seeing the awful terror that can be there is so repeatedly startling.

Brittany and I were flying. She had shocked me with her extraordinarily accurate appraisal of my defenses against intimacy: how well I take care of everyone else and how much frustration they sometimes have when they try to help me. This new episode began when, in response to her complaining about her depression, I left a message for her saying, ''Brittany you can't afford to get lost in this kind of swampland now; you've got to continue your writing.'' She claimed, and later proved to me, that not far below the surface of that message was my irritation. What I really was saying in that message was that her despair was a nuisance for me; I really did not want to hear about it. My message made her feel neurotic, like a complainer.

Fortunately, Brittany saved my phone message and wanted me to hear it. When I listened, I understood exactly what she was talking about. On the tape, I did come across as irritated and severe, opposite to the way I thought I sounded.

I had no choice but to admit to both Brittany and myself that my pending divorce was preoccupying and pressuring me. She admonished me, saying, "You would do so much better to tell me what you are going through. If you deny your distress, the interaction in here feels fake. If you're distracted and don't feel like being a shrink one day, you feel guilty and go on to do it anyway, but not nearly as well. I thought you trusted me enough to be straight with me." The lesson couldn't be more poignant: patients generally need openness and honesty. The alternative is for them to become confused, blaming themselves for the therapist's failures.

You're right Brittany, for me to say more, to complain, is inadmissible as a therapist, and generally risky, since I believe people might consider it a weakness in my character or a lapse of professional conscience. I wondered how she felt having a therapist with so many revealed imperfections? She reminded me of a comforting dream she had where she showed me her scars, and I showed her mine. I said that according to my training this degree of self-revelation was forbidden territory, and neither man nor angel should go there.

The next time I saw her, Brittany brought her most recent writing. I was pleased, but apparently still slightly distracted by events in my own life. In a later session, she said she again noticed my remoteness. Not really hearing her, I produced a ready-made interpretation wondering if she was compelled to undo the excitement of making such an impact on me in the previous session. Our dialogue became lackluster. While we kept talking about my taking her thoughts about me seriously, we did so with limited emotion. Finally, she said it was true, her excitement about our connection worried her, and she was afraid of spoiling it; still, this time the problem seemed to be with me. Uncharacteristically, she offered a hug and clung to me for a few moments.

By not dropping the subject, Brittany helped me become aware of my detachment. Once I caught on, I noted appreciatively that when we worked at this level of scrutiny, she became clearer, more articulate, as if we had excavated her healthy self, buried years earlier during her childhood when her family collapsed.

Secretly, the angels were up to their old tricks, this time putting my rapport with Brittany to a test. They probably knew what was coming. Brittany's beloved stepmother, Laura, found part of a diary note Brittany had written to herself in which Brittany was critical of Laura's behavior with Brittany's father. Brittany mattered a lot to Laura, and Laura was devastated. Laura called me, as she had done in the past with Brittany's permission, when she needed to talk over Brittany's problems with her birth father, and was quickly reassured when I told her that I felt she was taking the letter out of context. Brittany actually had endless praise for Laura. With this information Laura realized the note bothered her a lot less than a dispute she was having with her husband, and that Brittany was probably bearing the brunt of their problem.

My first thought was not to tell Brittany about her stepmother's discovery of the note and the phone call from her, taking refuge in the permission I had to talk to Laura. For the moment I had taken care of the problem, and I believed if she knew about it Brittany would beat herself up about Laura's discovery of the note. But what about our repaired authenticity? Could it stand to be compromised? Also, in the past I had always told Brittany about every contact with her stepmother. I held back for one session, but was troubled enough with the secret to tell Brittany in the next.

Brittany seemed all right with my confession, at least until the next day when I got a call saying that she was depressed about hurting her stepmother so badly. Heaven rapidly became no-man's-land, and there was no stopping Brittany's self-recrimination. All creative work stopped; golden bliss disappeared.

Alas, when Brittany appeared at my door on Monday, there were nothing but storm clouds. She scowled, and just like in the old days, could hardly talk. This time, also, she had stopped writing. While she eventually explained her mood to me, at first she had so much difficulty talking that I could not understand her, and assumed she was mainly reacting to my delay in telling her about Laura's finding the note and Laura's phone call to me. Brittany was saying something about it being fine for her to be depressed about hurting someone who was as decent to her as Laura. Mainly, she was irked by my attempt to suppress her remorse by withholding information about Laura's call and being reassuring that the crisis had passed. Her argument, what I understood of it at first, seemed so preposterous to me that I kept blocking it out. Why would she, to whom the prospect of writing as a career was everything, choose atonement through immobilization instead, even briefly? In contrast, her point was that, even if exaggerated, her concern about hurting Laura was ethical, part of what made her a decent human being. The people she grew up with never aspired to such a standard.

So, here Brittany was thinking I would never understand her intense caring for her stepmother, and I was believing she was misguided in the intensity of her self-blame. Moments of confusion like this had become familiar. These were the times when I needed to listen more intently, trying to understand our disjunction. When I did that this time her explanation made sense. I realized that Brittany and I were talking two different languages. In hers, obligations to others you loved always came first; in mine, in this case as Brittany's therapist, preservation of the self, Brittany's hopeful mood and her writing, were paramount. Brittany saw her worrying as legitimate, a trademark reflecting her decency, the kind of emotional integrity she never saw as a kid. In contrast I had advocated the easier path, bypassing the ethical obligation she felt toward Laura.

By this time, there weren't any angels in sight, just two people relearning the value of listening and struggling. Brittany began writing again, intensely, for the next several weeks. Her words came out clearly, painful muscle tension disappeared. Periodically, she called between sessions, but mainly to tell me she was doing fine, and she hoped I was also. She thought I could receive her good wishes for me. Earlier, the idea of welcoming her compassion for me would have made me feel corrupt. This time I accepted it with pleasure.

Brittany had been buried alive since childhood: no one in her family talked openly or admitted they felt very much during those hellish early years. Her mother withdrew from Brittany and the other four children, hardly even preparing meals. Her father disappeared, a brother had a psychotic break, and going unnoticed by anyone, her two sisters, one a twin, tortured Brittany. Inside, her world was fully alive with both painful and exquisitely beautiful images. Outside, Brittany felt and tried to assuage everyone's pain as if in her Godlike role she could redeem them all, keep them from burning up. Yet, Brittany's vitality became more inaccessible, no one was aware that she was anything other than perfect or bothered to inquire who she was until she was well into adolescence. By that time, to the point of our conjunction 20 years later, the real Brittany was out of reach. Then, as we made our discoveries, and Brittany slowly and writhingly emerged into the sunlight, we began to dance at the cliff's edge. At times, we lurched, at others we moved with grace. Sometimes Brittany led and at other times I did; it simply depended on who had the best moves in the moment.

The cliff-edge dance I am describing anticipates conjunction. The conjunctive process incubated Brittany's creative change, spawning creative development as precisely composed and reliable as it was surprising. At about the time of the stepmother incident, Brittany made the decision to undertake a methodical study of her muscle pain and headaches and to select her own treatments. She began by studying physiology. She read, attended lectures, and studied techniques, progressively learning how the muscles and nerves of the affected portions of her body worked, developing a theory about the connection between her early psychological trauma, the wear and tear of the endless hours of corporate office work, and her pain. Her studies took her to a Sufi healing practice, a philosophy and technique she says allowed her to integrate her writing with therapy. Impressively, the muscle pain and spasms dissolved over several months and have never returned.

During this period, Brittany took control of other aspects of her life. She made several new friends, all successful in their lives, and resolved to enter a commercial writing career, using my work as therapist and writer as a model for a more financially secure life. While at the beginning of her training she thought of little more than disaster, she soon began to receive encouraging feedback. The other students and her teachers were impressed with her uncanny ability to read people's emotions, just the quality that impressed me in our work. Classmates began to invite her to work and study with them. At this time, her mother paradoxically mounted a massive attack by threatening to cut off the financial supplements she provided for her medical care and education. In the past in response to such a threat, Brittany would have lost her balance and dropped off the ledge, lost for months; this time, she asked for my help in formulating a confrontational letter to her mother and went on with her studies.

Brittany's remarkable change, she says, was possible because I ultimately heard her and understood her suffering, staying committed through the early suicidal years: witnessing her siblings' decline, and recognizing the place of her parents' earlier disordered life in that process, advocating for her when she insisted she could no longer work in the field of public relations. Equally important, she said, was that she wanted to know how disruptions in my own life stopped me from being fully present with her in the therapy. Each one of these episodes required a wrenching readjustment on my part. As needed, we used Brittany's wisdom, transferring to her the authority to know and lead in our work. Added, was my introspection processed through controlled disorientation, helping us find our way. The result was that Brittany and I got to know each other ever more intimately, and our personal agendas and limitations were exposed. Brittany expected that I would grow tired of her as I got to know her better; I came to our therapy with traits that, at first, limited my involvement with her, undermining the fine-tuned rapport Brittany required for us to work successfully on her behalf and for my own creative change and development to proceed, along with hers.

I have said least about how my experience with Brittany changed me. When I began to work with Brittany years ago, I was more certain of my ability to read people, formulate their psychology, and intuit their emotional needs. My experience with Brittany made me far more aware of the distortions imposed on me by my own subjectivity. I have had an intimate experience with someone who, in ways, was more perceptive and sensitive than I am. More than with any other patient, my formulating the conjunctive process occurred with Brittany; she is the patient responsible for the most extensive changes in the way I view the therapy process. She knows how much she influenced me, and says she is delighted I took her so seriously.

Brittany and I changed in different directions, creatively, as a result of that therapy experience. I became acutely aware of some of my personal limitations and became committed to new areas of my own development, while Brittany became dramatically more confident, able to negotiate life in entirely new ways. The kind of change I am describing resulted significantly from our personal impact on one another. Driving this change from the inside, fueled by the struggle to understand one another and the disorienting discoveries we made, was the conjunctive process with its incorporated disjunctions building toward conjunction and our creative development.

Looking Back

When I reread this vignette, intending to use it to illustrate the conjunctive process, I was undone. It sounded choppy, bits of experience strung together: Brittany and I moving from a point just past her perceptive appraisal of my limitations, to her reaction to the critical and removed tone in my voice that Saturday morning, to her insistence that she be able to speak about her turmoil about having upset her stepmother without feeling judged as being neurotic. Each episode elicited confusion, pain, and, sometimes, awe in me. I wanted to wriggle out of the skin I was exposing everywhere, as I reread the case example. I pictured my critical colleagues deciding I was too unanalytical. Yet, as I reflect on it, this is exactly the kind of atmosphere I intended to create as I described my ideas about what makes therapy work, coming close to replicating the ever disrupting nature of a therapy, with possibilities of producing conjunction and sweeping creative change in the partners.

Brittany and I are now flying high above the cliff, discovering profound truths about ourselves, each other, and the world, in panoramic fashion. My prediction is that she will be finished with therapy sometime soon. A similar change process seems to be happening with many more of my patients as I use the conjunctive model, so I thought I would search for commonalities. Karen tells me that when Carl's therapist and I realized she understood Carl's deceitfulness better than we did it helped repair her self-doubts and her assumption that authority figures would always outclass her. Supported, she could then move on and attend to Carl in his illness. She was even more surprised and fundamentally validated that I set up a system where she could phone me any time she felt internally out of control, and then when I honored my promise without resentment. She talked about how important the depth of my commitment was to her, with us both sustaining it. It was not just my tenacity that mattered, but her discovery that she wanted to struggle to reengage me when she felt I was again becoming distant, as I had been earlier when I was uncomfortable with her unrelenting blaming of Carl. Then, when I mentioned to her that I had told a colleague that Carl and she were burning me out a bit, she said she found it helpful to hear the truth. The fact that I could tell her made her feel even safer, because I was less likely to store up my resentment and then explode later as her father always did.

Or, consider Russell, who, when Tom told him how angry and hurt he was about Russell's rude phone message, understood and simply explained what he really meant to convey. He said the move to a new house was harder than he expected, and he was short tempered during the week they exchanged calls. No big deal. Tom's calls were welcome. They got it all out and returned to their work unburdened, with Tom feeling closer to Russell than ever. At first, however, Tom was uncomfortable telling Russell about his dissatisfaction. Tom worried that his having established the ground rules for their treatment, insisting that Russell be self-revealing and the relationship heartfelt, was too stringent and may have alienated Russell. Russell listened carefully to Tom's concerns and reconfirmed that he was indeed committed to Tom's brand of therapy; he liked it and liked Tom, too. They then, in that session, went on with their "family of origin" study, as Russell answered Tom's questions about illness, using his own bout with cancer for background.

That therapy is over now. From the point of Tom's working through his dissatisfaction with Russell's detachment, it became so much easier, so less full of ceremony and compliance than his previous psychotherapy experiences. Tom realized he didn't even feel a need to be professionally allied with Russell, an obligation he had felt with his training analyst at the end of that analysis. Most interesting to me is that the effect of their work is so reliable, distinctly more impressive to me than the result of my own training analysis with Dr. Mark. When Tom entered the therapy, he was preoccupied with his recently treated cancer and found it hard to carry through with some life demands, like marketing his new book. Tom left the therapy restored, feeling vigorous.

There is a kind of love Tom says he feels for Russell, who nonetheless is so different from him. According to Tom, Russell is a funny mixture of moody and private, open and giving. They apparently aren't matched affectively, but Tom says their differences are, perhaps, just the formula for them to have influenced each other creatively, with Russell modifying the way he does therapy and Tom better able to deal with his illness.

Then there is Natalie, whose situation I reviewed extensively in the previous chapter. At first we thought the factor sustaining change after therapy was finished would be my promise to keep the path to her molestation memories from becoming impassable. Of course, my function in that role was not trivial, but there were two more jobs waiting for me before we could rest, each a surprise and each as urgent as the last. The first involved maintaining the therapy until we could deal with Natalie's morbid fears of abandonment, which we discovered when we began to discuss termination and were hidden previously by her fervent commitment to the therapy. That development was handled by extending the therapy by a year and a half. The second, the retraumatizing effect of my divorce-based distraction, tested our ability to use our therapy-developed collaborative skills to extricate ourselves from the crisis I created by withdrawing. In each instance our therapy result became more reliable, Natalie clearer about her vulnerabilities and me about the importance of my constancy, and with the last go around, Natalie becoming distinctly more able to manage her own life. Natalie is quite convinced that what mattered in each case was that I proved I cared and could be relied on once I understood the problem. She was right: a promise is a promise, compromise does not work. And in our case, depth was all about the relationship, testing its authenticity and its tenacity.

So far as I can tell, in each of these examples, the therapist, myself with Brittany, Karen, Marty, and Natalie, and Russell in his work with Tom, explores and exposes his own humanity. Irritability, distraction, attraction, elation are all part of the complex landscape, hence my extreme discomfort in committing these experiences to paper. But, not surprisingly, Brittany tells me that it is just that, the parts that make me most uncomfortable, which make therapy really work. Therapy, authentic connection, with the idea of being helping and helped in profoundly new directions implies depth: depth equals authenticity, at times, painful.

The conjunctive process with Brittany occurred all through those roller-coaster years of alternating disjunctions and conjunctions, eventuating in creative development. I loved her incisive observations of my barriers against paying attention to my own needs; no one had ever been quite that accurate. I was embarrassed, also, and confused about being so open with a patient and then receiving permission from her to attend to my own distress. When my divorce temporarily overwhelmed me, I simply couldn't keep up the introspective intensity Brittany required of me. But by that point Brittany felt she had some prerogatives and was scathing about my disappearance, "Authenticity is what matters, Steve, there are no substitutes." And then the diary note discovery incident where she needed me to understand and value a remarkable facet of her psychology: her exquisite ability to care for people who loved her, including, shockingly, me.

Conjunction is the consequence of repeated, radical readjustments of empathy and understanding. The fact is that Brittany and I were committed to keeping up our duet, playing with, off, and for each other. We noted the dissonances, and strived to move from one moment of consensus to the next so we could reestablish our harmony, even while on the narrow ledges of our precarious cliff. Our most striking insight was that we actually could perform each one of these demanding interpersonal tasks: confirming one's own personal competence, gaining conviction that the other person can be reliable and trustworthy, and recognizing that someone can comprehend your needs and motives accurately, assured that person gets great pleasure out of creating interpersonal music with you even during a perilous climb.

While patient and therapist are influencing each other creatively, ultimately they are working even more closely, toward conjunction. One of the unities in their experience involves the therapist facilitating shifts of authority and leadership, usually in response to reports from the patient about his subjective experience of their interaction. Another involves the profound trust, the familiarity, which grows between the two partners. They develop a sense for each other's style, limitations, needs, and capacities. They become ever more invested in the other's welfare, and most especially in the patient's, since that is the subject of their therapeutic contract. They get to know each other with a kind of honesty and precision not likely to be duplicated elsewhere. Here is the core of the conjunctive process: the indelible coming together of therapy partners for the enhancement of each other.

The real Brittany was exhumed and given a chance to live. At times holding Brittany's hand became part of the process, as a symbol of the safety rope that was never there for her before: the one attached between two people and then to a piton securely set into the rock of unconditional commitment. Had there been a human rope there earlier, securing her, she would never have tumbled so far in the first place.

For Alison, the counterpart of Brittany's authenticity was good will and love. She could never depend on receiving either before, and now she felt she had located a rich source and might have the basic resources to make it safe to search for more. For Tom with Russell, it was his lack of competition, his willingness to change his habits and embrace Tom's way of doing therapy. For Marty, it was honesty, brutal uncompromising honesty that finally assured him he could depend upon another person not to betray him. For Natalie, it was reliability, my heartfelt commitment to her causes: keeping vigil over the molestation memories, and then needing me to be introspective enough to recognize and reverse my abandonment of her.

Brittany facilitated insight and dazzling moments of psychological mindedness for me. Similarly, the experiences with Alison and Natalie, and apparently for Russell with Tom, were as powerful and mutative for me, as they were for the patient. Tom's work with Russell allowed Tom to tolerate and repair disappointments in relationships with men, without taking these as personal attacks or attempts to undermine him. But it also moved Russell to adopt a more personal style of psychotherapy. Alison showed me how far I could progress with another human being, helping me to overcome my natural tentativeness in the face of powerful invitations for nonsexual intimacy. Natalie taught me how to combat the hideous after effects of childhood terror and just how reliable a therapy partnership has to be to succeed under those circumstances.

Conjunction and Creative Development: What Happens to the Therapist?

Earlier in the book I mentioned that one block to the self-revelation and authenticity required in the conjunctive model is that the therapist does not come to therapy with the goal of changing. Yet, if he works as I have described, he will have no choice; he will undergo the most searching personal scrutiny as he finds himself tumbling into the deepest emotional chasms or floating in desolate personal and interpersonal space. I insist that without the kind of commitment that Russell with Tom; and Brittany, Alison, Marty, and Natalie with me, have shared; the therapist will never get to know the patient or himself with enough depth. The two will work in gross approximations, staying within the boundaries set out by theories and unstated agreements about how far they are willing to go together. Altogether, therapy conducted according to the conjunctive model is a remarkable adventure; there is no way of knowing exactly what will happen to you and your partner ahead of time, and if you try too hard to predict, you will never get off the ledge to which you are tethered. But ultimately, unnerving as it is to lose your footing at times and fly at others, the trip is exhilarating, especially with a progressively more experienced and unconditionally committed partner. In the end, there is an epiphany of self, and self joined to another, always promising more.

10

Extending the Conjunctive Model: Focused, Time-Limited Psychotherapy

Consider this chapter an epilogue. I wrote it as a challenge. If the conjunctive model makes a therapy more purposeful and powerful, if the principles found in the conjunctive sequence are valid, then they must have their place outside open-ended psychotherapy. What do we do, then, when patients face life constraints, such as an emergency due to emotional immobilization or influences that are wreaking havoc with their relationships or work, or when they are confronting a major move or other life change, such as marriage, childbirth, illness, or the impending death of self or a loved one? What if they have limited resources in terms of a network of family or friends, access to needed services, school problems, or financial limitations? What if they have to travel to get the help they need? Further, consider those people who cannot tolerate the open-endedness of traditional dynamic psychotherapy, who insist they need a bounded, practical procedure to help them through their personal turmoil. Then, a focused, time-limited assessment and intervention is the treatment of choice.

Psychotherapy certainly needs to be effective, that is, able to create lasting, deeply felt change. It also should be available to meet challenges in a timely, accessible, and affordable way, with special urgency when any of the patient's resources are limited. Hence my interest, in this chapter, on focused, time-limited approaches to conjunctive psychotherapy.

Let us return to the conjunctive model and ask how it can be applied on a focused, time-limited basis, while maintaining its collaborative essence. What therapy conditions allow for or require this modification of procedure? Are the results reliable, and how do they compare to those of an open-ended therapy? What special techniques can be used to improve the efficacy of the time-limited procedure? Should focused, time-limited psychotherapy necessarily end when its planned term is over? What is the place of follow-up? In addition to the use of conjunctive principles and technique, my time-limited version is unique in the introduction into the therapy of a psychologist consultant who administers assessment instruments for the psychological evaluation of the patient and to monitor the therapy's progress. In this view of time-limited psychotherapy, the therapist, and therapist and patient together, work collaboratively with the consultant during the initial assessment phase, and then again at intervals during and following the formal period of therapy. The introduction of this additional level of scrutiny sharpens the diagnostic process and provides a vehicle for therapist and patient to work their way purposefully out of disjunctions and toward conjunction.

Within the treatment itself, the collaborative aspect of the conjunctive method serves as the best bet for repeatedly putting the therapist and patient back on course. Progressively experienced depth and authenticity are their guides. Conjunctive therapy provides sequential revisions of impressions about what the patient needs and where the therapy should go next through interactively arrived at transfers of authority to know between therapist and patient and reciprocal knowing. Therapist's and patient's impressions are continually modified through the carefully structured and articulated, as well as subtle, nonverbal feedback each provides the other.

I support introducing into the time-limited therapy process two fresh and presumably relatively objective sources of observation. These consist of, first, the mentioned consultant who provides clinical observation, as well as administers and interprets normed questionnaires and psychological testing, including standardized psychological tests and projective tests (Finn, 1996a; Fischer, 1994a, 1994b; Marnish, 2002). Second are the variety of self-reporting questionnaires to be completed by patient and therapist (Clement, 1999; Cone, 2001; Hawkins, Mathews, and Hamdan, 1999). Which of these to use depends on carefully weighed clinical considerations, and should be based on a shared decision between the patient, therapist, and consultant.

By including a consultant, I am sanctioning the introduction of a third mind into the therapy process, a configuration I call the *three-person field,* a notion originally developed by myself and Philip Erdberg, and written about by Diane Engelman and myself (Engleman and Frankel, 2002). Our position is that when deployed thoughtfully, this model improves the accuracy of a therapy and enhances the therapeutic process.

In this chapter, then, we will consider this time-limited variation of psychotherapy conducted according to conjunctive principles, and its monitoring and enhancement through the three-person field.

Time-Limited, Focused Psychotherapy

Time-limited, focused psychotherapy is advocated by its proponents as effective in creating symptom relief and measures of sought after personality change (Budman and Steenbarger, 1997; Fosha, 2000; Neborsky and Solomon, 2001). The research on time-limited psychotherapy is equivocal, however, frequently identifying universal factors such as the therapist–patient bond to explain its effect (Garfield, 1994), and implying that when these are the relevant factors, similar results can probably be obtaincd with a variety of approaches. The depth and durability of results are, of course, a matter of heated controversy between advocates of time-limited psychotherapy (Davanloo, 1999a, 1999b; Fosha, 2000; Neborsky and Solomon, 2001) and those favoring open-ended therapy.

As a summary, in focused, time-limited therapies, as compared to more traditional open-ended formats:

1. The therapist tends to take additional responsibility for structuring, maintaining, and revising the therapy process.

2. Goals are repeatedly reformulated and made explicit, as much as they can be.

3. Key dynamic and transference issues, to the extent possible, are identified early. Thereafter, when feasible, they are dealt with head on and in the here and now as themes within the therapist–patient relationship.

4. Locating and unlocking core affect states is given particular attention, as it often is in open-ended treatments.

5. The therapist may find himself in the position of giving advice and assigning exercises with the objective of maintaining the therapy work outside of sessions.

6. Corrective interpersonal experience outside of therapy and education in areas pertinent to treatment are more likely to be seen as agents of change in time-limited therapy than in open-ended dynamic psychotherapy.

7. Throughout the time-limited psychotherapy literature, the type of intervention most valued varies according to author and ranges from corrective emotional experience (Alexander, 1956; Binder, 1984; Luborsky and Mark, 1991), to confrontation (Davanloo, 1999a, 1999b; Malan, 1979, 1986), to interpretive statements (Gustafson, 1995; Strupp and Binder, 1984). Explanation for change ranges from emotional or cognitive reworking (Horowitz, 1987, 1989) to the early and focused presentation of key transference themes (Luborsky, Crits-Christoph, Mintz, and Auerbach, 1988; Mann, 1973; Safron and Segal, 1990). However,

most authors seem to agree that the effective focus in time-limited psychotherapy is likely to be on the here and now, while not all agree on the value of looking for explanatory connections with the patient's early life. Apart from cognitive reworking, the major kinds of change that occur in most types of time-limited psychotherapy, as well as in some open-ended approaches, are largely assumed to be within an interpersonal framework, consisting of the revision of patterns within ongoing relationships, emphasizing the focused reengagement and revision of core affect constellations (Fosha, 2000). A major difference between time-limited and interpersonally oriented open-ended psychotherapy is the deliberate setting of goals, time restrictions, and the cognitive and emotional focusing, all of which may be required to move within a time-limited therapy framework.

On the surface, I find little to argue about when reviewing the guidelines for focused, time-limited psychotherapy summarized above. The idea that the therapist should be active and take ultimate responsibility for directing the treatment, the notion of collaborative goal setting with or without extratherapy assignments, the value placed on the therapist as a real person who engages affectively with the patient, the emphasis on learning about and finding ways of modifying behavior including that based on developmental delays and arrests, and the reliance on techniques that highlight the patient's personal strengths and adaptation, all make good sense to me—especially when there is a pressing personal need or the patient's tolerance, goals, or resources are limited.

The category of time-limited psychotherapy I describe in this chapter is also attractive in the extra measures of accountability that are built into it, both through its heightened collaborative emphasis and the use of a consultant who can offer psychological assessment. The fact of having a consultant allows the therapist to take more risks to not-know, and speculate, even when under the press to organize and lead the therapy within its time constraints. In open-ended psychotherapy, without the assistance of a consultant and testing, arriving at the kind of insight required to formulate a triumphant leap of inference is likely to come more slowly.

Of course, one needs to be aware of the potential limitations in a time-limited therapeutic undertaking, what may be missing, working against meaningful and enduring change. The patient's level of distress and need may not be fully addressable in a time-limited framework. Similarly, in time-limited treatment the depth of the therapy may be restricted, with the therapy partners diluting or avoiding critical emotional issues, such as those associated with attachment and separation, or opening up areas of trauma which cannot then be adequately worked out within a specific time frame. In making these points, I need to invoke the principles of the conjunctive method as I have articulated these throughout this book. Working according to the conjunctive method, while guarding its collaborative underpinnings, should protect against the therapy becoming perfunctory, with the therapist substituting wishful thinking about the practicality of time-limited therapy for its long-term success.

In refocusing on the conjunctive method, I am referring to all of the measures articulated throughout this book that are required in order to know and collaborate with a therapy partner. There is *controlled disorientation,* supporting *reciprocal knowing,* and *transfers of authority to know and lead,* requiring the therapist to endure periods of confusion about what the patient needs and intends and what influences are at work in the therapy. Applying controlled disorientation can be jolting for the therapist in part because it is so thoroughly predicated on complex and sophisticated *nonverbal* conversations, and dependent for its meaning on felt but often not articulated *discontinuity* in the therapy experience. All of the conjunctive events I describe are prerequisites for formulating the most commanding step in a therapy sequence, a meaningful *leap of inference.* The issue for the moment is how these processes can occur within a time-limited therapy structure. What do they look like? As I consider their applicability to time-limited psychotherapy, my ideas about how an effective therapy process works remain: Time-limited or open-ended, patient and therapist are the same animal. I am reminded of Natalie's insistence that authenticity simply cannot be compromised; it is an absolute requirement for an effective psychotherapy, and it is either there or not.

So, here we have our dilemma. There is every good reason, often an urgency, to make a therapy practical and accessible. And some people are prepared to work especially well in a goal-directed, time-restricted atmosphere. More than likely, a therapist working in this manner will be perceived by such a patient as working in his or her best interests. In this case, the time-limitation may further conjunctive involvement, enhancing the depth of the process. However, even in these time-limited therapies, the therapist's ability to suspend knowing, to be influenced and changed by the patient, needs to be preserved by his deliberate adherence to techniques of the conjunctive method. Here, controlled disorientation needs to be invoked even more rigorously to prevent its being sacrificed to the practical ends of the time-limited procedure. Techniques of focused psychotherapy cannot simply be placed in operation, in the form, for example, of cognitive–behavioral exercises, circumventing the emotionally trying conjunctive process that explains the depth and success of the conjunctive method. The challenge in focused, time-limited psychotherapy is to hold tightly to and make the best of the intense, emotionally rigorous, conjunctive sequence, knowing that it usually comes faster and harder in a time-limited framework.

No therapist, short- or long-term in orientation, can force emotional depth simply by imposing a structure on a therapy and insisting it move along. Necessary is the building of the patient's heartfelt trust and involvement as collaborator, as well as the kind of pacing a patient and therapist absolutely require to achieve enough depth to make their therapy meaningful. Further, for the transformative process I have described as the outcome of the conjunctive method to come to fruition, the therapist, not just the patient, needs to be an equal participant, recognizing how his needs influence the therapy; he also has to be deeply affected and changed by that experience.

Nonetheless, time-limited methods, even if conjunctive, may simply offer too little. In some cases, the patient may need additional treatment, at times converting time-limited therapy into a series of strategic interventions, each in response to a new, stressful life development. Others may be helped through a life crisis, but need to come back later in response to new developmental stress. And there are those who are in a time-limited psychotherapy for help with more personal issues associated, for example, with a medically related depression or an occupational dilemma, or require a therapist to assist them with interpersonal problems, such as those involving a child or a spouse. Finally, a time-limited course of treatment may serve as an entrée into an open-ended conjunctive psychotherapy. Time-limited therapy does not mean inflexible adherence to a formula. In the end, as therapists, we need to be led by the patient as our collaborator, regardless of how much efficiency and accountability we build into the therapy. These qualifications aside, focused, time-limited psychotherapy certainly has its place. Strategically positioned, the results can be impressive, catching the patient and therapist in just the right way, at the right time, and in a format that is time and cost efficient. Both open-ended and time-limited processes have their value, and each needs to be part of a contemporary psychotherapist's repertoire.

My Model: The Three-Person Field

For Whom?

Successful engagement in a collaborative therapy effort, time-limited or not, makes particular demands on therapist and patient for responsiveness and dedication. Regardless of the subtle yet powerful barriers to engaging meaningfully in treatment, each partner needs to be consciously committed to making the therapy succeed. Time and financial resources, enabling the patient or family to undertake a therapy process that, according to my model, ideally involves a focused psychological assessment, are, of course, required. The availability of a strong and reasonably healthy marriage or family unit, as well as other sources of ongoing support for social, emotional, and occupational needs during and after treatment, certainly count. So does the willingness to accept pharmacological, educational, or occupational counseling when required.

Regarding diagnosis, inclusion criteria for the studies reported in the time-limited psychotherapy literature (Barber and Crits-Cristoph, 1991; Greenberg, Rice, and Elliot, 1993) are often very strict. Generally, the more disturbed and less committed patients are excluded. Prominent criteria in these studies involve the patient's level of personal, and especially, social adjustment. Patients with significant character problems, for example, involving impulsivity, lack of conscience, or a thought disorder are usually eliminated from such studies. We are similarly discriminating in our work, selecting patients who by clinical interview and psychological testing are likely to tolerate and benefit from a time-limited psychotherapy process.

There are unique requirements for the patient if the therapy process is to proceed in a focused and time-limited manner. First, with the addition of a consultant, the patient needs to have the ability to welcome and work with an additional member of the therapy team, and tolerate and make use of the viewpoint he or she offers through clinical impressions and psychological testing. Second, establishing and maintaining some goals and excluding others means the patient must have a reasonably well-developed capacity to discriminate and select between conflicting choices. Third, the patient needs to have the willingness to tolerate the ongoing push to meet therapy goals. Pressure of this magnitude does not exist in open-ended, dynamically informed therapy. Overall, as compared with open-ended therapies, patient and therapist are more acutely dependent on each other to initiate and respond in time-limited therapy. When practiced according to the conjunctive model, the entire process hinges on this active and purposeful collaboration. Commitment and trust must be expeditiously established to fuel such a process, a tricky idea because neither commitment nor trust can be forced.

I hope I have not exaggerated the rigors of conjunctive, time-limited psychotherapy. In fact, in my experience most people who have a pressing enough personal reason to seek this kind of psychotherapy seem able to become involved, learn quickly, and put it to effective use. That is not the case with individuals who are too slippery characterologically, are frightened of therapeutic engagement, or come from a complex and failed early life. A different approach, one designed for the dedicated building of a therapeutic relationship and the filling in of developmental gaps, would be more appropriate for them. Also, the depth of the conjunctive process developed in the time-limited version, may of necessity be limited. After all, getting to know and trust another individual, and to create the kind of authentic bond I have described for the conjunctive process, takes time, and is extraordinarily demanding emotionally on both partners.

In time-limited, conjunctive therapy, most of the patients my colleagues and I encounter and work with comprehend and welcome its reciprocity. They are anxious to be understood and unravel the mystery of why they struggle in life. They move toward trust as the therapist reaches out, sharing relevant parts of his own reality with them. Finally, whatever its degree of effectiveness, the focused, time-limited, and monitored nature of that procedure is embraced and tried because it holds out the hope of results in the near future, and because the therapist takes active responsibility for optimizing the therapy and its outcome. When it succeeds, the results are gratifying; when it falls short of the mark, the time-limited work frequently becomes the beginning of a more extensive, open-ended psychotherapy.

The Time-Limited, Focused Assessment
and Intervention Procedure

The Center for Collaborative Psychology

Thus far, I have been talking in general terms about a time-limited assessment and intervention process, based on conjunctive principles. At this point I want to describe this procedure as it is used by my colleague Diane Engelman and myself at the Center for Collaborative Psychology, located in Marin County just north of San Francisco. At the Center, we implement the ideas I have evolved through my years of practice and have portrayed in my books: *Intricate Engagements: The Collaborative Basis of Therapeutic Change* (1995), *Hidden Faults: Recognizing and Resolving Therapeutic Disjunctions* (2000), and this current volume. Between the work we have done at the Center, and the roughly 25 cases Philip Erdberg, Ph.D. and I treated collaboratively as we developed the three-person field model, we have completed over 75 cases, reviewing 46 of them for this book.

The following paragraphs are excerpts from the descriptions we have created for the Center's activities, touching upon our orientation and methodology:

Most essentially, the evaluation is "open." That means both patient and therapist have constant and equivalent input into the process, each modifying the other's viewpoint.

There are many ways of helping people and each of these methods tends to be specific and different. Therefore, the outcome of our evaluation may or may not be to recommend psychotherapy. Other kinds of interventions, educational or pharmacological, for example, may be recommended instead or in addition. Also, the type of therapy, whether individual, family, or marital, and the technical bias of the therapy, psychodynamic as opposed to behavioral, for example, is not preset. Always, in our work, however, we are guided by the principle of the conjunctive method. We make these determinations collaboratively with the patient, therapist, and psychologist consultant, who is an integral member of the therapy team, using as much specificity and objectivity as possible.

The evaluative process may or may not conclude with the patient continuing in an extended psychotherapy. However, the evaluation will always include an initial implementation of the recommendations made, with the partial goal of refining objectives through this "trial run," and when possible, meeting therapy goals in a focused, time-limited psychotherapy with the therapist.

The time-limited services we offer are unique. They are practical, when possible self-limiting, and contain instruments for measuring the accuracy and appropriateness of what therapist and patient conclude and do. We believe that change can occur through experience and education, and that people in addition to therapists can be quite influential in the change process, so we advocate respectful attention to the entirety of the patient's life, including his home, work, social, and spiritual life.

The Assessment–Intervention Process

Our 6- to 24-month-long time-limited therapeutic protocol consists of four major phases. The first, the assessment phase, begins with a series of clinical interviews, which include taking a patient's history and setting initial goals with the therapist, who might also be thought of as the case manager because he or she takes ultimate responsibility for orchestrating the procedure from beginning to end. People may come to time-limited psychotherapy with a spectrum of needs, sometimes requiring advice from a variety of sources, all of which the therapist will have a hand in arranging. Helping to provide for these needs, whether they require a nutritionist or an educator, informs the patient that he or she is understood and cared for, key elements of therapeutic conjunction.

The second, the consultation phase, is initiated when the psychologist-consultant joins the team to offer both clinical input and testing (Engelman and Frankel, 2002; Finn and Tonsanger, 1997; Fischer, 1994a, 1994b).

In the third, the intervention phase, the therapist and patient implement their collaboratively derived understanding of what the patient requires. This is where the body of the time-limited psychotherapy is carried out, moving toward whatever level of conjunctive joining is possible within its time constraints. Often coupled with the therapy is an array of other therapeutic interventions, which may consist of meetings with family members, home visits, or consultants other than the psychologist, all according to a carefully formulated but openly evolving plan.

The final, concluding phase, seeks to consolidate gains made during the evaluation and treatment, effecting closure where possible. Requirements for ongoing work, in psychotherapy and otherwise, are identified and implemented during this period. Referrals are made to other professionals, such as psychotherapists, educators, and educational counselors, who are handpicked according to their skills, personal style, and professional commitments, including their willingness to work collaboratively according to the principles of the conjunctive method. The trust developed during the entire evaluation and treatment process establishes the therapist as a critical, ongoing resource, available past the term of the time-limited psychothcrapy for assuring therapeutic gains are maintained and new sources of help are introduced as needed. Also, at the end of regular sessions, periodic follow-up meetings are arranged making it most likely that this tracking will be carried out.

Throughout all phases, while the collaborative method supports dialogue with the psychologist consultant, the therapist is responsible for moving the entire process forward through the steps of the conjunctive sequence, enabling the progressive clarification and implementation of the patient's latent goals.

The Phases, Illustrated

The Initial Clinical Assessment

The therapist and patient meet together for two to five sessions to develop a plan for the assessment. When the client is a child or adolescent, meetings with parents precede and follow the patient assessment. When more than one family member is involved, reasonable precautions for the confidentiality of the participants are formulated. These guidelines are developed and made explicit early in the assessment process, reflecting the privacy requirements of each participant and the competing need to share information for the sake of countering a crippling family pattern. Factual information is collected by interview and through our own data gathering forms that the adolescent or parents or adult patient fill out, as well as through calls and meetings with collateral sources such as siblings, relatives, or teachers.

It may seem odd, but at this early point in the work the identity of the "patient" may be ambiguous to the evaluator. For example, a child or adolescent may be referred to the Center but the main therapeutic commitment throughout can be from one or both parents, or the spouse of a referred patient may come to have a similar, primary role. That person becomes the key participant in the developing conjunctive process, working tirelessly with the therapist to understand and resolve the psychological issues presented by the child or family, becoming the person most deeply involved with and affected by the intervention. In our experience, that person frequently continues in a working, ongoing therapy relationship with the therapist, after the therapist's work with the identified patient is finished. This kind of unanticipated shift, eventuating in therapy for the person who was originally the major collaborator, was, in fact, the situation in the work I will now describe with Mary and her family.

Mary   After a long phone conversation with her parents who lived in a different state, I met twice with Mary, age 22. In the first meeting, she was cooperative and articulate; to me, she seemed remarkably forthcoming. She emphasized her difficulty concentrating to explain her school failures beginning in the ninth grade, necessitating a move from one school to another. In college, she was in a constant struggle to focus and stay interested. In our meeting, though, Mary was clear and cogent. However, the second interview was particularly bewildering. Mary's thinking during that session seemed so tangential that I found myself thinking about organicity, or even a thought disorder. Her same pattern of inconsistency repeated itself through the third and fourth sessions. These sessions with Mary were flanked by meetings with her parents for the purpose of gathering history, making sense of my clinical observations, and formulating a plan for the extended evaluation. The clinical picture remained confused, framed by Mary's disarmingly cooperative manner in the midst of her fluctuating display of good and poor judgment, insightfulness and obtuseness.

Six weeks later, Mary again visited California, this time for testing with Dr. Engelman and several more sessions with me. During the intervening period I spoke with Mary on the phone several times a week, and, while I also had several phone conversations with both her parents, the main support for our work came from her stepfather. Mary's stepfather made the initial contact, insisted Mary keep her appointments, pushed Mary's mother to see Mary's problems as urgent, and progressively confided in me about his struggle to find a comfortable place for himself in this blended family, one where his concern for Mary as well as his own needs could be heard and taken seriously. It was his tireless efforts, his willingness to join with me, that fueled my work with Mary and then redirected me to his wife's parenting failures and serious deficiencies in the marriage. However, at the point of these initial meetings, all I knew was that Mary's school failures and seeming irresponsibility had her parents greatly concerned.

Consultation

In this phase of the assessment, the therapist's impressions are conveyed to the consultant verbally and in writing (Finn, 1996b, 1999). Ideally, the patient (at this point the identified patient was Mary) is given a copy of the therapist's note to the consultant. Also, questions for the consultant are formulated by both the patient, Mary in this case, and the therapist. The consultant takes the information she receives about the initial assessment, adds her clinical impressions, and decides which tests to use. In the interest of economy we prefer to use, when possible, an individualized, focused battery of psychological tests to a general, all-inclusive one.

Mary   After meeting with Mary once, Dr. Engelman gave her the following psychological tests and inventories: MMPI-2, TAT, Rorschach, Strong Interest Inventory (Harmon, Hansen, Borgen, & Hammer, 1994), Myers-Briggs Type Indicator Career Report (Hammer and Macdaid, 1992), Neo Five-Factor Inventory (Costa & McCrae, 1985), and the Millon Clinical Multiaxial Inventory III (Millon, 1994). She also had available for review an ADD battery that had been done by another psychologist a few years earlier.

In Mary's case, the results of the testing were eye-opening. Her inconsistent thinking and behavior had been documented clinically for years, but its explanation psychologically had remained mysterious. According to the testing, Mary was experiencing substantial levels of stress, and was so thoroughly separated from her feelings that she lacked the personal resources to find resolution. Drugs and alcohol were the only method she knew for finding relief, once her intellectual attempts to manage her dilemma were exhausted. In short, Mary was at the end of her rope emotionally, suffused with anxiety, and had no way out.

To cope, Mary had seized on substances as her most reliable means of relief. Using these, Mary had become slippery, clever enough to conceal her now exposed addiction to alcohol and marijuana from everyone, including her parents. Even on testing, Mary did her best to hide her addiction behind her substantial intelligence and charm. In interviews with me, Mary had likewise been disarming, but I had been alerted both by her history and my observation that her thinking intermittently became tangential.

Completing this picture was Mary's idealization of her mother, a highly principled and charismatic businesswoman with a stunning academic background. Unfortunately for Mary, fulfilling her mother's ambitions for her, especially considering the mother's disappointment with Mary's older sister who was genetically damaged, was a nearly impossible challenge. To compensate for her anticipated failures, Mary resorted to distancing herself from people and their judgments, and adopted "self-glorifying" defenses, designed to repair her chronic sense of deficiency. Left to her own resources from at least age 12, as her mother and father strived professionally, Mary became increasingly entrapped within her rigid, self-reinforcing defensive fortress, consolidating her attractive but impenetrable shield against personal involvement. To make matters worse, she was not just emotionally isolated but was becoming progressively cynical about life, and depressed as well.

In spite of the technical value of the assessment for Mary, it was becoming plain to me that the developing conjunctive process was primarily between myself and her stepfather. He and I were single-handedly exposing the family's problems and attending to them. While he was dutiful, he complained that his wife was unable to tolerate the stress of Mary's now revealed addictions, and that she tended to minimize their significance. He seemed relieved each time he talked to me, which generally was on the phone because he lived at such a distance.

As the next step, the stepfather asked for an "intervention" with Mary involving the entire family, including her biological father who lived in another distant city and even the stepfather's and mother's 5-year-old son. That meeting took place a month later. Everyone gathered in my office, as far as Mary knew, for detailed feedback about Mary's testing. Mary had met weeks earlier with Dr. Engelman for initial feedback, and agreed to this next meeting because she knew that her parents now regarded her school failure and her just exposed chemical dependency as an emergency.

Dr. Engelman and I began the meeting by reporting our findings. Soon Mary's mother and stepfather were in tears, her mother begging Mary to go into a chemical dependency rehabilitation program. The mother, who by nature was quiet and reserved, was overcome by the emotion in that moment. At this point, Dr. Engelman broke the stalemate, challenging the disjunction separating Mary and her family by using her authority as an outside "expert," the person who had tested Mary. Her presentation was compassionate but confrontational, emphasizing the seriousness of her findings. Mary yielded; she began crying, too. Yes, she would get treatment; she loved them all and was grateful for their help. During this time, Mary kept looking at her mother, amazed by the intensity of the mother's emotional display. We had one more meeting the next day when Mary reaffirmed her promise and agreed to have weekly phone sessions with me. For the term of our work, she would return to California to see me on a bimonthly basis. I also arranged for an outpatient drug rehabilitation program for Mary near her home and established a liaison with the staff there because Mary refused to go into a residential program.

That was the official version of the story. The as yet undisclosed version was that both the stepfather and I were terribly disappointed in Mary's mother. By the time the family left to return to their various distant homes, not much would have happened for Mary without his ongoing initiative. I had known very little about Mary's stepfather earlier, and now I felt drawn to his cause, inspired by his good judgment and sense of family duty. He and I had started to join, as partners, in a conjunctive process that would affect all family members.

Margie   In another case, the clinical interviews and testing of Margie were as dramatic as Mary's, but, unlike Mary, the testing in that case revealed unexpected psychological health. Margie, from childhood, had been treated as an intellectual and emotional cripple. She was adopted at birth by an angry and resentful father whose hostility toward Margie went unchallenged by his compliant wife. Margie's affluent parents covered their hostility toward her by placing her in the finest schools for educationally disabled children. Clinically, Margie, at age 18, indeed seemed impaired, acting the role of an immature, intellectually damaged young woman. And yet she was contemptuous, able to get away with her contempt by hiding her disdain behind apparent disability. Strikingly, the person most affected by Margie's hostility was her adoptive father, toward whom Margie took the liberty of saying the most insulting things, albeit in cleverly disguised ways.

After my initial meeting with Margie and a few history-taking sessions with her parents, I met with Margie on six occasions over a period of 2 months. I found myself intrigued with her because, although her tendency to talk nonstop could be tedious, I had the sense she was hiding something from me and the rest of the world. The history and clinical interview did not add up, making me wonder whether Margie might be using her disability as a foil to hide her own hostility. For example, Margie had invented an elaborate story about a boy she claimed was in love with her while she was in a boarding school for children with special education needs and who was killed in a skiing accident. The story accumulated extensive detail, and everyone, including Margie's parents and teachers, believed it was real; that is, everyone but me. When I asked Margie with confrontational humor whether she was "bullshitting," she grinned, and we both had a belly laugh. At this point, I discussed that impression with Margie and, while she was still noncommittal, I thought she was implicitly concurring with my observation.

We were ready for the consultant's input. Margie and I formulated our questions, a collaborative process where the authority to know changes hands repeatedly. Our questions were all directed at discovering the real Margie, our goal being to remove the veil of pseudo-emotional and intellectual retardation conditioned from early childhood. Margie was specifically interested in knowing the extent of her limitations and whether she could ever expect to be "normal," have a social life and hold a job. Clearly, in contrast with Mary, whose interest in our work was mostly based on compliance with her disappointed parents,

Margie was my committed patient in this therapy. However, because in a little more than a year Margie was scheduled to leave home for a small college with a program for students with academic disadvantages, as with Mary, we had a restricted time period in which to do our work.

Dr. Engelman and Margie got on well. Margie appreciated Dr. Engelman's interest in her. Dr. Engelman administered the MMPI-2, TAT, Rorschach, and the Strong and Myers-Briggs Type Indicator Career Report, adding to that group the WAIS-III. The similarity in the tests chosen by Dr. Engelman for Mary and Margie in part reflects the age of both young women, and in part the mixed emotional–cognitive nature of their presenting problems, as well as the availability of other recent testing reports. For Margie, Dr. Engelman also had several sets of prior testing available, including old educational and neuropsychological evaluations from 3 years earlier. According to each tester, the results of their cognitive testing had been equivocal because Margie was so anxious each time she was tested. Nonetheless, the testing, unreliable as it was, always did suggest that Margie was intellectually impaired, her verbal and performance IQ apparently in the low normal range.

Here, unlike Mary, Margie was the person waiting anxiously for the results. Margie also requested a second feedback session with Dr. Engelman, because she could hardly believe the message Dr. Engelman delivered in the first one. But no one was more surprised by the results of Dr. Engelman's cognitive assessment than Margie's father, when on every measure of cognition Margie at least equaled, if not surpassed, her non-impaired peers. Her verbal IQ was in the high average range, besting 81 percent of her peers; her performance score was in the average range ranking her above 55 percent of her peers. There was no significant scatter on the subtests of the WAIS, suggesting, for one thing, that the assessment was not contaminated by anxiety.

Clearly, the experience with Dr. Engelman, including the testing and feedback she provided, coupled with the fact that I went to more trouble than anyone before me to expose Margie's emotional and cognitive strengths, fueled the conjunctive bond between Margie and myself. Oddly, that bond began with the creation of a disjunction as I extricated Margie from her comfortable, but partially unconscious, hiding place. Margie was beginning to see me as the only one who ever really believed in her. From Margie's standpoint, the decision to do the testing constituted a critical act, a *leap of inference,* conveying my growing conviction about Margie's real identity and how it might have been obscured by her lifetime of victimization at her father's hand.

Regarding future treatment, the personality testing revealed significant emotional turmoil, consistently related to Margie's experience of devaluation within her family, in part having to do with Margie being the only adopted child out of four siblings. While major depression or even psychosis had been suspected by her parents, no major psychiatric disorder was identified. Depression and low self-esteem were prominent, as was self-absorption, serving to protect Margie against incessant experiences of degradation and disappointment in relationships. Retreat into fantasy, unique for its invention of an aristocratic biological family, was a major technique she used to counter her despair. According to the testing, Margie craved contact with others, and yet that kind of intimacy terrified her. Redemption through an exclusive, committed relationship with a therapist was clearly in order. That work could be time-limited to begin with, and extended if needed. Moving on to college and into an occupational track through which she could develop useful skills was also imperative for repairing Margie's battered self-esteem.

In both cases, feedback meetings between Mary, her family, the consultant, and myself, and, between Margie, the consultant, and me, enabled me to radically change our sense of where our therapeutic interventions needed to be directed. Mary's addictions, her underlying pessimism, and her defective relationship with her much admired mother were exposed in full, and both began to receive help, a move that powerfully supported her stepfather. Margie, after 9 months of therapy meetings with me, went on to college.

The dialogues with the consultant are just that, a forum in which new information can be received and taken in. The fact that the patient can tolerate this *collaborative* feedback process and use it for change is explained, I believe, by the conjunctive relationship developed between the patient and therapist. The patient's willingness to tolerate exposure of previously guarded personal secrets, to be curious enough to manage the disorientation provoked by the consultant's findings, are possible only on the bedrock of a trusting, committed relationship, even if it is early in its development. Without that kind of shared involvement in a developing conjunctive process, I posit that the consultant's influence would hardly scratch the emotional surface.

Here, I do not mean to contradict myself. While it is true that the identified patient may not be the person with whom the therapist develops the most powerful and enduring conjunctive bond, it is always necessary for the identified patient to join solidly in the therapy work. Mary's commitment to our effort, while more limited than her stepfather's, was substantial nonetheless. She progressively became a full participant, taking on increasing responsibility for overcoming her addictions.

In the face of the test results, Mary had to admit to her misuse of substances. Then she needed the motivation to begin her work with me as a support for the more extensive rehabilitation she undertook over time. Her cooperation required that she trust me first. Margie only dared to come out of hiding, because she believed I meant her no harm and was genuinely interested in understanding and supporting her true identity.

The Formal Intervention

The evaluation and consultative phases, with their collaborative formats, often have a powerful interpersonal and therapeutic impact (Finn and Fischer, 1997; Fischer, 2000). During the formal intervention, the findings from the first phases are implemented and elaborated as goals in focused, time-limited psychotherapy. As part of the treatment the therapist and patient continually search for ways that the patient's personal and interpersonal difficulties are reenacted in his life and psychotherapy. These themes are identified and discussed with an eye to expanding the patient's capacity to reflect, and to deepen the evaluation of his needs in treatment. Those involved, adult patient, parents, child, and, of course, therapist and consultant, are progressively organized according to the newly articulated therapeutic goals, with the therapist and the person or persons engaged in a conjunctive relationship with the therapist at the helm. The principle subject or subjects in this pivotal role may not be the identified patient but may instead be parents or other family members, with the effort always directed toward identifying and undoing the difficulties that brought the patient or family to the Center.

It is important to emphasize that the most powerful influence making this process work is the depth and committedness of the tie between the therapist and the person or people who are primarily, conjunctively, involved in the treatment process. The leverage achieved is reflected in their motivation for therapy to succeed, and their willingness to collaboratively explore and refine the therapeutic issues, as well as accept and engage assistance from outside sources to supplement the work of therapy. The collaborative therapeutic relationship, in time-limited psychotherapy especially, is used not just to grapple ever more effectively with personal, psychological issues, but also to find ways to enhance and maintain the treatment by engaging sources in addition to the therapist, whether these are family members, friends, or other professionals.

In our work at the Center we contract to pursue these therapeutic ends for up to 24 months, making it clear that decisions about more extensive psychotherapy will wait until we have a sense about what the patient still needs, and at that time, how effective our work has been. At first, manifest goals are articulated as a result of the evaluation, including both the clinical sessions and testing, with the procedures to be used in treatment as yet unidentified. Included in that list may be liaisons with family, spouse, and consultants other than the testing psychologist. We assume that during the formal intervention phase the patient's latent goals and psychology will be revealed through carefully managed therapeutic collaboration, allowing continual modification of the therapeutic plan. Creating the kind of collaboration necessary to support a true conjunctive, albeit time-limited, therapeutic therapy requires that the therapist be able to move with agility between a structuring and informing role, directing the therapy work, and a more receptive role processing feedback from the patient.

Mary   After the meeting with Mary's extended family, Mary enrolled in an outpatient drug rehabilitation program, staying in touch with me by phone on a weekly basis. She signed a statement agreeing to go into a residential program if she could not maintain her sobriety or failed to work consistently in the outpatient program. I collaborated with Mary's counselor at the rehabilitation program, and spoke with Mary's parents every week, the stepfather being the reliable contact. Family meetings occurred at my office every other month, each following individual meetings with Mary and at times feedback to Mary and myself by Dr. Engelman. Also, I prescribed antidepressant medication for Mary, a function that was later transferred to the medical consultant at the rehabilitation program she attended.

In family meetings, the relationship between Mary and her mother became a particular focus. Mary craved her mother's admiration, and her mother was anxious to understand and repair the relationship with her daughter. The surge of emotion the mother experienced in my office during our family "intervention" had been unprecedented in her life. She had never felt such sadness, matched with her relief at locating this well of emotion. She wanted to understand the source of these feelings, finally concerned she had been avoiding a major sector of her internal life. She began to see the match between her own "emotional deficit" and Mary's. In family meetings with me, and progressively through her work with the staff at the rehabilitation program, her mother's role in fostering Mary's emotional handicap was explored, as was the burden imposed on Mary by the expectation she would compensate for the parents' heartache with their older daughter. Further, there was a developing match between the work Mary and her mother were doing with their relationship and the repair her husband, Mary's stepfather, and I were identifying as needed in the marriage.

Mary's stepfather expressed enormous relief that he could, at last, share his burden with someone else, relieved that Mary was receiving the attention she required. Then, 3 months after the assessment and consultation were completed, he asked for a series of phone meetings of his own with me. The stepfather was ready, he said, to discuss his most painful problem. While he respected the ethical way his wife conducted her life, he had lived for several years with the private opinion that Mary's mother was rather shallow. Mary's stepfather admired the way his wife supported Mary's mildly retarded older sister, but had become progressively disillusioned when he watched her underestimate Mary's difficulties. Their intellectual and, then, sexual life had stopped a few years earlier. The stepfather wondered how he could have gotten into such an unsatisfying relationship, why and how he needed to maintain the illusion that it was richer, and what he should do about that. Mary's stepfather had avoided seeking psychotherapy earlier in his life, but now wanted to talk with me to decide whether psychotherapy might be of use to him. He said the fact that I could admit when I felt worried or stuck in my work with Mary made it easier for him to acknowledge his own confusion about what to do about his dissatisfaction with Mary and his wife, as well. He had been raised in a strict Germanic household, where the expression of feelings and admission of uncertainty were unacceptable and psychotherapy certainly was not an option.

Margie   After the assessment and consultation, Margie began to meet with me twice weekly based on Dr. Engelman's recommendations. We had only 12 months before she was scheduled to leave home for college. Margie began to dream, hideous dreams about being dead and aware of it, sinking to the bottom of the ocean and being aware of it, being in a crowd but totally ignored and being aware of it. As with her fantasy elaborations, in the beginning telling me these dreams constituted a test to see whether I would believe her and would get frightened. Out of interest in joining as fully as possible with Margie and facilitating our *reciprocal knowing* process, I decided to share my reaction with her. I told her that the dreams she was having did indeed frighten me, making me worry a bit about her safety, and that I was troubled by their morbid content.

When I added and demonstrated that I would not back away, Margie relaxed and showed me another side of her personality, a humorous one. She began to mimic people, most particularly her adoptive father. And she was good. All of a sudden Margie and I started to have fun, hilarious fun. Admittedly, the humor from Margie's side was often rather aggressive, with Margie deriding everyone who she ever perceived as feeling superior to her, again most particularly her adoptive father. I judiciously became her partner, a receptive audience, bringing us closer to one another. In parallel with the way we lived in and navigated her gut-wrenching dreams, I joined with her bitter humor, always going for the most vivid emotion. Soon Margie was dreaming with a new theme: how she did not belong in her adoptive family. Hidden in this new set of dreams was a picture of her imagined biological family as being Hungarian royalty. Strikingly, the father in that family looked a lot like me. What, she wondered, would it have been like if I had been her father? For Margie, there was a blissful, conjunctive victory in that idea, one that made life seem to her distinctly more worth living.

During this period, individual and conjoint meetings were arranged with Margie and her adoptive father, both receiving additional help from me as I attempted to mediate their rift. Critically, also, I established liaisons with Margie's occupational counselor and teachers. Unlike Mary, Margie was fully engaged with me. Mary, in contrast, was respectful and compliant but never as attached to me. Both Mary and Margie required a fo-cused, time-limited therapy procedure: Mary, because her addic-tions urgently threatened her health and welfare, Margie, because she was so close to leaving home. However, in Mary's case, the most powerful conjunctive process occurred between me and her stepfather, while with Margie, it occurred directly in my therapy with her and was supported by my corrective work with her adoptive father.

The Concluding Phase

The challenge when we enter this final phase, with 1 to 3 months to go, is to finalize the work and anticipate what lies ahead. Conceptually, this phase should contain or at least embody the results of the most definitive leap of inference attempted in the therapy. It has been the therapist's responsibility to progressively work with the patient to uncover the patient's latent goals, find ways to accomplish them using the interpersonal power of the conjunctive method, and be clear about which remain unad-dressed. The leap of inference leading to or organizing this phase occurs primarily as an action, directed at achieving relative clo-sure as therapy draws to an end, leaving the patient with an in-depth appreciation of the conjunctive work that has been done, and a sense for how to continue that work on his or her own.

It would be false to claim that Mary's addictions and her underlying desperation at being designated to be the successful replacement for her retarded older sister, or Margie's life-long struggle to feel she really belonged somewhere and her severe difficulties with her adoptive father, could be fully resolved within a 12- to 18-month time frame. Recall, however, that in both cases we had been anticipating and planning the conclusion of our formal work from the beginning, attempting to make sure key issues were not missed. Both patients and their families knew that at the end of our planned therapy further treatment of some sort might be required.

A major task of this period is to determine whether referrals of any sort are required, and to work in collaboration with the patient to evaluate and implement these. Referrals may be made for ongoing psychotherapy or for other services, such as complex psychopharmacology or systematic desensitization for the management of a persistent phobia. It is critical to my model of focused, time-limited psychotherapy to recognize and work within its limitations. Problem areas may be opened but only partially resolved; time restrictions usually mandate that the therapy couple focus on the most pertinent of the patient's difficulties. For a full therapy result people other than the therapist may need to be engaged to pick up the slack and provide technical assistance that the therapist cannot. Rather than being a detriment to the therapy, maintaining a focus and engaging others to do part of the work is, in my opinion, one of the strongest features of the time-limited model. Along with the three-person field, these are methods that serve to make treatment more efficient and pertinent to a patient's needs. It bears repetition, however, that the conjunctively developed therapist–patient dyad is at the center of this rather complex operation, and it is the depth of the respect, trust, and ability to collaborate achieved by both participants that provides the fuel that makes it succeed.

In our opinion, at the end of the work a termination period of at least 6 to 8 weeks is required, because the return of original anxiety and symptoms during this time is so common, and because the anticipation of the end of therapy tends to bring up concerns specifically associated with separation. The termination period has an additional purpose. It provides an opportunity to confirm for the patient that he or she has made an impact on the therapist, that he or she really matters to the therapist. If the results of this period of treatment are to last, the patient and the therapist need to have a unique sense of each other as human beings, a bond that can be built upon later either in treatment or with others who are similarly significant to the patient.

Finally, we consider follow-up visits to monitor treatment results, and then intermittent consultations with the therapist and repeat periods of treatment, when indicated, to be part and parcel of our conjunctive, time-limited psychotherapy model. Rather than corrupting an otherwise pristine time-limited therapy, follow-up meetings represent realistic acknowledgments of the persistent nature of psychological and interpersonal problems, and the limitations of the time-bounded psychotherapy process. Even more to the point, making these contacts readily available reflects an understanding of the depth and durability of a genuine conjunctive connection between therapist and patient. In our view, while psychotherapy can certainly lead to the resolution of a patient's current difficulties, there is no justification for reducing the power of a healthy conjunctive therapy connection that can be tapped if and when more contact is needed.

Mary   After 4 months of phone calls with me and two more visits, including several meetings with myself, Mary, and her mother, Mary fully embraced my concern about her addiction seriously for the first time and made the decision to commit herself to a 90-day residential program to deal with both her addiction and her now apparent depression. At her request, she has remained in touch with me and Dr. Engelman, and we both have had intermittent contact with the staff at the rehabilitation program. The family work now takes place as part of this program. We will participate in the referral for follow-up therapy when she finishes. Weekly phone sessions with me and Mary's stepfather continue with the blessing of his wife, the focus being mainly on the marriage. Whether he will enter a more extensive psychotherapy, individually or with his wife, is not yet settled. He has used our work to initiate discussions with his wife about their relationship, and, for the moment, both see the benefit of his conversations with me.

This situation illustrates the way in which collaboration with the person primarily involved in a conjunctive relationship with the therapist, when that person is not the identified patient, can be used to uncover and work with the issues most centrally affecting the identified patient. In this situation, the identified patient was Mary. However, because the conjunctive process, involving the most dedicated exchange, occurs between the therapist and collaborator, it is that person who is likely to experience the most profound and enduring gain. While Mary clearly benefited when I acted to enforce the suggestion that she enter the residential rehabilitation program, the most enduring impact of this work is likely to be on her stepfather. By entering therapy himself he will not just insure Mary's future, but even more powerfully, will be taking care of his own.

Margie   As for Margie, at the point we stopped our regular meetings, 3 weeks before she left home, Margie was working with tutors and slated to go to a small college where she would receive a reasonable amount of personal attention. Margie's adoptive father started to see a therapist, who planned to meet intermittently with the adoptive father and Margie together. Margie will check in with me periodically. Based on the power of our bond, and, I think, its authenticity, at my suggestion Margie has decided she will continue psychotherapy with a therapist near her new school. She now imagines a future for herself, one with a dignified occupation and a social life.

Ideally, at the inception of the concluding phase, the patient, or patient and family members, are again seen by the consultant and some of the original psychological tests and self-rating inventories are repeated to evaluate progress. Therapist, consultant, and patient share their impressions and the therapist organizes these into a collaboratively developed treatment summary (Finn and Fischer, 1997, Fischer, 2000), which also contains recommendations for the future. As noted earlier, following the conclusion of their treatment, patients and their families are offered periodic follow-up meetings with the therapist, and when possible the consultant, to assess the reliability of the gains of the treatment, and to see whether additional work is needed.

How Effective Is the Center's Focused, Time-Limited Treatment?

Patient Experience

Here I offer a distillation of clinical reports from our 46 reviewed cases utilizing the three-person field for assessment, treatment, and treatment monitoring, including the 21 that were time-limited. We have had at least 6 years to follow up the initial 25 cases using the three-person field without time-limitation, and at least 3 years of follow-up for 12 of the time-limited treatments. With few exceptions, our patients were ultimately gratified by the availability of a consultant, and convinced that the pace of the therapy was not only quickened but made more accurate by the consultant's clinical and testing-derived input. Some patients were initially uncertain about the relevance and value of the testing, but almost all ultimately found the test results illuminating, especially when processed together with the therapist and consultant. Apparently, the background of the therapist's dedicated clinical and personal commitment makes it possible for the patient to consider and use the consultant's input.

Certainly, open-ended psychotherapy, conducted according to the conjunctive principles developed in chapters 1 through 9, is likely to have the most profound personal impact on the patient, leading to creative change and involving personal and interpersonal transformation. However, when time-limited treatment is conducted according to the same principles, emphasizing collaboration and establishing an authentic connection, creative change most certainly can, and often does, occur. Our survey, with the frequent backing of repeat psychological testing toward the end of each time-limited therapy, supports this assertion. Further, the personal impact of such a therapy is enhanced as the therapist leads and monitors the therapy, takes responsibility for setting and revising its goals, arranges for ancillary supports for the patient whether educational with a tutor or occupational with a career counselor. He works with these people collaboratively in much the same way the therapist works with the psychologist consultant.

Change in the therapist, as it occurs in these focused, time-limited treatments, is illustrated by the surprising emergence of Mary's stepfather as my conjunctive partner and his part in shifting my thinking about how the time-limited arrangement works. From him I learned to look for subtle clues for how to identify my primary collaborator, and to give myself greater permission to think of the problems of the referred patient as possibly ancillary to a more central enterprise, organized around the actual conjunctive therapeutic relationship. In this way, Mary's stepfather distinguished himself as my teacher, engaged and inspired me, and eventually moved me toward a possible psychotherapy with him.

Collaboration with the Consultant
Combined with the Conjunctive Process
with the Therapist

In our work at the center, the new perspective offered by the consultant when reporting on the testing has frequently been astonishing for both therapist and patient, in part, we assume, because it has brought out dynamic themes and issues that might otherwise have taken months or even years to uncover clinically. Mary's addictions and Margie's above average IQ are examples of such discoveries. Of relevance was the provision that the patient and therapist could submit their questions and misgivings about the evaluation or therapy, or even about one another, to the psychologist consultant as part of the consultant's inquiry.

In our experience, the task of accepting and assimilating what the consultant has to offer is greatly enhanced when the patient has faith in and is working well with the therapist. As part of that experience, the patient witnesses the therapist taking the consultant seriously, expanding his ideas by using the consultant's input. From this vantage point, both patient and therapist are involved in a *collaborative* interaction with the consultant, while the patient and therapist are in a *conjunctive* relationship with one another, each influencing and transforming the other. Margie illustrates these principles, having used the information we gained in the consultation to deepen and enrich her sense of herself as intelligent and worthwhile. In parallel, my personal involvement with Margie developed as we moved through our therapy project, and placed me constructively in a role not unlike that of her fantasized biological father, which allowed me to be especially influential with her.

The Three-Person Field

The three-person field model has been tested by us in two incarnations: its value in ongoing, open-ended psychotherapy and as an integral component of a time-limited assessment–intervention process. The benefit of having an additional clinical and testing-derived source of information in both procedures has been profound. But why? Dynamic therapists have typically guarded the therapy field, concerned that introducing another voice might corrupt the transference, making it difficult to usefully uncover dynamic and genetic themes. And, of course, to an extent these considerations may be true. As in the case of injudicious self-revelation, the careless introduction of another person, a family member or a professional, may result in confusion or a split transference, for example. There is every reason to be concerned about contaminating an already complex therapy situation.

Countering these arguments is the observation that thoughtfully introducing new sources of clinical data via the psychologist consultant and at times other consultants, adds perspective to what is always a hard to decipher subjective and intersubjective therapy field. The consultant is not yet embroiled in the interpersonal pulls that are ever-present in therapy, and logically may offer a fresh, reliable clinical perspective. Normed psychological testing adds levels of pivotal information. Finally, having another clinician pay careful attention to the clinical process and assist in its planning, adds a layer of assurance for both therapist and patient, and a second level of review for each.

Certainly, the presence of the consultant may distort a therapy, making it more difficult to determine where a particular influence comes from. It is incumbent on the consultant to remain even-handed, and for all members of the therapy team to confirm that the consultant is in a noncompetitive, helping role. It is of benefit for the therapist and consultant to have previous experience working together successfully. Experience working within the conjunctive model, and, in particular, its collaborative aspects, is invaluable, so that the two do not work at cross-purposes due to ideological differences. The collaborative work I did with Drs. Erdberg and Engelman improved as we worked with and discussed more cases. The difficulties we encountered in our first three or four cases, before we learned each other's pacing and style, and filtered out hidden elements of competition, faded. Also making an important difference, we agree, was our friendship and respect for one another.

The Place of the Conjunctive Process in Focused, Time-Limited Psychotherapy

Of course, the results just cited could reflect the support and encouragement virtually everyone experiences in any reasonably committed psychotherapy. However, a more critical look suggests, I believe, something more. What encouraged Mary to sign on? Why did Margie give up years of subterfuge and self-deception, and go public, making it possible for her to discover her intellectual and social potential? With Mary and Margie, both, this dramatic switch happened within a few months after the evaluation was completed, and was catalyzed by the radically new perspective offered by the consultant, as therapist and patient worked committedly toward understanding and trusting one another. The issue in focused, time-limited work is for the therapy dyad to be dedicated to an active, vital, collaborative defining and redefining of therapy goals right from the beginning. The patient has someone she has come to trust who supports and validates this process and underwrites the new viewpoints collaboratively developed with the consultant and in the therapy itself. The ground rules of the conjunctive method, the thrust toward authenticity and away from interpersonal compromise, apply as much here as in dedicated open-ended psychotherapy. The therapist's struggle to know the patient, understand his or her latent needs and objectives, and connect in deep-reaching interpersonal ways, is no less critical in focused, time-restricted therapy.

Clearly, the evaluation–intervention attempt can fizzle, the victim of limited motivation and restricted vision. It is noteworthy that only four of our time-limited cases followed this pattern. The others gained momentum as the process went on, the patient unmistakably gaining ground. Most likely, these encouraging findings reflect the powerful conjunctive joining that can occur in these therapies, even if they are time-limited. Therapist and patient unite, facing the therapeutic challenges the patient brings to the table. As is true of the conjunctive process altogether, it is the therapist's willingness to not-know, to endure uncertainty, to rely on the patient for clarity, and to selectively turn control of the collaborative and conjunctive process over to the patient, that speak most loudly.

A Model Case: Katherine

Katherine, 52 years of age, contacted me with the encouragement of her husband, complaining that her life had become bland. Nothing concrete was missing. She could not be more successful as a financial consultant. In fact, people flocked to her, in part because she was known to be so compassionate with her clients.

She claimed to be happily married and devoted to her two sons, both in their early 30s. Her friends, mainly female, were thoroughly committed to her.

Katherine described herself as a "doer," not a "feeler." She liked having projects and felt lost when she did not have one. In fact, one of her current life problems was that she was out of meaningful projects; none she picked up made her feel excited.

My initial experience with Katherine was as unblemished as she described her life. No doubt about it, had we not met in this way, we probably could have been friends. We even shared the same political and ethical convictions, Katherine's direction in life always ultimately influenced by her desire to help others.

Katherine's parents had survived a concentration camp, remaining together throughout their ordeal. By Katherine's report, their experience was less malignant than that of most survivors, the only recognizable psychological consequences being their practical, unemotional bearing. Katherine described her relationship with them as dutiful, surmising that her main emotional sustenance during her childhood came from her older sister.

After three meetings with Katherine, I was ready with an opinion. I told Katherine I was suspicious. I had no doubt she was pleased with her life. I had friendly, in fact admiring feelings for her. However, I agreed that something emotional, something neither she nor I had yet put our fingers on, was missing for her. Whatever it was, the fact that it seemed so elusive must be a clue to its identity.

So far so good, but Katherine was not sold on psychotherapy as an antidote to her existential problem, especially because her life was already "quite good." Along with her "practical" orientation and her tendency to dismiss psychotherapy as "subjective and impossible to quantify," Katherine had been warned by friends that if she became attached to therapy it could become a way of life, a substitute for life itself. Nonetheless, she agreed to work with me for a period of 6 months, because she reasoned that the possible value of the therapy would become clear within that time period. She also recognized that, based on what we discovered, this interval might need to be extended. Finally, we concurred that our focus could develop most efficiently with the help of psychological testing.

Given our interest in Katherine's affective life, Dr. Engelman administered the Rorschach, adding the MMPI-2 and the 16PF. The results of the testing were quite informative. In stark contrast to the way I experienced her, and her view of herself as sociable and altruistic, the testing showed Katherine to be almost entirely cut off from her emotions and personally isolated. On the Rorschach, she scored low on measures of empathy and high on ratings associated with self-absorption and defensive self-aggrandizement, a pattern conveyed to her diplomatically through Dr. Engelman's report and in the feedback meeting in which the three of us participated. The general tenor of the report, underscoring Katherine's separation from her emotions and her egocentricity was as I anticipated, but the magnitude of both so far exceeded my expectations that I found the testing report hard to believe at first.

At this meeting to provide Katherine with the testing feedback, attended by Katherine, Dr. Engelman, and myself, a breakthrough occurred that provided a beacon for the rest of our therapy. Katherine was in the process of politely dismissing everything Dr. Engelman had to say, at each point subtly neutralizing the finding with the thought that it offered "nothing new" for her. I watched this activity with a growing sense of disappointment and frustration. After all, Dr. Engelman's report was exemplary and, I believed, her findings were important for Katherine to digest. What had more impact on me, however, was the growing effect of Katherine's disdain on Dr. Engelman. Her voice was quickening, and she seemed a bit worried that our meeting might be a failure. In retrospect, I am impressed that I was so aware of Dr. Engelman, empathizing with her distress and feeling so little of my own. After all, it was likely that Katherine's disinterest or disdain was at least as much directed at me as therapist. Or perhaps, Katherine was really emotionally out of touch with both of us, my presence no more important to her personally than Dr. Engelman's.

As a first attempt to make a therapeutic impact on the deteriorating situation, Dr. Engelman asked Katherine if she could describe her response to the feedback she, Dr. Engelman, was providing, adding a particular twist. That is, after inquiring about Katherine's personal reaction to her findings, Dr. Engelman wondered aloud whether Katherine had any idea how she, Dr. Engelman, was feeling at that moment. Apparently, Dr. Engelman and I had intuitively landed on the same issue: Katherine's stunning lack of empathy. Dr. Engelman in her role as consultant was attempting to arrange an *in vivo* demonstration of her test findings.

At that point, I seized the moment. Confronted with Katherine's unrelenting negation of the value of the testing results, I asked Katherine if, indeed, she did have any reaction to or thoughts about what Dr. Engelman might be experiencing. Katherine's response was that she hadn't even given Dr. Engleman's experience a thought. In fact, our asking that question stunned her. She realized that she was completely unaware that Dr. Engelman was feeling anything at all, underscoring a deficit in her empathizing that she was aware of but rarely thought about. In fact, her next comment was a disconcerted, "My God, that's exactly what is missing in my relationship with my sons. It's exactly what I don't know how to do. I don't know how to know what other people are feeling. I don't really know how to improve my relationships with my sons, but I desperately want to." Katherine then plied us with questions about relationships, how to understand them, how to "do them."

Remarkable. In that moment, Katherine, Dr. Engelman, and I made a discovery, potentially affecting all of Katherine's life, and fully illustrating Dr. Engelman's findings. Here was self-absorption, suppressed feeling, and truncated empathy in bold relief. Katherine was shocked, and the intuitive hunch I was discounting about Katherine's emotional deficit was verified and extended. To see the magnitude of Katherine's limitations, I needed to hear about the testing, and then see a clinical demonstration for confirmation. A situation external to Katherine and me, orchestrated by our consultant, was required to break the spell of minimization that was permeating our recently started therapy.

Following this session, almost 3 months into our work, a vigorous interactive and exploratory therapy took hold. Katherine moved from repeating her emotional obtuseness with me to exploring it. She began to recognize how thoroughly her traumatized parents had been forced to disavow their emotions; how they depended on their children to live and feel for them, always nonreflectively, as a repeat of their own need to avoid looking inward. In this work, we focused on the here and now: Katherine's feelings, her relationships, my reactions to Katherine, hers to me, and her blunted experiences with her children. I also asked Katherine to record in detail, between appointments, her immediate personal experiences, and when possible, to e-mail these to me so I could read them close to the time of their occurrence. Whenever Katherine complained that she was fading because she "already knew everything I was saying," I asked her to recall how deceptive this response could be. I reminded her of the feedback session with Dr. Engelman, when she seemed convinced that Dr. Engelman had "nothing new" to offer, and wondered whether she might again be using that kind of belief in her own "knowing" as a shield against intense, possibly disturbing feelings.

To understand the complexity of the conjunctive process at work here, we return to the question of how, despite my clinical impression that Katherine had an emotional deficiency, I managed to underestimate the extent of Katherine's disability. As I looked back at these sessions, here is what I discovered. From Katherine's side, her commitment to therapy was ambivalent. There was Katherine not buying in, subtly insisting that what we had discussed made no difference. Her life had become no more emotionally interesting, regardless of our efforts. Here,

Katherine was being like her parents, seemingly dutiful but entirely remote. On the other hand, during these first months I was paradoxically growing fond of Katherine, more than likely a response to her hidden but passionate desire for us to succeed, for us to rouse her from the nearly dead.

In these two interpersonal constellations, we were enacting different scenarios. In one, Katherine would always be the same. She would never abandon the parents who had suffered so much, who needed to forget their denied but considerable suffering during World War II, and who tasted whatever life they could through their emotionally captive children. In the second, Katherine had joined me in coaxing her into a hopeful life. This second rendition reflected an *incipient conjunctive process,* a facilitating relationship in very newly developing form, with me altering my reality to protect the emerging Katherine (and myself) from reexperiencing just how bleak life according to her parents had been. These were the two poles; there was nothing in between. However, for a true conjunctive development, we needed to break the unrealistic spell enveloping both of us, and move to emotional depth. That path was opened by the psychological testing and the event where Dr. Engelman, by being willing to risk a challenge to Katherine's reenactment of her discouraging experience with her parents, offered a first and powerful demonstration of Katherine's missing emotion.

The following clinical hour provides a closer look at the conjunctive process as it developed after 6 months of work with Katherine. At this point, Katherine was becoming self-reflective but, at the same time, she regularly failed to acknowledge this shift, and undid her participation in it especially when she perceived I was excited about the change she was making. By this point, she was keeping fairly regular company with the alive, hopeful version of herself. Further, I now could usually bring Katherine back to this hopeful, conditionally reflective self by deliberately joining her in her newfound pleasure with emotions, her own and those of others. But acknowledging that our interaction was responsible for these shifts and that she was definitely changing, was still problematic for her. In taking this stance, Katherine was alternately identifying with her parents' insistently bleak view of life, and being obstinate with me, possibly repeating her feelings during her developing years when her parents could not move beyond their concentration camp created emotional prisons. In spite of Katherine's contradictory attitudes, both moving ahead and simultaneously being unwilling to admit progress, the conjunctive process was alive and growing. She resisted acknowledging it, but she was emerging from her personal isolation, experiencing empathy, and becoming more interested in her own and other people's emotional experience.

In this particular clinical hour, Katherine was describing her disappointing relationship with her father. Previously, she had been content to experience but not think about how repelled she felt by her father's cynicism. To begin, Katherine reported that her father uncharacteristically had been trying to "reach out" to her, but that she was not extending herself in response.

Katherine said, "He was trying to be [she struggled with the word] er . . . emotional. He even tried to be physical. He hugged me for the first time in years. I hugged him back; of course, he's getting more vulnerable as he gets older. He's always been this rock of Gibraltar type person; if you fall off a horse, you get back up again."

I asked how this exchange with him made her feel. She answered that it made her feel "bad" because it highlighted how different they were. If he was not family, they wouldn't be interested in one another. "I'm thinking about that for the first time," she said. "I wonder how I developed my values, my interest in social justice. But, I can empathize. They lost everything. Well, maybe it's just the Jewish ethic, my training, nothing I feel so deeply."

I responded, saying I found it hard to believe that her emotional depth was as limited as she reported. In a flash of what felt like inspiration, I had the thought that Katherine's emotional limitations were yielding to our ongoing conversation and that my belief in her essential humanity was instrumental to that shift.

I told Katherine that after each hour I could recall everything she said almost perfectly, and that I did not remember that kind of detail unless I formed a strong emotional connection to a person. I made this statement to Katherine based also on information from the test findings about the extent of her detachment. I was almost defiant as I said these things to her, in effect, insisting we affirm her hopeful self.

Suddenly, there was a shift in Katherine's tone. She went back to the topic of empathizing and said with great emotion that she felt bad for her kids, also. For the first time in 6 months of our meeting she told me that both boys had real problems, one, social problems, and the other, with his weight. She desperately wished she could talk to her oldest son with real feeling, but their conversations always became stilted. Speculating for the first time that she might be implicated in her son's remoteness, as her parents had been implicated in hers, she wondered if her son's emotional inaccessibility might be caused by her.

At this point in our dialogue, I could feel the life in Katherine and confirmed her insight and her headway in recognizing and using her emotions, in this case in relating to her son and understanding her father. She replied that when she awoke that morning she thought, I'm making no progress in therapy. She continued, "I often feel excited about coming to see you and spoil it with a thought like that."

Prior to her last statement, I noticed that I suddenly felt alone in Katherine's presence, not heard by her. I told her that she seemed to become vacant at the moment we both were becoming most enlivened. What could have happened? She worked to hear me, and for the most part succeeded, saying she didn't want to lose the thread we were developing.

After 4 months of our initial 6-month work, Katherine extended our time frame for an additional 9 months, for a total working time of 15 months. In my opinion, having a time frame supported our work in at least two ways: in addition to urging it forward, it helped to secure our therapy against discouragement. It also supported a fragile early conjunctive process by giving us an agreed-upon objective, however contrived.

The time frame appealed to Katherine stylistically. Katherine liked being efficient, task oriented, and having goals. It also induced us both to work vigorously to keep alive Katherine's "hopeful" constellation, the one in which we felt fond of one another and optimistic. Being purposeful competed with her existential ennui, which as a repetition of Katherine's parents' emotionally vacant lives, always threatened to reenvelop her. However, it wasn't only Katherine who could be thrown off course by too much discouragement; it was me, as well. Without the time focus, I suspect I may also have succumbed to the lifelessness in our therapy and at points lost my spirit.

Over time, as we got our bearings and the conjunctive process was well under way, with Katherine's hopeful self secure, we could work together in a more typical exploratory therapy. By then, our facilitating and analyzing constellations were in place. But getting the process started, especially on a time-limited basis, required the boost offered by our experience with Dr. Engleman and the security afforded by knowing that we were assured of working together for at least a designated period of time.

At Katherine's request, Dr. Engelman returned to our sessions twice, the first time to expand on the clinical observations we made in our first meeting and the second time, 2 months before we stopped, to repeat the testing. In her second Rorschach, Katherine was less self-absorbed. Her capacity for empathy had improved and her affective life was richer. Altogether, a significant affective breakthrough had occurred.

Concluding Thoughts

My experiences doing focused, time-limited therapy with Mary and Margie and their families, and with Katherine, were anything but commonplace. In each case, we quickly made a discovery that entirely surprised us, forcing the patient and myself in new and dramatically more profitable directions. The *radical discontinuity* in each situation hurried the sequence of *controlled disorientation* and *collaboration* required to formulate a uniquely effective *leap of inference.* The new ingredient in each case was the psychological consultant who delivered information in the presence of a therapist and patient engaged in a committed conjunctive effort with the patient.

How likely is it that Katherine would have noticed her lack of comprehension of how others think and feel without the test data and in the absence of her trusting relationship with me? How far would we have come within our time constraints had I not been willing to confide how shocked I was by her lack of empathy with Dr. Engelman and insist she pay attention to that observation, an example of what might be termed instructive self-disclosure? How meaningful would our relationship have been without my insistence that we talk in personal ways about our feelings, including our friendly, even fond, feelings for one another? What if I had not yielded to the inexplicable pull I felt to affirm Katherine, at first joining her in minimizing her barriers to empathizing and later doggedly insisting we foster her hopeful self-experience. And what about the future? As we approached the conclusion of our work, Katherine suggested we get back together once every 3 months for the first year or so. She wanted Dr. Engelman to join us again toward the end of that period. If her gains did not last, she said, she was more than willing to undertake a more extensive psychotherapy.

The Place of Time Limitation and Focus in a Therapy's Success

It seems safe to say that the time limitations and goal directedness in these therapies, with the therapist accountable for its progress, offered clear benefits in each of these three cases. Katherine insisted the therapy be time-limited from the start, before she would commit herself to it. Mary and Margie had only limited time to work with me: fighting Mary's addictions was medically urgent, Margie was leaving to go to school within months. In both cases, the consultant made a critical discovery early in the course of treatment enabling us to direct our focus.

I became a uniquely important figure in Margie's and Katherine's, and, in a sense, in Mary's, life. In the end, Margie liked the idea of my being a fill-in for her pictured birth father. For Katherine, the reality we created together substituted for the awful bleakness carried by her parents. In Mary's case, I became that catalytic person for her stepfather after I first joined with him to rescue Mary from her addictions and then to repair his own marriage. He discovered in me someone with whom he could "actually talk." Each person, Margie, Katherine, and Mary's stepfather, joined with me conjunctively, and in each case, a monumental personal shift occurred.

Where was I personally in each of these cases? Did the changes recorded occur unilaterally? Less explicit, partially obscured by the practical nature of my time-bounded charge, is the effect each of these people had on me.

For Margie, admittedly, I became a surrogate father, especially given her adoptive father's enmity toward her. However, I contend that development was absolutely dependent on the process, transformative for both of us, of my finding and believing in an entirely different Margie than anyone else had previously seen.

With Katherine, there were at least two factors at work in her becoming committed to our venture: my willingness to see the best in her, and the fact that I agreed to be task-oriented. I contend that if we did not have the time limitation pushing us, creating a sense of purpose, movement, and protection for her against unlimited personal exposure, I could have been swept with Katherine for some time into the meaninglessness that originally caused her to detach herself and live in an empty world of claimed perfection. To achieve both of these ends, however, I had to bend the truth, as I knew it, toward an affirmative view of Katherine's psychology. My new perspective contradicted the consultant's findings, and clashed with my training as a psychoanalyst, a frame of reference mandating that her test-exposed lack of depth would require long-term intensive psychotherapy to remedy. But, my desire to join with Katherine to retrieve her full participation in life went even deeper. As I told her on several occasions, I had the sense that if we were not involved in our therapy project, and knew each other socially, that she, my wife, and I would probably have been friends. Katherine got that close to me personally, causing me to resist the implications of the testing that she was likely to lead a life-course of superficiality, and firming up my faith in my clinical judgment that she could do much better.

Mary's stepfather was willing to organize his family to travel 1000 miles every other month to see and work with me, an extraordinary vote of confidence. He believed fervently that he and I together could work on each compromised segment of the family, ultimately dealing with his own needs. Together, we felt a powerful rapport that still keeps us working in conjunctive harmony, his part coming from his first-time experience of being heard and valued. I have already described how this work and the guidance he provided substantially added to the sophistication with which I now approach time-limited psychotherapy. Indeed, his effect on me as a strategist of time-limited psychotherapy has been profound.

As I consider these profiles, they could seem less psychologically complex than those from the long-term treatments described in the first nine chapters. Indeed, conjunctive, time-limited psychotherapy is more solidly action-based than extensive, open-ended therapies, usually generating less detail to get one's teeth into. On the other hand, the results of our time-limited therapies were substantial. Important goals, critical to each subject, were achieved in most of the cases, at times setting the stage for later work, whether through brief post-termination consultations or renewed psychotherapy. In Mary's case that work will occur with Mary and her stepfather separately, in Margie's case with a therapist close to her school. Katherine will return for follow-up visits, assessing each time whether she requires more therapy sessions.

The Future

Thinking about the versatility and power of the conjunctive method turns us toward the future, pointing us in new and exciting directions. In writing this book, I wanted to find ways to make the theory and the practice of psychotherapy ever more practical, the therapist more accountable for progress in treatment. My more than 30 years of practice, many of them as an independent-minded psychoanalyst, have led me to make collaboration my unwavering emphasis in this book, focusing on therapist and patient continually informing each other about what they believe and know, on the patient's intermittent prerogative to lead, and on authenticity and self-disclosure.

When thinking about the conjunctive method I can still lose my bearings, wondering why the fuss? Isn't it true that with love and commitment anyone can be conjunctive with another? All you have to do is bring him or her closer to you. Yet, that's where the difficulty begins. Like it or not, you have to consider which parts of you and that person are being brought together. What about incompatibilities of style and temperament? Do you both use the same verbal and nonverbal language? How about timing and pacing? Add innumerable other considerations, not the least of which is the subjective haze we all live in, and conjunction, usually borne of disjunction, becomes a stunningly complex and challenging achievement.

Orchestrating conjunctive movement in psychotherapy is anything but easy. It is the same with the charge that we deliver the most powerful and reliable service to our patients. The self-monitoring and self-correcting capability built into the conjunctive method through its collaborative aspect, if used assiduously, should go far in providing the feedback required to tighten up the therapy process. Further additions, like the three-person field, in both open-ended and time-focused work, can dramatically enhance this process by bringing out therapy themes early that might otherwise take months or years to identify.

And, from there? Given its collaborative nature, isn't it true that each therapy becomes a research project in itself, with both therapy partners stretching to find new, radical angles to further the patient's progress? After all, it is the creative edge of the conjunctive process that makes it so exhilarating. And, in the end, I believe that is the point. Whether breaking new ground or furthering the bounds in an open-ended individual therapy, the conjunctive method reliably generates an inspiring result. The possibilities for creation and progress are limitless, providing that both therapist and patient maintain a probing edge and in-fluence each other to make sure he or she, in being fully commit-ted and passionately involved, changes and grows.

References

Alexander, F. (1956). *Psychoanalysis and psychotherapy.* New York: Norton.

American Psychiatric Association. (2000). *Diagnostic and statistical manual of mental disorders* (4th ed. text. rev.). Washington, DC: Author.

Aron, L. (1992). Interpretation as expression of the analyst's subjectivity. *Psychoanalytic Dialogues, 2*(4), 475–508.

Aron, L. (1996). *A meeting of the minds: Mutuality in psychoanalysis.* Hillsdale, NJ: Analytic Press.

Auerhahn, N., & Peskin, H. (in press). Action knowledge, acknowledgment, and interpretive action in work with Holocaust survivors. *Psychoanalytic Quarterly.*

Bachant, J., Lynch, A., & Richards, A. (1995). Relational models in psychoanalytic theory. *Psychoanalytic Psychology, 12,* 71–88.

Bachrach, H., Galatzer-Levy, R., Skolnikoff, A., & Waldron, S. (1991). On the efficacy of psychoanalysis. *Journal of the American Psychoanalytic Association, 39,* 871–914.

Bader, M. (1996). Altruistic love in psychoanalysis: Opportunities and resistance. *Psychoanalytic Dialogues, 6,* 741–764.

Barber, J. P., & Crits-Christoph, P. (1991). Comparison of the brief dynamic therapies. In P. Crits-Cristoph & J. P. Barber (Eds.), *Handbook of short-term dynamic psychotherapy* (pp. 323–355). New York: Basic.

Bass, A. (1996). Holding and the fate of the analyst's subjectivity. *Psychoanalytic Dialogues, 3,* 361–378.

Beebe, B. (2004). Faces in relation: A case study. *Psychoanalytic Dialogues* 14(1):1–52

Beebe, B. & Lachmann, F. (2003). The relational turn in psychology and relational psychoanalysis: bi-directional influence and proposed syntheses. *Contemporary Psychoanalysis* 39(3):379–410.

Beebe, B., Jaffe, J., & Lachmann, F. (1992). A dyadic systems view of communication. In N. Skolnick & S. Warshaw (Eds.), *Relational perspectives in psychoanalysis* (pp. 61–82). Hillsdale, NJ: Analytic.

Beebe, B., Jaffe, J., & Lachmann, F. (1997). Mother–infant interaction structures and presymbolic self and object representations. *Psychoanalytic Dialogues, 7,* 133–182.

Beebe, B., & Lachmann, F. M. (1988). Mother–infant mutual influence and precursors of psychic structure: In A. Goldberg (Ed.), *Progress in self psychology* (Vol. 3, pp. 3–25). Hillsdale, NJ: Analytic.

Beebe, B., & Lachmann, F. M. (2002). *Infant research and adult treatment: Co-constructing interactions.* Hillsdale, NJ: Analytic.

Benjamin, J. (1992). Recognition and destruction: An outline of intersubjectivity. In N. Skolnick & S. Warshaw (Eds.), *Relational perspectives in psychoanalysis* (pp. 43–60). Hillsdale, NJ: Analytic.

Benjamin, J. (1995). *Like subjects, love objects: Essays on recognition and sexual difference.* New Haven, CT: Yale University Press.

Bergin, A., & Garfield, S. (1994). *Handbook of psychotherapy and behavior change.* New York: Wiley.

Binder, J. L. (1977). Modes of focusing in psychoanalytic short-term therapy. *Psychotherapy: Theory, Research and Practice, 14,* 232–241.

Bion, W. (1955). Language and the schizophrenic. In M. Klein, P. Heimann, & E. Money-Kyrle (Eds.), *New directions in psychoanalysis* (pp. 220–239). London: Tavistock. (Original publication 1952)

Bion, W. R. (1967). *Second thoughts.* London: Heinemann.

Blechner, M. (1995). The analyst's dreams and the countertransference. *Psychoanalytic Dialogues, 5,* 1–26.

Bollas, C. (1987). *The shadow of the object: Psychoanalysis of the unthought known.* London: Free Association Books.

Bollas, C. (1991). *The forces of destiny: Psychoanalysis and human idiom.* London: Free Association Books.

Bowlby, J. (1969). *Attachment.* Vol. 1. New York: Basic.

Bromberg, P. (1991). On knowing one's patient inside out. *Psychoanalytic Dialogues, 1*(4), 339–422.

Bromberg, P. (1995). Resistance, object-usage, and human-relatedness. *Contemporary Psychoanalysis, 31,* 173–191.

Bromberg, P. (1998). Standing in spaces: The multiplicity of self and the psychoanalytic relationship. *Contemporary Psychoanalysis, 32,* 509–536.

Bromberg, P. (2000). Potholes on the royal road: Or is it an abyss? *Contemporary Psychoanalysis, 36,* 6–27.

Budman, S. H., & Steenbarger, B. N. (1997). *The essential guide to group practice in mental health: Clinical, legal, and financial fundamentals.* New York: Guilford.

Casement, P. (1985). *Learning from the patient.* New York: Guilford.

Charles, M. (2002). *Patterns: Building blocks of experience.* Hillsdale, NJ: Analytic.

Clement, P. W. (1999). *Outcome and incomes.* New York: Guilford.

Cone, J. D. (2001). *Evaluating outcomes: Empirical tools for effective practice.* Washington, DC: American Psychoanalytic Association.

Costa, P., & McCrae, R. (1985). *The NEO personality inventory manual.* Odessa, FL: Psychological Assessment Resources.

Cozolino, L. (2002). *The Neuroscience of Psychotherapy: Building and rebuilding the Human Brain.* New York: Norton.

Davanloo, H. (1999a). Intensive short-term dynamic psychotherapy—Central dynamic sequence: Phase of challenge. *International Journal of Short-Term Psychotherapy, 13*(4), 237–260.

Davanloo, H. (1999b). Intensive short-term dynamic psychotherapy—Central dynamic sequence: Head-on collision with resistance. *International Journal of Short-Term Psychotherapy. 13*(4), 263–280.

Ehrenberg, D. (1992). *The intimate edge.* New York: W. W. Norton.

Emde, R. (1988a). Development terminable and interminable, I. Innate and motivational factors from infancy. *International Journal of Psycho-Analysis, 69,* 23–42.

Emde, R. (1988b). Development terminable and interminable, II. Recent psychoanalytic theory and therapeutic considerations. *International Journal of Psycho-Analysis, 69,* 283–296.

Emde, R. (1990). Mobilizing fundamental modes of development: Empathic availability and therapeutic action. *Journal of the American Psychoanalytic Association, 38,* 881–913.

Engelman, D., & Frankel, S. (2002). The three person field: Collaborative consultation to psychotherapy. *The Humanistic Psychologist, 30,* 49–62.

Ferenczi, S. (1955a). The elasticity of psycho-analytic technique. In M. Balint (Ed.), *Final contributions to the problems and methods of psycho-analysis* (pp. 97–101). London: Hogarth. (Original work published 1928).

Ferenczi, S. (1955b). Child analysis in the analysis of adults. In M. Balint (Ed.), *Final contributions to the problems and methods of psycho-analysis* (pp. 126–142). London: Hogarth. (Original work published 1931).

Finn, S. E. (1996a). *A manual for using the MMPI-2 as a therapeutic intervention.* Minneapolis: University of Minnesota Press.

Finn, S. E. (1996b). Assessment feedback integrating MMPI-2 and Rorschach findings. *Journal of Personality Assessment, 67,* 543–557.

Finn, S. E. (1999, March). *Giving feedback to clients about "defensive" test protocols: Guidelines from therapeutic assessment.* Paper presented at the Midwinter Meeting of the Society for Personality Assessment, New Orleans, LA.

Finn, S. E., & Fischer, C. (1997, August 8). *Therapeutic psychological assessment: Illustration and analysis of philosophical assumptions.* Paper presented at the Annual Meeting of the American Psychological Association.

Finn, S. E., & Tonsager, M. E. (1997). Information-gathering and therapeutic models of assessment: Complementary paradigms. *Psychological Assessment, 9,* 374–385.

Fischer, C. T. (1994a). *Individualizing psychological assessment.* Mahwah, NJ: Erlbaum.

Fischer, C. T. (1994b). Humanizing psychological assessment. In F. Wertz (Ed.), *The humanistic movement: Recovering the person in psychology* (pp. 202–214). Lake Worth, FL: Gardner.

Fischer, C. T. (2000). Collaborative individualized assessment. *Journal of Personality Assessment, 74,* 2–14.

Fosha, D. (2000). *The transforming power of affect: A model for accelerated change.* New York: Basic.

Fourcher, L. (1992). Interpreting the relative and absolute unconscious. *Psychoanalytic Dialogues, 2,* 317–329.

Frank, K. (1997). The role of the analyst's inadvertent self-revelations. *Psychoanalytic Dialogues, 32,* 281–314.

Frankel, S. (1995). *Intricate engagements: The collaborative basis of therapeutic change.* Northvale, NJ: Aronson.

Frankel, S. (1997). The analyst's role in the disruption and repair sequence in psychoanalysis. *Contemporary Psychoanalysis, 33,* 71–87.

Frankel, S. (2000). *Hidden faults: Recognizing and resolving therapeutic disjunctions.* Madison, CT: International Universities Press.

Frankel, S. (2001). New and creative development through psychoanalysis. *Contemporary Psychoanalysis, 37,* 523–550.

Freud, S. (1955). Totem and taboo. In J. Strachey (Ed. & Trans.), *The standard edition of the complete psychological works of Sigmund Freud* (Vol. 13, 1–162). London: Hogarth. (Original work published 1913)

Freud, S. (1964). New introductory lectures on psycho-analysis. In J. Strachey (Ed. & Trans.), *The standard edition of the complete psychological works of Sigmund Freud* (Vol. 22, 1–182). London: Hogarth. (Original work published 1933).

Frie, R. (2002). Modernism or postmodernism? Binswanger, Sullivan and the problem of agency in contemporary psychoanalysis. *Contemporary Psychoanalysis, 38,* 635–674.

Fromm, E. (1960). *Crisis in psychoanalysis.* Greenwich, CT: Fawcett.

Fulmer, R. H., Cohen, S., & Monaco, G. (1985). Using psychological assessment in structural family therapy. *Journal of Learning Disabilities, 18,* 145–150.

Gabbard, G. (1994). Sexual excitement and countertransference love in the analyst. *Journal of the American Psychoanalytic Association, 42,* 1083–1106.

Gabbard, G. (1995). Countertransference: The emerging common ground. *International Journal of Psycho-Analysis, 76,* 475–485.

Garfield, S. L. (1994). Research on client variables in psychotherapy. In A. E. Bergin & S. L. Garfield (Eds.), *Handbook of psychotherapy and behavior change* (4th ed., pp. 190–228). New York: Wiley.

Gerson, S. (1996). Neutrality, resistance and self-disclosure in an intersubjective psychoanalysis. *Psychoanalytic Dialogues, 6,* 623–646.

Ghent, E. (1995). Interaction in the psychoanalytic situation. *Psychoanalytic Dialogues, 5,* 479–491.

Goodman, A. (1995). Containing and responding. *Contemporary Psychoanalysis, 31,* 557–574.

Greenacre, P. (1971). *Emotional growth.* (Vol. 2). New York: International Universities Press.

Greenberg, J. (1991). *Oedipus and beyond: A clinical theory.* Cambridge, MA: Harvard University Press.

Greenberg, J. (1999). Analytic authority and analytic restraint. *Contemporary Psychoanalysis, 35*(1), 25–41.

Greenberg, L., Rice, L., & Elliot, R. (1993). *Facilitating emotional change: The moment-by-moment process.* New York: Guilford.

Greenspan, S. (1981). *Psychopathology and adaptation in infancy and early childhood.* New York: International Universities Press.

Greenspan, S. (1997). *Developmentally based psychotherapy.* Madison, CT: International Universities Press.

Greenspan, S., & Lieberman, A. (1988). A clinical approach to attachment. In J. Belsky & T. Nezworski (Eds.), *Clinical implications of attachment* (pp. 387–424). Hillsdale, NJ: Analytic.

Grigsby, J., & Stevens, D. (2000). *Neurodynamics of personality.* New York: Guilford.

Gross, E. (1985). Modulation of affect and non-verbal communication by the right hemisphere. In M. Mesulam (Ed.), *Principles of behavioral neurology* (pp. 239–259). Philadelphia: F. A. Davis.

Grossman, L. (1996). The analyst's influence. *Psychoanalytic Quarterly, 65,* 681–692.

Grossman, L. (1999). What the analyst does not hear. *Psychoanalytic Quarterly, 68,* 84–98.

Gustafson, J. P. (1995). *Brief versus long psychotherapy, when, why, and how.* Northvale, NJ: Aronson.

Hammer, A., & Macdaid, G. (1992). *Meyers-Briggs career report manual.* Palo Alto, CA: Consulting Psychological Assessment Resources.

Handler, L. (1995). The clinical use of figure drawings. In C. Newmark (Ed.), *Major psychological assessment instruments* (pp. 206–293). Boston: Allyn & Bacon.

Harmon, L., Hansen, J., Borgen, F., & Hammer, A. (1994). *Strong interest inventory applications and technical guide.* Palo Alto, CA: Consulting Psychologists Press.

Hart, A. (1999). Reclaiming the analyst's disruptive role. *Contemporary Psychoanalysis, 35,* 185–211.

Hawkins, R., Mathews, J., & Hamdan, L. (1999). *Measuring behavioral health outcomes: A practical guide.* New York: Plenum.

Herman, J. L. (1992). *Trauma and recovery.* New York: Basic.

Hirsh, I. (1994). Dissociation and the interpersonal self. *Contemporary Psychoanalysis, 30,* 777–799.

Hoffman, I. (1983). The patient as interpreter of the analyst's experience. *Contemporary Psychoanalysis, 19,* 389–422.

Hoffman, I. (1991). Discussion: Toward a social–constructivist view of the psychoanalytic situation. *Psychoanalytic Dialogues, 1,* 74–105.

Hoffman, I. (1992). Some practical implications of a social–constructivist view of the psychoanalytic situation. *Psychoanalytic Dialogues, 2,* 287–304.

Hoffman, I. (1994). Dialectical thinking and therapeutic action in the psychoanalytic process. *Psychoanalytic Quarterly, 63,* 187–218.

Hoffman, I. (1996). The intimate and ironic authority of the psychoanalyst's presence. *Psychoanalytic Quarterly, 65,* 102–136.

Hoffman, I. (1998). *Ritual and spontaneity in the psychoanalytic process: A dialectical–constructivist view.* Hillsdale, NJ: Analytic.

Horowitz, M. J. (1987). *States of mind: Analysis of change in individual personality* (2nd ed.). New York: Plenum.

Horowitz, M. J. (1989). *Nuances of technique in dynamic psychotherapy. Selected clinical papers.* Northvale, NJ: Aronson.

Jacobs, T. (1991). *The uses of the self.* Madison, CT: International Universities Press.

Jacobs, T. (1999). On the question of self-disclosure by the analyst: Error or advance in technique. *Psychoanalytic Quarterly, 68,* 159–183.

Johnson, B., & Hugdahl, K. (1993). Right hemisphere representation of autonomic conditioning to facial emotional expressions. *Psychophysiology, 30,* 274–278.

Jung, C. (1968). The structure and dynamics of the psyche. In H. Read, M. Fordham, & G. Adler (Eds.), *The collected works* (Vol. 8, pars. 317–321). Princeton, NJ: Princeton University Press. (Original work published 1927/1931)

Kantrowitz, J. (1996). *The patient's impact on the analyst.* Hillsdale, NJ: Analytic.

Kernberg, O. (1995). *Love relations.* New Haven, CT: Yale University Press.

Kiersky, S., & Beebe, B. (1994). The reconstruction of early nonverbal relatedness in the treatment of difficult patients: A special form of empathy. *Psychoanalytic Dialogues, 4,* 389–408.

Klein, M. (1975a). Some theoretical conclusions regarding the emotional life of the infant. In *Developments in psychoanalysis* (pp. 198–236). New York: Delacorte Press/Seymour Laurence. (Original work published 1952)

Klein, M. (1975b). Envy and gratitude. In *Envy and gratitude and other works, 1946–1963* (pp. 176–235). New York: Delacorte Press/Seymour Laurence. (Original work published 1957)

Kohut, H. (1977). *The restoration of the self.* New York: International Universities Press.

Kraemer, G. W. (1992). A psychobiological theory of attachment. *Behavior Brain Science, 15,* 493–541.

Kumin, I. (1996). *Pre-object relatedness: Early attachment and the psychoanalytic situation.* New York: Guilford.

La Barre, F. (2001). *On moving and being moved: Nonverbal behavior in clinical practice.* Hillsdale, NJ: Analytic.

Langs, R. (1978a). *Technique in transition.* Northvale, NJ: Aronson.

Langs, R. (1978b). *The listening process.* Northvale, NJ: Aronson.

Levenson, E. (1972). *The fallacy of understanding.* New York: Basic.

Levenson, E. (1996). Aspects of self-revelation and self-disclosure. *Contemporary Psychoanalysis, 32,* 237–248.

Levenson, E. (1998). Awareness, insight and learning. *Contemporary Psychoanalysis, 34,* 239–249.

Levin, F. (1991). *The mapping of the mind.* Hillsdale, NJ: Analytic.

Lichtenberg, J. (1989). *Psychoanalysis and motivation.* Hillsdale, NJ: Analytic.

Lieberman, A., & Pawl, J. (1988). Clinical applications of attachment theory. In J. Belskey & T. Nezwarski (Eds) *Clinical implications of attachment* (pp. 327–351). Hillsdale, NJ: Analytic.

Loewald, H. (1960). On the therapeutic action of psycho-analysis. *International Journal of Psycho-Analysis, 41,* 16–33.

Loewald, H. (1977). Reflections on psychoanalytic process. In H. Loewald (Ed.), *Papers on psychoanalysis, 1980* (pp. 372–393). New Haven, CT: Yale University Press.

Luborsky, L., Crits-Christoph, P., Mintz, J., & Auerbach, A. (1988). *Who will benefit from psychotherapy? Predicting therapeutic outcomes.* New York: Basic.

Lubrosky, L., & Mark, D. (1991). Short-term supportive-expressive psychoanalytic psychotherapy. In P. Crits-Christoph & J. P. Barber (Eds.), *Handbook of short-term dynamic psychotherapy* (pp. 110–136). New York: Basic.

Mahler, M. (1971). A study of the separation–individuation process and its possible application to borderline phenomena in the psychoanalytic situation. *The Psychoanalytic Study of the Child, 26,* 403–424. New Haven, CT: Yale University Press.

Malan, D. H. (1979). *Individual psychotherapy and the science of psychodynamics.* London: Butterworth.

Malan, D. H. (1986). Beyond interpretation: Initial evaluation and technique in short-term dynamic psychotherapy. Parts I & II. *International Journal of Short-Term Psychotherapy, 1*(2), 59–106.

Mann, J. (1973). *Time limited psychotherapy.* Cambridge, MA: Harvard University Press.

Marnish, M. (2002). *Essentials of Treatment Planning,* New York: Wiley.

Maroda, K. (1991). *The power of countertransference.* New York: Wiley.

Maroda, K. (1999). *Seduction, surrender, and transformation: Emotional engagement in the analytic process.* Hillsdale, NJ: Analytic.

Maroda, K. (2002). No place to hide: Affectivity, the unconscious, and the development of relational techniques. *Contemporary Psychoanalysis, 38,* 104–120.

Meissner, W. (1981). *Internalization in psychoanalysis.* New York: International Universities Press.

Meissner, W. (1991). *What is effective in psychoanalytic therapy: The move from interpretation to relation.* Northvale, NJ: Aronson.

Meissner, W. (1996). *The therapeutic alliance.* New Haven, CT: Yale University Press.

Meltzoff, A., & Moore, M. (1992). Early imitation within a functional framework: The importance of person identity, movement. and development. *Infant Behavioral Development, 15,* 479–505.

Meltzoff, A. N., & Moore, M. K. (1999). Persons and Representations: Why infant imitation is important for theories of human development. In J. Nadel & G. Butterworth (Eds.), *Imitation in Infancy* (pp. 9–35). Cambridge, U.K.: Cambridge University Press.

Meyerson, P. (1994). Expressions of countertransference and the curative process. *Contemporary Psychoanalysis, 30,* 213–235.

Miller, L. (1986). Some comments on cerebral hemispheric models of consciousness. *Psychoanalytic Review, 73,* 129–144.

Millon, T. (1994). *Millon clinical multisocial inventory-III (MCMI-III) manual.* Minneapolis, MN: National Computer Systems.

Mitchell, S. (1991). Contemporary perspectives on self: Toward an integration. *Psychoanalytic Dialogues, 1*(2), 121–147.

Mitchell, S. (1993). *Hope and dread in psychoanalysis.* New York: Basic Books.

Mitchell, S. (1997). *Influence and autonomy in psychoanalysis.* Hillsdale, NJ: Analytic.

Mitchell, S. (1998). The analyst's knowledge and authority. *Psychoanalytic Quarterly, 68,* 1–31.

Modell, A. (1984). *Psychoanalysis in a new context.* New York: International Universities Press.

Modell, A. (1990). *Other times, other realities: Toward a theory of psychoanalytic treatment.* Cambridge, MA: Harvard University Press.

Modell, A. (1991). The therapeutic relationship as a paradoxical experience. *Psychoanalytic Dialogues, 1,* 13–29.

Moore, R. (1999). *The creation of reality in psychoanalysis.* Hillsdale, NJ: Analytic.

Natterson, J. (1991). *Beyond countertransference.* Northvale, NJ: Aronson.

Natterson, J. (2003). Love in psychotherapy. *Psychoanalytic Psychology* 20(3):509–521.

Neborsky, R. J., & Solomon, M. F. (2001). Attachment bonds and intimacy: Can the primary imprint of love change? In M. Solomon, R. Neborsky, L. McCullough, M. Alpert, F. Shapiro, & D. Mahan (Eds.), *Short-term therapy for long-term change* (pp. 155–185). New York: Norton.

Ogden, T. (1982). *Projective identification and psychotherapeutic technique.* Northvale, NJ: Aronson.

Ogden, T. (1986). *The matrix of the mind: Object relations and the psychoanalytic dialogue.* Northvale, NJ: Aronson.

Ogden, T. (1994). *Subjects of analysis.* Northvale, NJ: Aronson.

Orange, D. Atwood, G., & Stolorow, R. (1997). *Working intersubjectively: Contextualism in psychoanalytic practice.* Hillsdale, NJ: Analytic.

Pine, F. (1993). A contribution to the analysis of the psychoanalytic process. *Psychoanalytic Quarterly, 62,* 185–205.

Pollock, L., & Slavin, J. (1998). The struggle for recognition: Disruption and reintegration in the experience of agency. *Psychoanalytic Dialogues, 8,* 857–873.

Racker, H. (1968). *Transference and countertransference.* New York: International Universities Press.

Renik, O. (1993). Analytic interaction: Conceptualizing technique in light of the analyst's irreducible subjectivity. *Psychoanalytic Quarterly, 62,* 553–571.

Renik, O. (1995). The ideal of the anonymous analyst and the problem of self-disclosure. *Psychoanalytic Quarterly, 64,* 466–495.

Renik, O. (1998). Getting real in analysis. *Psychoanalytic Quarterly, 67,* 567–593.

Renik, O. (1999). Playing one's card face up in analysis: An approach to the problem of self-disclosure. *Psychoanalytic Quarterly, 68,* 521–540.

Rorty, R. (1991). *Objectivity, relativism, and truth* (Vols. 1&2). Cambridge, U.K.: Cambridge University Press.

Roth, A., & Fonagy, P. (1996). *What works for whom?: A critical review of psychotherapy research.* New York: Guilford.

Safron, J. (2003). The relational turn, the therapeutic alliance, and psychotherapy research: Strange bedfellows or postmodern Marriage? *Contemporary Psychoanalysis* 39(3):449–476.

Safron, J., & Muran, J. (2000). *Negotiating the therapeutic alliance: A relational treatment guide.* New York: Guilford.

Safron, J. D., & Segal, Z. V. (1990). *Interpersonal process in cognitive therapy.* New York: Basic.

Sandler, J. (1976). Countertransference and role responsiveness. *International Review of Psychoanalysis, 3,* 32–37.

Schachter, J. (2002). *Transference: Shibbolith or albatross?* Hillsdale, NJ: Analytic.

Schafer, R. (1976). *A new language for psychoanalysis.* New Haven, CT: Yale University Press.

Schafer, R. (1983). *The analytic attitude.* New York: Basic.

Schafer, R. (1997). *Tradition and change in psychoanalysis.* Madison, CT: International Universities Press.

Scharff, J. (1992). *Projective and introjective identification and the use of the therapist's self.* Northvale, NJ: Aronson.

Schore, A. (1994). *Affect regulation and the origin of the self: The neurobiology of emotional development.* Hillsdale, NJ: Erlbaum.

Schore, A. (1997). A century after Freud's project: Is rapprochement between psychoanalysis and neurobiology at hand? *Journal of the American Psychoanalytic Association, 45,* 807–840.

Schore, A. (1997). Interdisciplinary development research as a source of clinical models. In M. Moskowitz, C. Monk, C. Kaye, & S. Ellman (Eds.), *The neurobiological and developmental basis for psychoanalytic intervention* (pp. 1–72). Northvale, NJ: Aronson.

Schore, A. (2003). *Affect Regulation and the Repair of the Self.* New York: Norton.

Schwaber, E. (1996). Toward a definition of the term and concept of interaction: Its reflection in analytic listening. *Psychoanalytic Inquiry, 16,* 5–24.

Searles, H. F. (1975). The patient as therapist to his analyst. In P. Giovacchini (Ed.), *Tactics and techniques for psychoanalytic therapy* (Vol. 2, pp. 95–151). Northvale, NJ: Aronson.

Seligman, S. (2003) The developmental perspective in relational Psychoanalysis. *Contemporary Psychoanalysis* 39(3):477–508.

Settlage, C. (1992). Therapeutic process and developmental process in the restructuring of object and self constancy. *Journal of the American Psychoanalytic Association, 41,* 473–492.

Settlage, C. (1993, May 1). *On the contribution of separation individuation theory to psychoanalysis: Developmental process, pathogenesis, therapeutic process and technique.* Paper presented at the 24th annual Margaret Mahler Symposium on Child Development, Philadelphia, PA.

Shane, M., & Shane, S. (1989). Prologue. *Psychoanalytic Inquiry, 93,* 333–339.

Shane, M., Shane, E., & Gales, M. (1997). *Intimate attachments.* New York: Guilford.

Siegel, D. (1999). *The developing mind: Toward a neurobiology of interpersonal experience.* New York: Guilford.

Shill, M. (2004) Analytic Neutrality, Anonymity, Abstinence, and Elective Self Disclosure. Journal of the American Psychoanalytic Assn. 52:151–188.

Silverman, D. (1992). Attachment research: An approach to a developmental relational perspective. In N. Skolnick & S. Warshaw (Eds.), *Relational perspectives in psychoanalysis* (pp. 195–216). Hillsdale, NJ: Analytic.

Slavin, J. (1994). On making rules: Toward a reformulation of the dynamics of transference in psychoanalytic treatment. *Psychoanalytic Dialogues, 4,* 253–274.

Slavin, M., & Kriegman, D. (1998). Why the analyst needs to change. Toward a theory of conflict, negotiation, and mutual influence in the therapeutic process. *Psychoanalytic Dialogues, 8,* 247–284.

Slochower, J. (1996a). *Holding in psychoanalysis: A relational perspective.* Hillsdale, NJ: Analytic.

Slochower, J. (1996b). Holding and the fate of the analyst's subjectivity. *Psychoanalytic Dialogues, 6,* 335–360.

Spence, D. (1987). *The Freudian metaphor: Toward paradigm change in psychoanalysis.* New York: Norton.

Spence, D. (1993). The hermeneutic turn: Soft silence or loyal opposition? *Psychoanalytic Dialogues, 3*(1), 1–10.

Spezzano, C. (1993). *Affect in psychoanalysis.* Hillsdale, NJ: Analytic.

Spillius, E. (1992). Clinical experiences of projective identification. In R. Anderson (Ed.), *Clinical lectures on Klein and Bion.* London: Tavistock.

Stern, Daniel (1985). *The interpersonal world of the infant.* New York: Basic Books.

Stern, Daniel (2004). *The Present Moment in Psychotherapy and Everyday Life.* New York: Norton.

Stern, Donnel (1997). *Unformulated experience: From dissociation to imagination in psychoanalysis.* Hillsdale, NJ: Analytic Press.

Stolorow, R. D. (1995). Introduction: Tensions between Loyalism and Expansionism. In: Progress in Self Psychology, 11:xi–xvii, ed. A. Goldberg. Hillsdale, NJ: Analytic Press.

Stolorow, R., Brandchaft, B., & Atwood, G. (1987). *Psychoanalytic treatment: An intersubjective approach.* Hillsdale, NJ: Analytic Press.

Stone, L. (1961). *The psychoanalytic situation: An examination of its development and essential nature.* New York: International Universities Press.

Strenger, C. (1991). *Between hermeneutics and science: An essay on the epistemology of psychoanalysis.* Madison, CT: International Universities Press.

Strenger, C. (1998). *Individuality, the impossible project: Psychoanalysis and self-creation.* Madison, CT: International Universities Press.

Strupp, H. H., & Binder, J. L. (1984). *Psychotherapy in a new key: A guide to time-limited dynamic psychotherapy.* New York: Basic.

Summers, F. (1994). *Object relations theories and psychopathology* (pp. 345–380). Hillsdale, NJ: Analytic.

Tansey, M., & Burke, W. (1989). *Understanding countertransference.* Hillsdale, NJ: Analytic.

Toronto, E. (2001). The human touch: An exploration of the role and meaning of physical touch in psychoanalysis. *Psychoanalytic Psychology, 18,* 37–54.

Tronick, E. (1989). Emotions and emotional communication in infants. *American Psychologist, 44,* 112–119.

Van der Kolk, B. (1988). The trauma spectrum: The interaction of biological and social events in the genesis of the trauma response. *Journal of Traumatic Stress, 1*(3), 273–290.

Van der Kolk, B. (2002). Posttraumatic therapy in the age of neuroscience. *Psychoanalytic Dialogues, 12,* 381–392.

Viderman, M. (1991). The real person of the analyst and his role in the process of psychoanalytic cure. *Journal of the American Psychoanalytic Association, 39,* 451–490.

Wallerstein, R. (1986). *Forty-two lives in treatment: A study of psychoanalysis and psychotherapy.* New York: Guilford.

Wallerstein, R. (1992). Psychoanalytic pluralism: The resolution of the issue? In R. Wallerstein (Ed.), *The common ground of psychoanalysis* (pp. 3–62). Northvale, NJ: Aronson.

Weston, D., S. Gabbard, G. O. (2002). Developments in Cognitive Neuroscience. I. Conflict, Compromise, and Connectionism. *Journal of the American Psychoanalytic Association, 50,* 53–98.

Weiss, J. (1993). *How psychotherapy works: Process and technique.* New York: Guilford.

Winnicott, D. W. (1958). Metapsychological and clinical aspects of regression within the psychoanalytic set-up. In *Through paediatrics to psycho-analysis.* London: Hogarth. (Original work published 1954)

Winnicott, D. W. (1963, May). *Communicating and not communicating leading to a study of certain opposites.* Presentation to the British Psycho-Analytic Society.

Winnicott, D. W. (1965). The theory of the parent–infant relationship. In *The maturational processes and the facilitating environment: Studies in the theory of emotional development* (pp. 37–55). New York: International Universities Press. (Original work published 1960)

Winnicott, D. W. (1968). The use of the object and relating through identifications. In *Playing and reality* (pp. 86–94). New York: Routledge.

Winnicott, D. W. (1971). *Therapeutic consultations in child psychiatry.* New York: Basic.

Wolf, E. S. (1983). *Aspects of Neutrality, Psychoanalytic Inquiry,* 3:675–689.

Wolstein, B. (1983). The first person in interpersonal relations. *Contemporary Psychoanalysis, 19,* 522–535.

Wolstein, B. (1987). Experience, interpretation, self-knowledge. *Contemporary Psychoanalysis, 23,* 329–349.

Name Index

Subject Index